Economic Theology

Economic Theology

Credit and Faith II

Philip Goodchild

ROWMAN & LITTLEFIELD
Lanham • Boulder • New York • London

Published by Rowman & Littlefield
An imprint of The Rowman & Littlefield Publishing Group, Inc.
4501 Forbes Boulevard, Suite 200, Lanham, Maryland 20706
www.rowman.com

6 Tinworth Street, London SE11 5AL, United Kingdom

British Library Cataloguing in Publication Information Available

Library of Congress Cataloging-in-Publication Data
Names: Goodchild, Philip, 1965– author.
Title: Economic theology : credit and faith II / Philip Goodchild.
Other titles: Credit and faith II
Description: Lanham : Rowman & Littlefield, 2020. | Includes bibliographical references and index.
Identifiers: LCCN 2020007282 (print) | LCCN 2020007283 (ebook) | ISBN 9781786614261 (cloth) | ISBN 9781786614278 (paperback) | ISBN 9781786614285 (epub)
Subjects: LCSH: Economics—Religious aspects—Christianity. | Credit—Religious aspects—Christianity.
Classification: LCC BR115.E3 G647 2020 (print) | LCC BR115.E3 (ebook) | DDC 261.8/5—dc23
LC record available at https://lccn.loc.gov/2020007282
LC ebook record available at https://lccn.loc.gov/2020007283

Human history is simply the history of the servitude that makes men – oppressors and oppressed alike – the plaything of the instruments of domination they themselves have manufactured, and thus reduces living humanity to being the chattel of inanimate chattels.

– Simone Weil, *Oppression and Liberty*

Contents

Preface
A memoir offered in lieu of a literature review

The quality of a human mind may be measured – if not simply by its capacity for rigorous thought nor simply by its capacity for scholarship – for reading, citing, mastering, deploying, and occasionally misconstruing as many other authors as possible – then at least by its capacity to be shaped and moulded by the ideas it encounters and the books it reads. I mean this quite literally, for an active reader is an unconscious electrician or electrician of the unconscious, busy rewiring his or her own brain. Invisible footnotes are written on one's soul, yet, for all that, they might still be legible on occasion. The crucial question, then, is which books providence places in one's path. The great Cambridge economist J.M. Keynes has left a beautiful memoir of the combined early influence of G.E. Moore's *Principia Ethica* and Bertrand Russell's *Principia Mathematica*.[1] By contrast, the books that shaped my own student days were not nearly so august and rigorous, and in fact not even on the Cambridge Faculty of Divinity reading list. My uncle lent me three books which epitomised the mid-twentieth-century Anglican formation that he and my late father had shared: William Temple's *Readings in the Gospel of St John* (which I largely read at the local launderette, washing my thoughts with my laundry), W.H. Vanstone's *Love's Endeavour, Love's Expense*, and John A.T. Robinson's *Honest to God*. Subsequently, he also lent me Dietrich Bonhoeffer's *Letters and Papers from Prison* and Kosuke Koyama's *Waterbuffalo Theology*, recounting what a Japanese Lutheran could learn from Theravada Buddhism as a missionary in Thailand ('the crucified Christ has open hands', Koyama used to say) – a set of books less influential and renowned than those of Keynes' formation, no doubt (perhaps some are hardly read any more), but a set that oriented a young idealist who, like Keynes, loved understanding for its own sake, onto the path of a spirituality of receptivity – unlike Keynes' 'religion' that consisted in taking pleasure only in a present state of consciousness. In other words, blithely unconcerned by any assessment of my learning by others, I started scribbling notes, blots and smudges on my soul.

After devouring Vanstone's subsequent *The Stature of Waiting*, I was attracted by a title that I found in Mowbray's bookshop, which then stood in King's Parade in Cambridge, from an author of whom I had not previously heard: it was *Waiting for God* by Simone Weil. This was my first encounter with a trained French philosopher. The book did not speak to me: I did not recognise Weil's description of a rather Stoic Christian faith which she had always possessed. Likewise, the description of struggling with mathematical exercises at school as a preparation for prayer bore no relation to my perplexed preparations for weekly supervisions as a rather pious first-year mathematics undergraduate. The analysis of the Lord's Prayer in terms of attitudes to time left me cold. Whatever impression the book had made, it was not one that I could grasp. I rapidly moved on, engaged only by authors concerned with heart and soul: John Howard Yoder, M.K. Gandhi, Jürgen Moltmann, Erich Fromm, E.F. Schumacher, C.G. Jung, and Roberto Assagioli, leading to my initiation into philosophical thinking by reading Friedrich Nietzsche, and a decade later my initiation into economic thinking by reading Karl Marx. After the Anglican theology of Temple and Vanstone, then, my brain was wired by the critical thinking of Nietzsche and Marx rather than by the analytic thinking of Moore and Russell. And once I had at last turned from the soul to the economy, my thoughts were further formed by reading Karl Polanyi, Vandana Shiva, Maria Mies, Mike Rowbotham, Paul Robertson, and Frances Hutchinson.

Now, for two decades after taking up philosophy, my work was haunted by thoughts developed in a similar way by Weil – on matters, such as suffering, attention, and atonement – and yet each time I picked up her work, I was soon repelled by what I found. It was only later, under the remote influence of a friend in California, Lissa McCullough, and the closer influence of a doctoral student, Stuart Jesson, that I was persuaded to read Weil properly and thoroughly. *Oppression and Liberty* not only crystallised my reservations about Nietzsche and Marx (see my previous *Credit and Faith*) but also held out my promise of something further – a further rewiring of the brain. The philosopher I now encounter in her essays and notes bears little resemblance to the Platonic, ascetic, spiritual writer of popular imagination and of my previous misconceptions. In some ways, this whole project on credit and faith could be taken as an attempt to further develop and crystallise Weil's thought in our contemporary context – albeit with a major reservation: I have rejected key Platonic and Kantian assumptions that the good should be conceived as either an object of desire or as an assent to an obligation; I conceive it instead as an act of offering through the theological virtues of faith, hope, and love. What I have received instead, by contrast, may be more a matter of style: there is a kind of academic prose which seeks to appropriate a full complement of theoretical equipment – it wishes to teach how one should be oriented if ever one were to set out on the journey towards the kingdom of justice and truth. These are no doubt worthy motives, but they do tend to render every consideration merely hypothetical: 'if one is to think correctly, one should . . .'. Weil and I have been granted little time for such constraints; we have broken out of the chains of theory; for ordinary life is itself more thought-provoking. We are called to put our hands to the plough, to begin the task of thinking, ill-prepared as we are, irrespective of whom we might offend, and uncertain of where we might arrive.

But I will mention just a few more preparations. I remember as a fresh graduate student being asked to read a weighty book by Martin Heidegger, *What Is Called Thinking?* I was stunned. Starting from the premise that we are not yet thinking, he pursued this single question relentlessly, digging deeper and deeper into the foundations of human thought. One who has not read Heidegger simply cannot imagine either the exertion involved or the thinking achieved. 'If he continues like that, he'll reach the Antipodes!' I thought. The question seemed to me sound and pertinent. The inquiry was formidable, resolute, and heroic. And yet I could not help but suspect that the materials were unyielding, the tools inappropriate, and the destination – a fragment from Parmenides – too obscure, too opaque, and too ambiguous to be held in mind with anything like the clarity that was sought. Heidegger may have invoked the image of entering a forest clearing, there or elsewhere, but I was not convinced – he was mining deeper and deeper into the darkness. This was not a way to escape the cave.

A little later in the course, the young and relatively unpublished lecturer, a Vico scholar by the name of John Milbank (later to become a colleague at the University of Nottingham), asked us to read an even longer book, one by Gilles Deleuze and Félix Guattari: *A Thousand Plateaus*. I was captivated. The question of what is called thinking was not explicitly posed – or at least, the authors' final collaborative book that did pose the question had not yet been written. And yet a strikingly fresh answer was offered on every page: contrasted with Heidegger's toil and depth, their voices were so creative and light. What captivated me about this image of thought was laid out at the start of their first collaborative project, *Anti-Oedipus*:

> A schizophrenic out for a stroll is a better model than a neurotic lying on the analyst's couch. A breath of fresh air, a relationship with the outside world. Lenz's stroll, for example, as reconstructed by Büchner. This walk outdoors is different from the moments when Lenz finds himself closeted with his pastor,

who forces him to situate himself socially, in relationship to the God of established religion, in relationship to his father, to his mother. While taking a stroll
outdoors, on the other hand, he is in the mountains, amid falling snowflakes,
with other gods or without any gods at all, without a family, without a father or
a mother, with nature.[2]

This is how I learned to think – looking across Morecambe Bay towards
the mountains amid falling raindrops – a more modest experience than
Nietzsche's alpine wanderings – without situating myself in relation to
Heidegger or Deleuze or even Milbank's Augustine. I still have not read
Büchner, but this paragraph is sufficient to state what is essential: to think
is to engage in a relation with what is outside. It is to think with a series of
objects, to assemble and to synthesise – or, perhaps at the very least, to offer
a memoir in place of a meditation on the ontological structure of the histori-
cality of being. As Weil put it, 'We should like everything which is of value
to be eternal. Now, everything which is of value is the result of a meeting
(myself, in the first place: what chance was it that in the past brought about
the meeting between my father and mother!)'.[3] A thoughtful book records the
minutes of meetings. It is not a matter of clarifying or meditating on the ideas
that have formed one – these are, after all, unconscious – but of thoughtfully
engaging with the world from the perspective that they afford. If closeted
in a quadrangle with a pastor from the academic establishment, I would, of
course, be obliged to situate this work in relation to its immediate predecessors by offering a kind of literature review – but no, my role is now better
described as an entrepreneur in the knowledge industry (the university title of
'professor' has recently become somewhat anachronistic), and, as such, I live
by taking risks. Credit, critique, and creation are what I profess. But despite
the apparent difference in subject matters discussed, the fathers from whom
I diverge would be Heidegger, Deleuze and Milbank, the mothers Arendt and
Weil. For orienting the inquiry in this trilogy, there is but a single question,
'What is called thinking?' The substance of these books is a meditation on the
meaning of the temporality of being, the exteriority of being, and the divinity of being. And the conclusion, articulated in terms of credit and faith, is
everywhere yet nowhere – everywhere else but the paragraph you are reading,
and yet now here.

Part I

INTRODUCING ECONOMIC THEOLOGY

Chapter 1

Global Modernity: Economics and Theology

Human prosperity and wellbeing depend in large measure upon ongoing cooperation: mutual trust is the principal source of wealth. While trust in one's immediate neighbours is straightforward if it is deserved, trust in those whom one rarely meets or does not even meet at all is a far more momentous, yet rather more fragile, affair. The twentieth century has witnessed the extension of a cumulatively more momentous and yet increasingly fragile apparatus of trust: economic globalisation. Distant people may be trusted to the extent that they are incorporated into a framework for guiding conduct based on contract and exchange, monetary transactions, audited accounting, regulation and enforcement of trading standards, stable government, employment in corporations, and an infrastructure for transport and communication – all contributing towards the free movement of goods and services, workers and consumers, and capital investment. Such social institutions, consistent conduct, and allocations of trust make markets possible.[1] At the same time, such mobility also has the effect of uprooting people from previous frameworks of trust: when products, people, and investment capital are scattered far from the living communities in which they first emerged, modernisation and rationalisation tend to replace the prior customs that gave identity and orientation to human conduct. Trust in living traditions is undermined, being replaced by trust in products, procedures, systems, governments, and money.[2] Although economic globalisation offers utility, it may not, for all that, fulfil human needs for meaning and belonging. It is therefore hardly surprising that the twentieth century has also witnessed another momentous transformation of frameworks for trust throughout the majority world: the spread of world religions, or more specifically, Pentecostal Christianity, Roman Catholicism, indigenous Christianities, Sunni Islam, and neo-Hinduism, as well as minor religious movements. Whatever processes of secularisation may have been

2

operative in Europe, North America, China, and Japan, the twentieth century has largely witnessed the triumph of religion – a cultural transformation which, emerging from much longer histories, may perhaps prove to be rather more stable and enduring than economic globalisation. Moreover, in situations where the very existence of trust and community has been under threat, whether as a result of war or as a by-product of the disruptions wrought by economic globalisation, world religions have proved effective in re-establishing a basis for organised, meaningful conduct and mutual trust.

Nevertheless, for all the vibrant success of economic and religious globalisations, the intellectual disciplines that underpin them, economics and theology, have recently been less successful at inspiring trust. While mistrust of the religious motives of others has been a defining feature of both militant atheism and militant religion, mistrust within markets is the defining feature of financial crisis. For a generation that expects a poorer standard of living than that of its parents, the economic promise of the free market as the route to stability and prosperity is no longer quite so credible – free markets seem rather to generate inequality. Similarly, for a generation that experiences ethnic and cultural diversity on a daily basis, the religious promise of a common heart and mind united through a comprehensive theology no longer inspires quite so much faith – religious commitment only seems to generate, fragmentation and conflict. In the case of both economics and theology, then there is a notable gap between the consciousness of their savants who extol the powers of the market or the virtues of the true faith and the recalcitrant majority who remain unconverted and mistrustful of such promises. Economics and theology are disciplines in crisis, albeit crises often unacknowledged by their practitioners: economics aspires to scientific status basing its models on evidence, but it is largely unable to predict major economic events and so inspire stability and confidence; theology aspires to provide a universal and comprehensive vision of life, yet finds it impossible to unite believers from the same tradition in a single vision, let alone the wider world. Each of them offers an inadequate guide to the conduct of everyday life. Where economics fails to attract credit, theology fails to inspire faith. Even their own natural constituents may ignore them: firms and finance institutions seek out knowledge of economic life that is not yet grasped by the market, while religious movements endeavour to reinvent themselves with just a Bible or a Qur'an and a few borrowed insights from the reformers of previous centuries.

A COMMON DOMAIN

The principal idea motivating this study is that, in spite of appearances, economics and theology do indeed share a common domain: the ordering of trust.

It is not merely the case that all economic activity is dependent on trust. It is also the case that when economics describes human behaviour as regular, reliable, predictable, and automatic, it gives grounds for future expectations, enabling people to make rational decisions – that is to say, such rational expectations are the condition for enabling people to behave in ways which are themselves regular, reliable, predictable, and automatic, so confirming the grounds for trust. Moreover, initiating any economic activity is an offering of credit, whether as a monetary advance or as a gesture or token signifying that the value, significance, response, and reliability of things may be taken for granted. What actually happens in economic life depends on what is given credit. At the same time, religious traditions, for all their variety, transmit ordered ways of offering time and attention, care and evaluation, trust and cooperation. Whatever the explicit place of faith within such traditions, such ordered ways are adopted in faith, since there can be no possible verification of the value of an ordering of time. Credit and faith offer frameworks for trust. At times these might be relatively compatible; at times these might enter into direct competition.

This assertion of a common domain may at first seem counter-intuitive. Where economics is concerned with determinism and causation, theology is concerned with meaning and intention. A common sense view is that their realms cannot collide any more than the realms of facts and values. A difficulty with such common sense is that one only verifies facts if one has first decided they are valuable; one only adopts values if one hopes that they might be later instantiated in what is the case. A further difficulty is thrown up by the entities whose side of the boundary is hard to determine: God, truth, reason, trust, money and power, for example. However carefully one orders the framework of one's thinking to keep fact and value distinct, one still trusts that, in existence itself fact and value have been and may be reconciled. The distinction between them rests on certain questionable assumptions about what it means to think propagated by David Hume and Immanuel Kant; yet both of these authors still attempted to overcome the rationalist Enlightenment by means of a critique of knowledge in order to make room for belief or faith.

For our purposes, the distinction between economics and theology is historically rooted in the Enlightenment project of the conquest of nature. Starting from the assumption that human physiology has determinate needs and human labour has relatively uniform productive capacities, then the production, distribution, and consumption of goods and services might be known through its regularities like nature; it could be managed for the sake of health, satisfaction, and power.[3] Nevertheless, the very success of the conquest of nature constructed an economy which became less and less natural: the physiological model of the economy was disrupted by increased production enabled by inventions and the organisation of labour, by developing consumption preferences beyond natural needs, and by significant changes in the distribution wrought by management for the sake of profit.[4] To preserve the appearance of mastery, a restriction of attention to distribution alone, where labour only appears under the form of supply and need only appears under the form of preference or demand, was far more promising for the constitution of an economic science – and with a few assumptions about marginal changes in production and preference, equations could be constructed to represent the laws of the market, operating according to an inner necessity, like a machine. As a self-regulating machine, the economic realm would function independently of the theological realm of human meaning: economics could start to regard itself as a positive science. Having consolidated the separation between fact and value in the practical sphere, it was then a providential boon that such a machine appeared to reunite them: the market promotes human values – it provides opportunities for freedom to exchange as one wishes; it enacts justice by enabling the choice of exchanges that meet the wishes of all parties; and it ensures the most efficient distribution of resources by compensating the most those who create the most wealth. It was a further providential boon that such a market tended towards equilibrium between supply and demand, ensuring a stable order. If the market is a fact, it may also become a value: hence economics could start to regard itself as a normative science.

If such a pure market was more of an ideal rather than a reality,[5] trust in its perceived benefits created a moral and political obligation to extend and restructure economic life to conform more closely to this market: enclosing land; colonising near and distant places; ensuring the right to property; allowing freedom to trade and price fluctuations; removing prior social obligations that had restricted the mobility of people, goods, services, and capital; supplying an appropriate quantity of the means of payment as well as tax obligations; encouraging prudent self-management through bookkeeping; and erecting state authorities to oversee development as the march to freedom. In particular, landscapes and society were reconstructed to yield fuel, resources, food, and labour which could be extracted without payment – just as one does not offer monetary payment to a forest for timber, nor to a mine for metal, nor to land for crops, neither does one offer payment to a mother for bearing and raising the worker one employs or drafts into service. Promoting relations of trade, impossible without political preconditions, led first to colonialism. For those who were colonised in the service of economic extraction, the outcome was often landlessness, unemployment, illiteracy, poverty, disease, transportation, and servitude.[6] The political disruptions brought to prior social configurations, often advanced through bribery, patronage, slavery, debt, taxation, and military force, may have produced some chaos and instability, but the just and peaceful ideal of the pure market ensured that any blame for such chaos could be attributed to the remnants of non-market factors – thus justifying coercion in the name of liberty.[7] In all this, construction of the free, rational, public space of the market consisted in setting it free from the constraints of religious obligation: the independence of economics from theology has been a political value rather than a verifiable scientific or metaphysical fact.

Nevertheless, what is intended to guarantee the independence of the market is its machine-like necessity: as an immanent, self-regulating system, it needs no external guidance (beyond ensuring its freedom to operate), while it, in turn, may regulate the conduct of the material life of production and consumption.[8] Just as God was no longer appealed to in order to explain the natural order discovered by science, so God was no longer appealed to in order to legitimate the practical order regulated by economy. Yet, more recently, the ideal fact and value of a self-regulating market have started to collapse – one might mention economic crises in advanced market economies that were supposed to feature the stability of pure markets, advances in the discipline of economics itself to take into account behavioural, knowledge-based and financial factors,[9] deconstructions of the metaphysics of subject and object, the lessons learned from the historical experiences of developing countries, among many other factors. Perhaps it is time for the imagined independence of the economic and theological spheres to fall with it.

ECONOMIC LIFE

Economic life has never been consistently structured as a market because instead of instantaneous exchanges it is ordered by enduring temporal relations of credit and debt. Of course, in bookkeeping, these are subsumed under the model of exchangeable property as definite quantities due at definite times. This is, however, an illusion generated by the mode of representation: when I have issued credit, I no longer have mastery over what I might nominally consider my property; when I am in debt, I no longer have mastery over my own conduct because I am under obligation. As a network of credits and debts, the economy is less a distribution of private property than a set of contracted, mutual obligations. Bookkeeping records obligations not facts. Moreover, the act of offering credit is not ontologically reducible to the material advance, or the debt, because it involves a judgement that the recipient is creditworthy. Such creditworthiness consists in the recipient's intrinsic value, capacities to repay, sincere intentions and economic opportunities – factors which are a matter of trust, rather than reducible to facts or values (despite attempts to represent these as a credit score).

On this account, the modern economy is not simply an ordered exchange of private property, but an ordering of credit and trust by means of debt. The key idea to be explored in what follows is that in modern economies trust, instead of being enabled and structured by religious traditions, has come to be structured by debt.[10] A debt is a contractual obligation that imposes the expectation of settlement, usually for a specified sum of money and before a specified time. Where credit marks an investment in an uncertain future, and faith is trust in another's unforeseen conduct, these are ordered by debt when investment and trust are delimited to a precise expectation of money and time. The institution of debt builds trust where it is lacking: it extends credit and faith to relations where otherwise they would be absent. Moreover, the institution of debt extends the transmission of abstract value, as embodied in money, across societies, cultures, and institutions. For when a debt is transferred, it may function as a means of exchange: the same sum is still owed by the same debtor, but the creditor to whom it is owed has changed. Once ordered by debt, then, credit is usually conceived as simply its converse: for every creditor there is a debtor. Balancing each other out, credits and debts may be created out of nothing more than mutual promises. On this account, the vast sums of debt owed by households, corporations, financial institutions, and governments are simply a measure of the overall level of credit, of contracted trust, that is present in a society. Transferrable debts can be used effectively as money, and so constitute a measure of the liquid wealth present in a society. Trust and obligation, in practice, are mediated by debt. This has immense significance for both economics and theology.

While the phenomena of debt may be as ancient as human civilisation itself, their increasing usage as mobile vehicles for trust and obligation has wrought fundamental and ongoing transformations within modernity. In economic life, successive fundamental transformations have taken place since the time of Adam Smith, each facilitated by a massive injection of credit – that is, fresh promises – which have distanced advanced economies from any ideal model of a market:

- Capital investment has led to the emergence of large corporations, so that, instead of an economy consisting of a multitude of individual economic agents interacting solely through free market exchange, the conditions of economic life for suppliers, customers, and employees are significantly determined by the planning decisions taken within corporations.
- Following the World Wars I and II, the Great Depression, and the rise of the welfare state, government spending as a proportion of gross domestic product (GDP), funded significantly by borrowing, has increased to around 40% in many advanced economies.[11] Government decisions on allocating resources and rationing spending impact directly upon that proportion of the economy, while setting the market conditions for the wider economy.

- Deregulation in financial markets since the 1970s and 1980s, while intended to employ the market in place of the state in the allocation of scarce credit, has led to a substantial increase in the financial, insurance, and real estate sectors, funded by speculation based upon borrowing, so that a significant proportion of economic activity involves neither production nor consumption.[12]
- Consumer credit, supported by a widespread rise in asset prices due to increased borrowing, has rapidly increased over the same period, leading to expectations of a higher standard of living funded by debt: spending exceeds income.
- Finally, following the Great Financial Crisis of 2007–2008, government borrowing has increased once more, accompanied by massive injections of lending into the economy by the major central banks: financial stability rests purely on the interventions of these pivotal institutions.

As a result of these changes, what actually happens in economic life looks less and less like any classical model of a market: it is determined to an increasing extent by people and institutions paying their debts and fulfilling their obligations rather than by them simply expressing their preferences through exchange.

Much recent research on contemporary finance-dominated capitalism exposes, alongside any free market, a system of governing the conduct of others through their own self-government in line with external demands. Kathryn Tanner, cogently summarising such research in *Christianity and the New Spirit of Capitalism*, offers a bleak picture of a culture of self-exploitation in order to survive within a framework of ever-tightening competition and economic stagnation, at odds with those sunny celebrations of prosperity and liberty theoretically enabled by free market competition. The decisive difference can be found here: 'Unlike simple commercial markets for exchange (of the sort Adam Smith talked about), it is not just that one does not intend the good of others; what one does out of self-interest is not in fact good for them when markets are organized by direct personal rivalry'.[13] The pertinent difference between financial and other markets is that in finance, there is only one broad kind of good – expected profit measured against perceived risk – such that all exchanges involve a degree of direct rivalry. The current era is finance-dominated, not merely because finance occupies an increasing proportion of economic life or that it is often the most profitable, but because finance is decoupled from being an intermediary in the 'real economy' of goods and services while at the same time regulating conduct within such an economy through debt. Finance-dominated capitalism is debt-driven capitalism, controlling the conduct of corporations, governments and individuals alike. Tanner exposes the dark underside of 'market' discipline: efficiency savings are in fact achieved by shifting exposure of risks onto others while at the same time requiring more from them. Corporations are disciplined by finance in the form of both debt and equity, meeting interest payments or driving up shareholder value; individuals are disciplined by finance in the form of student loans, mortgages, car loans, credit cards, and payday loans; governments are disciplined by finance in the form of their costs of borrowing to fund their basic provision of services. Instead of corporations conducting themselves in the interests of all stakeholders or individuals conducting their lives in line with their preferences or governments conducting their policies in line with the will of the people, the demands of economic necessity – that is, the capacity to maintain and repay debt – takes priority over any other considerations. Even so, the demands of debt service may be so high as to destroy economic activity through bankruptcy. Profits are made by extracting wealth from others. Michael Hudson has explained the core dynamic in these terms:

> The financial business plan is to turn economies into a set of rent traps, carving out privileges to extract monopoly rent – and for banks to finance the purchase and sale of such rights at interest. Instead of lowering the cost of basic services to make economies more competitive, the effect is to load them down with debt to extract interest, fees, and *rentier* overhead. This destructive policy inflates the economy's cost structure by building in higher user fees for privatized monopolies and a rising flow of debt service to bankers, while imposing debt and rent deflation on the core economy.[14]

In other words, a debt-driven economy is neither a pure market, characterised by unrestricted rights of private property and freedom in exchange, nor purely capitalist, characterised by the accumulation of the means of production.[15]

On the one hand, then, the spread of markets is the spread of those political institutions under which trade can take place – themselves, like all state institutions, propagated by the threat of force. On the other hand, once markets are established, they undermine their organising principle of coordinating supply and demand through price signals alone. For markets coordinate relations between strangers; they operate through competition; competition leads to winners and losers; success leads to capture of market share; numbers of participants in the market shrink; and the remaining relationships are forged as contracts between privileged competitors. Enduring relationships of contract, debt, and obligation replace instantaneous relationships of free exchange; force is exercised by governance over oneself. When the winner-takes-all, the market is exclusively appropriated by a few, and the investment and creativity of all other agents is driven out. In this respect, an economic 'science' that consists in reducing the essentially temporal and collective phenomena of cyclical needs and enduring obligations to the expression of instantaneous individual preferences – primarily so that these might be quantified for the sake of constructing mathematical correlations – becomes further and further divorced from reality.[16] Even the reaction in economics against deductive theory, which consists in gathering extensive data for the sake of constructing more accurate models, merely amounts to a matter of 'curve-fit back-testing':[17] it seeks out consistent relations and behaviour to be found in the past, a local and unstable consistency that may collapse with each environmental, social, political, and technological change – not to mention the effects of changing conditions of credit, trust, and obligation. Under such conditions, economic models and theories may generate useful rules-of-thumb but fail to produce knowledge that can be confidently extrapolated. If the statistical correlations discovered by economists are signs that there are significant stories to be told about the interactions of resources, labour, corporations, regulations, governments, and financial products, the models themselves may only be a small part of such stories.[18] Economists may be well placed to tell these stories, but their stories often widely diverge; furthermore, geographers can tell different stories of the maximisation of unpaid work by humans, other living beings, landscapes, and ecosystems.[19] Economic knowledge, in such a context, does not consist in the models but in the integration of the diverging stories. For whatever relations endure between economic variables, they are accompanied by a set of practices where money does not change hands: extracting wealth from nature, from society, and even from people's souls.[20]

RELIGIOUS LIFE

In religious life, the phenomena of debt, modernisation, and rationalisation also change the context for the expression of commitment. For although religious commitment requires complete devotion of heart, mind, and soul, the task of providing for one's household requires undertaking employment or debt contracts that impose obligations on the conduct of everyday life. While theologies place emphasis on both the ultimate goals of human endeavour and the character, virtues or laws that should guide its conduct, economic life is largely a matter of fulfilling the objectives set out by one's employer by means of following specified routines, procedures, systems, and processes. Such institutionalised obligations are regulated by the demand for efficiency and effectiveness; traditional religious and moral teaching simply has little purchase here. Many of these roles and processes did not exist a century ago, and the heritage of past religious teaching, focused on building a community and its traditions of mutual care and hospitality, is not adapted to daily interactions with strangers in the modern workplace. Since the communal dimensions of life are already organised and institutionalised, all that remains for religion and morality to shape is the individual dimension of life. Even here, since one cannot offer anything if one has nothing to offer, the maximisation of self-interest in the form of the acquisition of monetary wealth, whether to accumulate profit or to repay debt, tends to take precedence. In the developed world, where social and economic lives are tightly structured by modern institutions, theology suffers a crisis of relevance during the working week to the extent that believers and conscientious workers become largely indistinguishable – guiding their conduct by the same principles and procedures. While a religious faith might contribute towards making one a trustworthy employee or a motivated economic agent, it does not give complete shape to that employment or economic conduct. Under such conditions, religion is reduced to the ordering of leisure time. In this respect, it becomes an option rather than an obligation, like the expression of a preference in consumption. To consciously choose to submit your life to Allah or to Christ is already to express an implicit disbelief: for, according to religious belief, Allah or Christ already own your life – any act of commitment would be merely a recognition of a pre-existing obligation. Yet in practice, even the most devout believer's life may be owned and regulated, in separable components, by family, school, employer, firm, team, state, lender, prison, hospital, or nursing home; by contracts, debts, advertising pressures, and social media sites; or by a few consumption preferences expressed through purchasing. Under such conditions, even the most devout believers largely commit themselves in imagination alone.

The time has come, therefore, to reconsider economic life no longer simply as a self-regulating market, nor simply as a set of political commitments enabling trade, but according to its theological dimension of the ordering of trust. Likewise, the time has come to reconsider religious life according to its economic dimension of offering credit.

Chapter 2

A Precursor

Economic life is produced, maintained, and regulated through words. Such words are not simply those of knowledge and understanding, following after events, explaining what, how, how much, and why. On the contrary, rituals, promises, property rights, contracts, signed documents, standards, certificates, debts, money, markets, and derivatives in some sense construct the reality to which they refer: they create wealth. Faith in such instituting words, whether spoken by oneself or by others, empowers the construction of economic reality. Taking words for granted, often unspoken ones, combines their power with efficiency: once credit is granted, one no longer needs to monitor and attend to the whole unfolding course of events. Rather like religious life, economic life is also conducted through credit and faith. Words construct our lives, whether for good or ill. At times, such words create wonderful opportunities, possibilities, experiences, and realities; at times, such words create collective fantasies that inspire or justify ignorant and reckless behaviour. Sometimes, both good and ill issue from the same words: the prospect of living inside a collective fantasy may seem wonderful; once the rules of the game are agreed, one is constrained to seek the specified objectives irrespective of other concerns; beyond the borders of one's attention chaos may be stirred. A critical philosophy of religion may seek to expose misplaced trust.

Words hold the power to create, judge, and occasionally redeem. On the one hand, they determine what we count as significant, how we direct our attention, what becomes visible to us, what we record, and what we trust. On the other hand, they also create the reality to which we subsequently pay attention. Yet when it comes to the life that is lived, collectively or individually, economically or religiously, there is perhaps a more urgent question than that of the nature, grounds, or techniques of creative power: it is a question of orientation towards the future. What life are we to construct through our words? Or, rather, how are we to reconstruct our actual lives through our words?

OPPRESSION AND LIBERTY

For here, the 'future destinies of humanity are not the sole object worthy of consideration', as Simone Weil wrote in 1934. Reality itself is more worthy of consideration than any imaginary future. If fanatics devote the meaning of their existence towards the progress of a collective cause, by contrast, words of critical analysis enable those who deploy them 'to escape the contagion of folly and collective frenzy by reaffirming . . . the original pact between the mind and the universe'.[1] That philosophy should seek to connect thinking to reality is hardly unusual; what is distinctive here is that this connection is treated like a pact as a matter of affirmation on the part of the mind. The task is not merely to represent reality; it is to affirm it and construct it through our instituting words.

Affirmation is a matter of trust: without investing in the existence of some bond between the mind and the universe, both mind and universe may be left to their own separate devices and may go their separate ways. Trust and investment establish a relation in practice. Yet what is affirmed is a relation that is original, one which already exists prior to affirmation. That there exists some prior relation may be inferred from the innumerable phenomena in which the world affects thought and thought affects action in the world.[2] Nevertheless, this is merely an inference: how well the mind and world relate, how much truth subsists in any thought, is not an immediate experience. Thinking is not the same as being. The relation between them, so pivotal to human existence, is at once beyond the power of immediate human knowledge and at the same time given to us and, moreover, given to us to the extent to which we, in turn, invest in it. The mind encounters reality in economic life: in living not merely in knowing. Credit and faith in some sense construct the reality to which they refer; yet, perhaps unlike collective fantasy, truthful credit and faith construct this relation to reality only by submitting to it and repeating it. Truth is to be affirmed.[3] The affirming mind gains power and efficiency to the extent to which it is oriented towards truth. A philosophy of religion may seek an ordering of trust that restores the mind to reality.

The predicament to be explored in this volume is helpfully set out by Weil who, in commenting on tendencies observable in the 1930s, offers an account all the more applicable to our own times now that such tendencies have achieved greater fruition. Nowadays, the pact between the mind and the universe is increasingly conceived in terms of success rather than in terms of value. The mind demonstrates its relation to reality when success is achieved;

but this relation is at best partial – there is little consideration of the value of
the endeavour in question.

> In short, in all spheres, success has become something almost arbitrary; it seems
> more and more to be the work of pure chance; and as it constituted the sole rule in
> all branches of human activity, our civilisation is invaded by an ever-increasing
> disorder, and ruined by a waste in proportion to that disorder.[4]

The diagnosis, here, is that the human mind, increasingly uprooted, has
achieved success at the expense of becoming less capable of recognising,
understanding, articulating, and affirming value. We go through the motions
of reasoning and reason more proficiently, but all the while our reasoning is
hollowed out and we pursue it frantically and desperately, somehow aware
that our reasoning is no longer oriented by that which matters.[5] Mission
statements and objectives are often arbitrary and thoughtless postulates of
value; while we may reason well about the means, we have largely lost the
rational expertise for evaluating ends. The notions that the highest values
devalue themselves, that Western modernity is the progress of nihilism, that
even philosophy itself has achieved clarity and rigour at the expense of any
thoughtful way of orienting itself by what matters have been a commonplace
of European philosophy since Friedrich Nietzsche and Martin Heidegger.[6]
Weil, however, located the cause of the problem not in the historical progress
of ideas but in their external conditions, not in metaphysics but in work:

> Everywhere, in varying degrees, the impossibility of relating what one gives
> to what one receives has killed the feeling for sound workmanship, the sense
> of responsibility, and has developed passivity, neglect, the habit of expecting
> everything from outside, the belief in miracles. . . . The worker has not the feel-
> ing of earning his living as a producer; it is merely that the undertaking keeps
> him enslaved for long hours every day and allows him each week a sum of
> money which gives him the magic power of conjuring up at a moment's notice
> ready-made products, exactly as the rich do. . . . Generally speaking, the rela-
> tion between work done and money earned is so hard to grasp that it appears as
> almost accidental, so that labour takes on the aspect of servitude, money that
> of a favour.[7]

Once one no longer grasps the relation between the mind and the universe,
action that claims to be rational constructs an alienated world. Dependent on
social and economic processes they do not understand, people lose orientation and forget how to live. Willing is replaced by wishing. Instead of directly
relating actions to their effects, the mind relates to the universe, whether in
production or consumption, through the medium of money. Yet money does
not think and is itself poorly understood. Its power to command labour and

purchase products appears magical: a wish is transformed into reality as if money endowed wishes with a mysterious power. The outcome for those deprived of action, Weil saw, was an age of superstition:

> On all hands one is obsessed by a representation of social life which, while differing considerably from one class to another, is always made up of mysteries, occult qualities, myths, idols and monsters: each one thinks that power resides mysteriously in one of the classes to which he has no access, because hardly anybody understands that it resides nowhere, so that the dominant feeling everywhere is that dizzy fear which is always brought about by loss of contact with reality. Each class appears from the outside as a nightmare object. In circles connected with the working-class movement, dreams are haunted by mythological monsters called Finance, Industry, Stock Exchange, Bank, etc.; the bourgeois dream about other monsters which they call ringleaders, agitators, demagogues; the politicians regard the capitalists as supernatural beings who alone possess the key to the situation, and *vice versa*; each nation regards its neighbours as collective monsters inspired by a diabolical perversity.[8]

With less and less direct contact with reality, political decisions are grounded on mirages and the shifting sands of rumours. If another formulation of the task of modern philosophy of religion is the critique of superstition, its task is not complete when the world is exorcised of occult powers, spirits, and gods: there may still remain unreasoning fear of the imagined powers of others or of institutions. Perhaps superstition today includes the hopes and fears invested in celebrities, foreigners, or people of sexual, cultural, and religious difference; yet it also includes the hopes and fears invested in institutions such as money, businesses, banks, universities, governments, nations, and social media platforms. If in the chapters that follow there will be an endeavour to demystify money, markets, and banking denuding them of imagined occult powers, our task will also be to re-mystify them: to expose how they belong among the words and rituals which construct the reality in which we dwell. They express and may be understood by an economic theology.

Weil's diagnosis went further: when irrational opinions take the place of clearly understood ideas, acquiring force acquires much greater urgency than knowing the truth.[9] Concerns about value are set aside in favour of more urgent concerns about success: this is the root of oppression. An ultimate outcome of such fear is that the economic struggle is far less about building up than of conquering:

> The means employed in the economic struggle – publicity, lavish display of wealth, corruption, enormous capital investments based almost entirely on credit, marketing of useless products by almost violent methods, speculations with the object of ruining rival concerns – all these tend to undermine the foundations of our economic life far more than to broaden them.[10]

Likewise, she warns that the extension of credit undermines any tendency of markets to establish equilibrium, while the extension of speculation separates profit from capital accumulation.[11] Instead of being a free market capitalist system – an imaginary system of liberty – economic life is ruled in practice by an insatiable quest for power. In other words, the institutions that we have taken as those regulated by liberty may in fact be driven by quite different principles and dynamics. Our aim, then, is to offer a different ontological description of economic reality: to use words creatively to change what we count as significant, how we direct our attention, what becomes visible to us, what we record, and what we trust, in the hope of restoring some relation between thinking and being.

PHILOSOPHICAL METHOD

Weil proposed a philosophical solution to this problem of success without value: one must distinguish that which is directed by force without under-standing from that which is directed by understanding without force. This is the Platonic philosophical task of the pursuit of a metaphysics of value, where what is valued is understanding in and for itself (a task to be undertaken in *Metaphysics of Trust*). If this task has traditionally been pursued in terms of abstract metaphysical concepts, the danger, here, is one of constructing an autonomous system of signs and concepts which loses all meaningful rela-tion to the reality that is signified. Weil attributed the origin of a different approach to philosophy to Francis Bacon:

> he substituted in a flash of genius the veritable charter expressing the relations between man and the world: 'We cannot command Nature except by obeying her'. This simple pronouncement ought to form by itself the Bible of our times. It suffices to define true labour, the kind which forms free men, and that to the very extent to which it is an act of conscious submission to necessity.[12]

Truth, in Weil's philosophy, is not acquired through reflection but through purposeful action within the world – it is here that one engages with reality.[13] The specific feature of 'true labour', here, is that one takes a mechanical necessity, indifferent to human interests, and uses it as an instrument of one's own ends. Weil's favourite example is Descartes' discussion of a blind man's stick in the introduction to his *Optics*: it is at once an obstacle that separates the individual from what is to be perceived and a tool of perception, such that a practised hand will no longer notice the resistance and vibrations in the stick but will perceive the object encountered through the stick itself.[14] When it comes to action, Weil's preferred example is the lever, for by means of a lever, the smallest force can overcome the greatest: through ingenuity, that that separates can become a tool enabling reconnection.[15] Understanding can overpower and reorient force.

Now our dependence on Weil here will be somewhat metaphorical: our concern is with reasoning at work rather than 'pure' reason fixed under a microscope. Reality does not only consist in the physical environment which we may perceive or interact with using our tools but also contain all that we construct through our words, credit, and faith. Yet the truth about any ritual or right, any promise or contract, any institution or financial instrument – and, indeed, any metaphysical concept – is not necessarily to be gleaned from those words which construct it. Its reality also consists in its conditions and consequences, its orientations and values, the experiences it gives and the possibilities it offers. All this becomes invisible when words are treated in abstraction. Even while actively thinking, the mind, directed by the words used, may not pay attention to the wider reality. G.W.F. Hegel offered a useful analogy for this often-overlooked truth:

> Let us imagine a man who, from motives of revenge – perhaps justified revenge, in that he may himself have suffered unjustly – set light to someone else's house; this at once means that a connection is established between the immediate deed and a train of circumstances, albeit external circumstances, which have nothing to do with the original deed regarded purely in isolation. The deed as such consisted, let us say, in applying a small flame to a small portion of a beam. What this deed itself does not accomplish takes place of its own accord; the ignited portion is connected with further sections of the beam, these in turn are connected with the timberwork of the entire house, which is itself connected with other houses, and a widespread conflagration [results]; this conflagration destroys the property of many other people apart from that of the individual against whom the revenge was directed, and it may even cost many of them their lives. All this was not part of the original deed itself, nor of its perpetrator's intention. But the same action contains yet another general implication: in the intention of its instigator, it was purely a means of gaining revenge on an individual by destroying his property; but it is also a crime, which carries its punishment with it. The perpetrator may not have been conscious of this, and it may not have been his remotest intention, but it is nevertheless the universal and substantial essence of the deed itself, and a necessary consequence of it.[16]

In this example, the truth about the deed only arrives with the universal point of view which condemns it as a crime; for Hegel, truth is known through judging falsehood, wrong, and illusion. One has to build a perspective on a perspective, a thought about thought – for human, life is not built out of houses and fires alone, but out of the creative power of words and our thoughts about them.[17] For our purposes, if money and the economic system are that which separate reality from understanding, success from value, being from thinking, then an understanding of the necessary operation of money and the economic system might serve as that that helps to re-establish the relation.

Philosophy may be pursued by the use of tools, even if it starts out blind, unable to grasp all the conditions and consequences. Essential thinking does not require a complex system of signs, but a series of striking or homely examples invoked to address a problem.[18] Once pure concepts alone have proven inadequate for the task of noticing what matters, then one may turn to entities that are at once points of contact with reality and obstacles to understanding: in this case, the actual episodes of thinking performed by others, which are already the product of reality, as well as to actual economic institutions, which connect thinking to being in practice – such may become the units and tools of thought, its occasions, provocations, or cases to explore. As a philosophical inquiry, the method adopted here is in a certain sense dialectical: the material to be handled is not economic life as such, but views and perspectives on it; moreover, enlightenment consists in shifting to a different level by forming a perspective on a perspective – exploring the trust which can be placed rather than the truth-claims themselves. While much philosophy is pursued through conversations with other philosophers, and so is largely reliant on agreement or intuition to check whether thinking is grounded on being – an intuition which too often takes place in the relative vacuum of an office or seminar room rather than out and about in the world – an attempt has been made to ground philosophy here, ironically, by engaging largely with the thought of economists. Yet this one-way conversation is not strictly a matter of economics since there is no attempt to give a working model of economic life; the discourse is not at the same level. Our concern is not with the given but with thought about the given. Moreover, our aim is not to produce judgements for some economic views and against others, but to use economic thought, in its convergence and divergence from reality, as a lens through which to understand the vicissitudes of thought itself. Unlike Hegelian dialectic, our method is not primarily negation or critique – it does not stand above economists to judge them but below them to learn from them. Yet the method is a selective appropriation, participation, and offering of thought insofar as it shows glimpses of a relation to reality. Handling such objects, blind as one may be, may facilitate perception of the world through the resistance it offers to thought; yet this is an acquired skill, for the reality felt always differs from what is said. The work of thinking is not the same as any content of thought. Gilles Deleuze puts it like this:

> What we're plagued by these days isn't any blocking of communication, but pointless statements. But what we call the meaning of a statement is its point [literally: the interest it presents]. That's the only definition of meaning, and it

comes to the same things as a statement's novelty. You can listen to people for hours, but what's the point?. . . That's why arguments are such a strain, why there's never any point in arguing. You can't just tell someone what they're saying is pointless [literally: it is of no interest]. So you tell them it's wrong. But what someone says is never wrong, the problem isn't that some things are wrong, but that they're stupid or irrelevant. That they've already been said a thousand times. The notions of relevance, necessity, the point of something, are a thousand times more significant than the notion of truth. Not as substitutes for truth, but as the measure of the truth of what I'm saying.[19]

The dimension of reality for which one is groping here is value itself: the point or interest of something, in relation to some problem or circumstance. While values can be directly represented, the value of such values cannot. Yet value may be perceived indirectly through disvalue. Trust may then be allocated through appropriation and synthesis of very partial insights.

BRIEF OUTLINE

The brief discussions that follow aim to shed light on the divergence between mind and world. Taking up matters of considerable controversy, they do not seek to settle questions of fact: on these matters, entire book-length studies usually offer insufficient grounds for fully trusting the opinions expressed. Philosophy has a more urgent task than establishing evidence and argument. For our premises and perspectives are grounded in what we have noticed and counted as significant. Before we can argue and part company, I need to take you on a tour of this city of caves in which we live, to show you what I have noticed in the perspectives of others, whether familiar or unfamiliar. Yet this is no journalism, gathering sights by location, chronology, or theme: the path to be taken is determined in advance by the problems to be addressed. Thoughtfulness is expressed in structure. Argument can largely be postponed until the conclusions: a philosopher is better understood as someone who understands what matters in things rather than as one who wins arguments, or as someone with who evaluates real problems rather than someone who engages in abstract reasoning. A philosophical gadfly merely seeks to provoke thought, not produce knowledge; to cultivate a different understanding and expose a different dimension of reality, not empower particular opinions. The intention here is to discover tools through which the relation between the mind and world can be felt and affirmed, even if not adequately stated. Thinking through the causes of the separation of the mind and the world may offer a way of understanding and affirming its prior connection. Our task is to understand how, in economic life, mind and world have gone their separate ways.

The predicament is this: thoughtlessness rests in equilibrium. One extends credit to instituting words because they are given, familiar and facilitate stable functioning within a wider ecological, economic and cultural environment. It is not that a thoughtless person lacks words, self-expression or imagination, combining thoughts as they wish; it is rather that these words are produced in line with an unspoken set of deep presuppositions which are produced out of necessity. A television host or anchor freely chatters to all, but their speech is highly regulated so as not to challenge or offend the full diversity of viewers (except, perhaps, a few philosophers or theologians). There is no possibility of engaging with the actual conditions of existence or the vested interests maintained by these. Thoughtless words are uttered or repeated rather than deeply understood; they lack sense. Some may even go in search of the sense that should belong to such words by right, given that intuitively one feels compelled to grant them credit or repeat them; yet making explicit what is implicit is not sufficient to escape thoughtlessness – the compulsion to credit such words may remain unchanged. Words are spoken or trusted for reasons that remain unconscious. This condition of shallow consciousness is helpful and necessary in nearly all circumstances and respects – until it is necessary to exercise real agency when the world itself provokes a crisis.

Thoughtfulness involves escape from an automatic process which produces trust in a cycle of clichés, presuppositions, concepts, maxims, principles, rituals, and promises. The free mind does not easily achieve its freedom by theoretical reflection, but rather by spending itself by engaging with the conditions of reality and the problems they pose. The philosophical method advanced here works like this:

1. Find what is problematic in life: some lived tension which disturbs equilibrium and demands thought.
2. Seek to suspend some of the given clichés, presuppositions, and norms which structure and reproduce an inherited consciousness.
3. Explore how those whose words instituted such presuppositions may also have articulated an awareness of the lived tension.
4. Rethink inherited presuppositions as practical yet imperfect solutions to lived problems.
5. Observe what new problems and tensions arise from each solution.

This method is far clearer when it is practised rather than merely theoretically articulated. For example, Part II 'Markets and Money: Dynamics of Thought' is structured according to the following rationale:

1. Economic problem: How can trust and cooperation be extended among strangers for the sake of economic welfare? A common solution: promises,

debts, and obligations facilitate a market. Yet how can such obligations and liabilities be trusted? How to resolve the tension between extending credit and making it trustworthy? Solution: payment is valid when it is made with the debt of a trustworthy authority whose very existence depends on the maintenance of its own reputation: a bank. Yet banking consists in the activity of borrowing in the short-term to lend in the long-term – while the books are balanced at any one time, a bank itself is far from equilibrium over time. Economic life is characterised by a lived tension: the condition of possibility of an extended market, which theoretically tends towards equilibrium, is a banking and financial system that simulates balance while itself being far from equilibrium.

2. Suspension: economics should not be exclusively concerned with market exchange, 'the economics of stuff', but also with the changing conditions of credit, 'the economics of stuff happens'.

3. Exploration: if Adam Smith instituted the idea of markets as self-regulating systems, what did Smith say about economic conditions far from equilibrium? What can his account show us of the tension between the market as a machine in which to participate and the market as a machine to be carefully tended and managed? How is this theoretical tension lived out in practice by those whose conduct is at once freely chosen (or far from equilibrium) and determined by market forces (or adapted to equilibrium)?

4. Solution: counting values in terms of prices offers a solution by which chosen conduct can conform to external forces. The world can be rationally managed and controlled to the extent that it can be quantified.

5. New problem: the effort towards universal quantification is the product of an automatic process consisting of money, banking, finance, and debt, which reproduces a thoughtless consciousness of life in terms of success and without regard to value or its conditions of existence. Thoughtlessness is actively produced and sustained by a machinic process far from equilibrium.

Part III 'Exploitation and Constraint: Dynamics of Conduct' is structured according to the following rationale:

1. Political problem: What real conditions of possibility of economic life are excluded from consideration by a restriction of attention to what can be traded in markets?

2. Suspension: quantification and modelling, which give an account of those aspects of life that can be managed and controlled, should be suspended when it comes to handling perspectives and ideas, those aspects of life in which one participates (where philosophy offers more appropriate reasoning), and the investment of trust and credit, those aspects of life which can

only be offered, not appropriated (where theology offers more appropriate reasoning).

3. Exploration: if Pierre-Joseph Proudhon was the first modern thinker to articulate that 'private property is impossible', that an increase in value cannot be appropriated without contradiction, how did he articulate the theoretical tension between production and appropriation? How did Weil extend his analysis of the lived tensions and contradictions within capitalism? How can one reconcile being a master of one's own private property with the dependence of that property on inherited and social conditions as well as participation within a finite ecosystem?

4. Solution: a way of evading consciousness of such lived tensions is achieved through abstracting from reality by appropriation, substituting for reality by exchange, and anticipating value solely in the form of profit. This thoughtless solution is achieved at the cost of environmental destruction, inequality, and shallow consciousness.

5. New problem: a thoughtless economic system, under these conditions, is bound by conflicting constraints. Private appropriation of wealth must grow exponentially, yet it has insuperable limits. Wealth is to be extracted from others, yet wealth can no longer be extracted from those who no longer have any. Short-term interests take priority, yet they cannot be maintained if long-term interests are not served.

Part IV 'Finance and Salvation: Dynamics of Faith' is structured according to the following rationale:

1. Theological problem: What is a reliable basis for the exercise of trust within economic life?

2. Suspension: if markets are imperfect and far from equilibrium, neither practices of exchange nor regulations governing exchange offer a sufficient basis for trust.

3. Exploration: if John Maynard Keynes was the first to articulate how collective behaviour under conditions of mistrust undermines the functioning of markets, what did he say about finance as the set of institutions designed to extend and intensify markets? How did the successors to Keynes articulate the role and function of finance in shoring up trust?

4. Solution: an exclusive, mutual credit relation between commercial banks (as institutional representatives of the economic dimension of life), governments (as institutional representatives of the political dimension of life), and central banks (as institutional representatives of creditworthiness) makes trust possible in the wider financial and market systems.

5. New problem: these institutions are caught in the dilemma between inflating overall debt (and with it constraint) to maintain the failing stability of

the current system or inflating currency and losing the creditworthiness (and with it obligation) which enables the entire economy to function.

A problem remains outstanding: what is a truly secure basis for trust and cooperation, one that is adapted to the real conditions of existence? What are the conditions of existence for trust? For that problem, another book will be needed.

Chapter 3

Economic Theology

In one respect, the role of money in modern life is utterly mundane: money is passive, sterile, lifeless, and lacking in distinctive qualities of interest. In another respect, money symbolizes value: the accomplishments and trans-formations of the modern world facilitated by money would seem little short of miraculous to anyone of former generations called back to life to witness the modern spectacle. Economic theology is the endeavour to consider these apparently incompatible dimensions of contemporary existence together. The conception of economic theology to be explored here derives, in distinction from some other recent versions,[1] from a deconstruction of Karl Marx's early writings.[2] With a heavy dose of irony, Marx described the power of money in a property-owning society based around market exchange in theological terms as divine. It is worth quoting parts of his notes at length since they constitute the first substantial intervention in the field:

> By possessing the *property* of buying everything, by possessing the property of appropriating all objects, money is thus the *object* of eminent possession. The universality of its *property* is the omnipotence of its being. It is therefore regarded as omnipotent. Money is the *procurer* between man's need and the object, between his life and his means of life. But *that which* mediates my life for me, also mediates the existence of other people for me. For me it is the *other* person. . . .
>
> That which is for me through the medium of *money* – that for which I can pay (i.e., which money can buy) – that am *I myself*, the possessor of the money. The extent of the power of money is the extent of my power. Money's properties are my – the possessor's – properties and essential powers. Thus, what I am and am capable of is by no means determined by my individuality. I *am* ugly, but I can buy for myself the most beautiful of women. Therefore I am not *ugly*, for the effect of *ugliness* – its deterrent power – is nullified by money. I, according to

my individual characteristics, am *lame*, but money furnishes me with twenty-four feet. Therefore I am not lame. I am bad, dishonest, unscrupulous, stupid; but money is honored, and hence its possessor. Money is the supreme good, therefore its possessor is good. Money, besides, saves me the trouble of being dishonest: I am therefore presumed honest. I am *brainless*, but money is the *real brain* of all things and how then should its possessor be brainless? Besides, he can buy clever people for himself, and is he who has power over the clever not more clever than the clever? Do not I, who thanks to money am capable of *all* that the human heart longs for, possess all human capacities? Does not my money, therefore, transform all my incapacities into their contrary?. . . Money is the alienated *ability of mankind.*

That which I am unable to do as a *man*, and of which therefore all my individual essential powers are incapable, I am able to do by means of *money*. Money thus turns each of these powers into something in itself it is not – turns it, that is, into its *contrary*.

If I long for a particular dish or want to take the mail-coach because I am not strong enough to go by foot, money fetches me the dish and the mail-coach: that is, it converts my wishes from something in the realm of imagination, translates them from their meditated, imagined or desired existence into their *sensuous*, *actual* existence – from imagination to life, from imagined being into real being. In effecting this mediation, [money] is the *truly creative* power.

No doubt the *demand* also exists for him who has no money, but his demand is a mere thing of the imagination without effect of existence for me, for a third party, for the [others], and which therefore remains even for me *unreal* and *objectless*. The difference between effective demand based on money and ineffective demand based on my need, my passion, my wish, etc., is the difference between *being* and *thinking*, between the idea which merely *exists* within me and the idea which exists as a *real object* outside of me.[3]

Marx explores how money miraculously emancipates its bearer from the constraints of their individual nature as well as their social bonds. Others may not be inclined to respond to me as a person, my powers of persuasion, or the urgency of my needs, but they will respond to my money insofar as it offers to bring the means of life to meet their needs. Money promises redemption from want. Yet, even more than this, money appears to possess the divine power of turning ideas into reality. It appears to hold a complementary role to truth: while truth is that in respect of which thinking may be conformed to being, money is that through which being is conformed to thinking. As such, money, as a measure of value, could become as significant to philosophy as truth. One may think whatever one wishes to no effect; spending money, however, may change reality in line with one's wishes. The question before us, then, is that of the nature of this power.

A Marxist might say that money has no such power: to assert that it does is a matter of mystification. No one really believes that money accomplishes anything; people merely act as if it does. For whether money is treated as a commodity itself which may be owned and exchanged or as a unit of account in terms of which prices may be measured or as a store of value for the purpose of saving purchasing power between exchanges, money itself is a lifeless tool having no power beyond that which humans do with it. As Marx puts it, money is the alienated ability of mankind: one can only accomplish with money something which in fact is accomplished by other human beings. The dish and the mail-coach are prepared and offered by others: the power represented in money is the creative power of human labour. The power of money is easily demystified. One can simply distinguish between class perspectives: for the owner of money, it appears as though money accomplishes one's wishes, so having access to money remains a priority; by contrast, the one who works for money knows full well that it is their own efforts which convert another's wishes into realities. The power of money is an ideological fantasy of the bourgeois; reality is properly understood by the working class. In reality, one supposes, there is only the power of person over person, or human over nature.

The matter cannot be resolved quite as simply as this. It is not the possession of money, as if it were some badge of authority, which achieves deference: it is handing it over, spending, or investing it. When hoarded, money is a lifeless tool; when transferred to others, it exercises its power. In the ideal market, class perspectives become alternating roles: the money for which I work, I will come to spend in turn. Furthermore, labour alone cannot explain reality: the labour and creativity of others do not realise my wishes unless I have money to pay for them: they do not suffice alone. Likewise, reality cannot be explained by the causal power of preferences: as Marx points out, my wishes remain unreal while I have no money to fulfil them. Money facilitates cooperation between the preferences of some and the goods and services offered by others. Without money, neither preferences alone nor labour alone, nor even their combination (without the agreement of a common mind), can ensure that ideas are converted into realities. Money, therefore, does indeed have a distinctive power: the power to command labour. People produce goods and services for the sake of money. Money can extend cooperation beyond shared intentions and objectives and even beyond any mutual complementarity of wants as found in barter exchange. Money makes a market possible. It facilitates participation in a common institution, economic life organised as a market, beyond individual intentions to appropriate particular goods and services. The power of money is a social power, the power of cooperation: it facilitates agreement expressed through practice. Money really does, in faith and truth, possess an extraordinary transformative power.

What needs to be explained, then, is why people produce goods and services for the sake of money. A free market advocate might say that there are many possible reasons for seeking money according to different circumstances: one may seek money in order to spend it in turn on realising one's own preferences in the purchase of goods and services. One may seek money in order to pay one's obligations, such as rents, tithes, bills, taxes, or fines. One may seek money in order to pay one's debts. One may seek money as a store of value for the sake of its liquidity, its ability to be used for whatever unforeseen need arises in the future. One may seek it in order to gift it or spend it on others. Each of these, in different circumstances and proportions, contributes to the demand for money, ensuring that money retains its value by being in demand. There will always be some demand for money in a market economy, even if a particular currency may fall out of favour. Money, on this account, has the power to command labour because it is itself in demand.

This account is also incomplete, for money is not only a commodity within a market; it is what makes a market possible. One cannot easily exchange things without money as an intermediary. In one respect, the power of money is reducible to the power of exchange. In another respect, the capacity to exchange is facilitated by the power of money. To explain the demand for money within a market is not to explain the power of market exchange itself, facilitated by money. Taking the market as a given presupposition, explanations run in circles. For whatever reason, people demand money because they expect that money will be acceptable by others: in market exchange, in meeting obligations, in the payment of debts, or for its liquidity. The power of money derives from its acceptability; its acceptability derives from the power of money. When it comes to explaining the existence of a market itself, it is difficult to explain how such a circuit arises. Experience tells us that money is accepted; accepting money is a matter of trust.

A market society does require a common mind in one respect: it requires a generalised trust in markets and money. Money holds value, remains in demand, and facilitates market exchange to the extent that money is trusted. Moreover, as a matter of trust, people do not simply trust money in general nor money as a concept, let alone trust the concept of market exchange which emerges after the fact. People trust specific currencies and specific representations of such currencies, whether in the form of coins, notes, bank records, payment cards, cryptocurrencies, or whatever. People trade in highly specific markets devoted to particular goods and located in particular institutions. Such trust is grounded in the prudent conduct of the specific institutions charged with responsibilities for issuing, maintaining, and regulating each currency and market. Money as an abstract concept bears no particular power: one cannot spend the concept of money. The power one wields when one spends money is the trust which is invested in specific institutions responsible for money. In this respect, the power of money does not simply rest on a mystification; it lies within the power of trust. Money and markets offer a framework for ordering trust.

It is at this level that one encounters an overlap between the domains of religion and economics. Religious life offers a framework for orienting the distribution of time and attention, care and evaluation, trust and obligation. Likewise, economic life offers a support or infrastructure for orienting trust and obligation, which, in turn, have effects upon care and evaluation, as well as time and attention. Where faith makes life into an ascesis, a continual process of reorientation of trust, credit offers a support for life, a framework which can be taken for granted. In both cases, trust is not merely something to be appropriated, something which can be bought with money, nor is it merely something in which to participate, to be entered into as a privilege or right. Trust is something that must be actually offered and earned. Such an offering of trust, in conditions of uncertainty, is the theological dimension of life.

Marx himself conceived of this theological dimension of economic life in terms of alienation: money is the alienated ability of humankind. Purchase with money exchanges ownership: it alienates what the person has done from the person herself. His model, here, was Ludwig Feuerbach's theory of religious projection:

> All these consequences are implied in the statement that the worker is related to the *product of his labour* as to an *alien* object. For on this premise it is clear that the more the worker spends himself, the more powerful becomes the alien world of objects which he creates over and against himself, the poorer he him-self – his inner world – becomes, the less belongs to him as his own. It is the same in religion. The more man puts into God, the less he retains in himself. The worker puts his life into the object; but now his life no longer belongs to him but to the object. Hence, the greater this activity, the more the worker lacks objects. Whatever the product of his labour is, he is not. Therefore, the greater this product, the less is he himself. The *alienation* of the worker in his product means not only that his labour becomes an object, an *external* existence, but that it exists *outside him*, independently, as something alien to him, and that it becomes a power on its own confronting him. It means that the life which he has conferred on the object confronts him as something hostile and alien.[4]

The starting point, here, is the assumption of the classical economists that labour is the 'soul of value': the life of the worker is objectified in his prod-uct, and his product belongs to his employer. In this way, the product appears as something alien, something which might need to be purchased. Marx's main concern, in these passages, is how the endeavours of the workers increase the quantity of products on the market, so decreasing their prices and consequently the wages of labour: workers produce their own poverty. This, of course, is an effect of market relations on supply and demand; it does not explain how a market is possible nor the specific power of money. One must go further: objectification and alienation are achieved by exchange itself, by selling one's labour. It does not matter whether one's subjective ideas are objectified by being represented outside of oneself, as in religious life, or whether one's vital power is objectified by means of the product of labour, as in economic life: a similar logic is perceived to hold. On this account, money is the alienated ability of humankind. Recovering that ability, so Marxist reasoning goes, workers in a communist society would inevitably produce prosperity in place of poverty. Released from its weakening through alienation, the creative will or labour power of humanity could presumably accomplish truly wonderful things if it could be liberated from money. Yet there is little evidence that this has ever been the case.

There are good reasons for suspecting that this theological picture that retracts creative power back into humanity is rather incomplete: humanity rarely displays such creativity, whether as single individuals or as a collective based around a shared mind, unless money is involved. The contents of the human heart, whether expressed in thought, labour, or art, rarely show much propensity for truth, morality, justice, or beauty. Self-mastery is insufficient as a condition for power. As Marx himself puts it, 'That which I am unable to do as a *man*, and of which therefore all my individual essential powers are incapable, I am able to do by means of *money*'. That which we are unable to do as a species, and of which our collective essential powers are incapable, we have been able to accomplish by means of money. It is not simply the case that I can employ all the essential powers of humanity which are on the market. On the contrary, the market facilitates the creation of goods and services which would not have been possible without it. Far from being an obstacle, money amplifies powers which are barely noticeable without its assistance. The theological model of alienation is inadequate to account for such enhancement: it is not the case that all the essential powers of humanity are present from the outset, implicit within the human subject, essence, or species, awaiting expression. Money offers a support for human endeavour which does not derive straightforwardly from human capacities: it catalyses and extends trust. This is the creative power of money which requires a theological investigation.

What happens in a market is not merely alienation: it is committing one's cares to the responsibility of others. One may find within religion other models than alienation and projection; one may find models for credit and faith. Economic life also involves offering credit: handing over one's cares and responsibilities to others. Three voices from the gospels may exemplify this religious model of credit. Upon Jesus' baptism, a voice came from heaven, 'You are my Son, the Beloved; with you I am well pleased' (Mark 1.11). The origins of this heavenly voice are rather obscure; the authority which it delegates cannot be authenticated. Nevertheless, the message itself, devoid of context as it is, conveys the endowment of trust from an unknown source – a trust that made a decisive difference to Jesus who endeavoured to live up to it in his ministry. It is an offering of credit. A fuller context is available in our next example, the good Samaritan who gave two denarii to the innkeeper saying, 'Take care of him; and when I come back, I will repay you whatever more you spend' (Luke 10.35). The Samaritan entrusts the innkeeper with responsibility to care for the wounded man, including determining what expenditure may be appropriate. In this case, the money handed over expresses trust. Whether the innkeeper is inclined to trust in heavenly voices or those of Samaritans is less relevant; the innkeeper at least trusts the value of money. At the same time, the Samaritan endows the innkeeper with trust by handing over money. A third example comes from the story of Zacchaeus, the chief tax collector, addressed in his vantage point of a sycamore tree by Jesus: 'Zacchaeus, hurry and come down; for I must stay at your house today' (Luke 19.5). In this case, the expenditure falls on Zacchaeus alone, who is entrusted with responsibility to host and care for the needs of Jesus and his travelling band of followers. Jesus entrusts himself as a guest in the house of another, dependent upon Zacchaeus's capacity to assess and provide whatever care is appropriate.

These are examples of an elementary economic relation which is neither a simple exchange nor a contract nor a debt: it is endowing one's cares to the responsibility of another. Such trust is present, to one degree or another, in every act of purchase, every investment and every gift. There may be further mechanisms for extending the endowment of such trust, such as trading standards and regulations, pledges of collateral, audited accounts, and reports accounting for expenditure. Yet, whatever the preconditions for trust, economic activity is initiated by such an endowment of trust. The creative power of money is not simply its ability to command labour, endowing its possessor with authority to specify the precise good or service to be provided. The creative power of money derives from the fact that it is handed over – that, without a common mind achieved through command or persuasion, the recipient may be persuaded to take responsibility for that about which one cares. At the limit of human relations, in the form of a bequest, the recipient is entrusted to care about that which matters, irrespective of whether the donor has a grasp of what needs to be done. Such trust is often necessary in old age as well as childhood. Finally, beyond human relations, supreme trust is expressed in worship, entrusting the deity to care about that which matters, placing oneself at the mercy of a heavenly host. In this, as well as in the most commercial of relations, one does effectively place oneself as a guest in another's house. There are three dimensions of such credit:

- One endows another with a power over oneself in the form of a capacity to affect what one cares about.

- One entrusts another with the responsibility to care about what one cares about, even though one is aware that the other may fail in some respect, or that one may fail oneself in caring about what matters.
- One forgives the other for their failures of responsibility, just as one forgives oneself for failing to care about what matters, in the hope that nevertheless, among the failures and false starts, something good may be done.

It is this dimension of economic life, the offering of credit, which is the focus for the economic theology at stake here. The creative power of money lies in its role as a symbol of the power of trust facilitating cooperation.

This creative power of trust was exposed by its absence in the Global Financial Crisis of 2007–2008. Following the crisis, the world experienced no immediate shortage of resources, skills, machinery, businesses, institutions, educated workers, or even money. Nevertheless, the global productive capacity could not be fully utilised due to a lack of trust. What had seemed entirely ephemeral and insubstantial turned out to be the most significant factor of production. Few were willing to borrow and fewer were willing to lend. The money that existed in the economy, which was already credit, started to expire – it had a due date for repayment. Since there was a shortage of new loans entering the economy, there was a shortage of money with which to repay loans. Credit suddenly converted from the source of wealth that drives the economy into the obligation of debt that impoverishes all. Repayment of debt became urgent because debts come due and can no longer be rolled over. Without credit one cannot enter any economic transactions at all. When faced with a choice between increasing austerity or failing to honour debts, then the loss of credit consequent upon default or bankruptcy overrode all other considerations. Yet as each economic agent sought to repay its debts, at the same time as banks sought to increase their capital ratios, there was no longer any source of credit in the wider economy that could fund the repayment of debt. This is a key problem for an economic theology: Under such conditions, which institution will step in as the creditor of last resort?

Chapter 4

A Recapitulation

One may still quite reasonably doubt that this power of credit offers a complete determination of the power of money in a bourgeois society. Trust is often misplaced, and subsequently given only grudgingly; cooperation is often lacking. People fail to care about that which matters. Responsibilities are shirked. If credit is in certain respects a universal economic phenomenon, the actual frameworks for supporting, guiding and extending credit determine what kind of economy exists in practice. In *Credit and Faith*, I charted the emergence of certain key frameworks for extending credit which have stamped their character on what is habitually called contemporary capitalism. These frameworks coexist with many others which are recognised within economic and critical theory, but the determining role of these particular frameworks is often overlooked. Each involves changing practices as well as conceptual shifts.

In the first place, with the rise of the medieval merchants, money started to be regarded not simply as a valuable commodity or a means of exchange, but as capital: as a repository for intentions and possibilities which may be realised by another. Peter of John Olivi argued that while lending money at interest was usurious and exploitative, lending capital at interest was not, for such money in the form of capital facilitated productive investment which would not be possible without it. The truth about money was not to be found in its substance or function, but in the possibilities that may be drawn from it. One person may look at a sum of money and see only its metal content; another may see the dignity and authority of the ruler stamped upon it; a third may look at a sum of money and see the possibility of a Gothic church erected for the worship of God. Such major projects, relying on craftspeople and materials brought from elsewhere which could have been dedicated to other projects and uses, were facilitated by the use of money. Likewise, medieval merchants, investing in some productive enterprise, could justify paying for the money they had borrowed by the expectation of future wealth to be gained by such investment.

Future wealth became the basis for a promise to pay, and so facilitated investment. Nevertheless, investment was limited by the extent of trust in promises, restricting credit offered only to those known in person or by reputation. In the second place, with the rise of banking practices, debts became transferable: one could do business with a stranger who presented a bill of exchange which might be redeemed by a trusted bank. Trust was extended by being centralised around trusted authorities. In this way, future wealth itself could act as a guarantee of present credit.

In the third place, as a merchant economy came to predominate in the sixteenth and seventeenth centuries, trade was mainly conducted through deferred payment, yet held back by a shortage of coins and a lack of trust. Given the importance of money as more trustworthy and liquid than one's word, coins were hoarded for important transactions because they were scarce, holding back the growth in trade. William Potter argued that the problem should be addressed at a collective level: if one could pay with the promises of a bank, rather than with one's own promises of future payment, then there would no longer be a reason to hoard coins and they would circulate much faster, facilitating growth. The future collective prosperity this could achieve would, in various ways, underwrite the value of the current promises made by such a bank. In a virtuous circle, the power of such money to be trusted consisted in its power to facilitate general prosperity.

In the fourth place, once such a bank was established, its promises, unlike coins, were truly uniform and fungible: they could offer a measure for prices, a true unit of account, facilitating calculations to regulate conduct, ensuring efficiency and equity and enabling auditing. Trust could be further extended to those who maintained books to demonstrate their probity and solvency.

Each of these transformations is a mechanism for supporting, guiding, and extending credit. While the mechanisms themselves do not elicit wealth creation directly, they facilitate the acts of investment and purchase which stimulate economic growth. They are conditions for economic trust, comprising distinctive institutions which determine how trust is in practice distributed. Economic theology is equally concerned with credit itself, handing over responsibility to others based on perceptions about what matters and how it might be addressed, and the conditions of credit, the support and extension of trust. Money is such a support: it is a truly creative power when it designates the possibility of future wealth, as a transferable and liquid debt, underwriting collective trust through the institution of banking, and serving as an abstract measure of value. These are the neglected yet constitutive features of capitalism.

THE DIRECTION

The determining idea to be explored in these volumes is that problems of economic credit and religious faith meet and are indeed two sides of the same human experience. While the first volume explored a theology articulated in terms of the economic dimensions of life, a theological economics, the task for this volume is to explore the theology implicit within contemporary economic thought, life, and practice, an economic theology. The previous volume distinguished between goods of appropriation, things that money can buy, goods of participation, social and cultural institutions, which only exist insofar as people participate in them, and goods of offering, things – such as life, time, care, attention, love, and credit – which are only lived out to the extent to which they are offered. Such goods may be distinguished as constituting the economic, moral and political, and theological dimensions of life, respectively. Actual human life is constituted by the interaction of these distinct realms. Nevertheless, there is a tendency within modern thought to represent only what can be appropriated, and to consider as appropriate only what can be represented – it short-circuits being itself. When goods of participation are considered in terms of goods of appropriation, the result is estrangement; when goods of offering are considered in terms of goods of appropriation, the result is constraint to debt obligations.

Now, where mutual trust is lacking, as in the encounters between strangers, an expression of a common religious faith, implying subordination to a just future judgement, may offer some grounds for trust. Such measures are a little less effective, however, than passing on a credit note issued by some known and trusted authority such as a bank. One no longer needs to trust the stranger; one trusts the institution whose very existence depends on its reputation for honouring its debts. Indeed, a stranger who can regularly pay their dues in paper money gains a reputation for trustworthiness by that very act. This is immensely useful as a practical measure; it can, however, produce an ideological confusion – one treats the abstract conception of value promised by the credit note as the embodiment of true value, as it is that which can be trusted, while one treats the trust and cooperation generated as merely ephemeral. In the modern market economy, money replaces credit as the principal medium of exchange. Since the value of money can be appropriated, the nature of that value as an object of participation and offering becomes obscured. Moral, political, and theological concerns are replaced by purely economic concerns by means of a metaphysical illusion about the nature of reality. Even though the modern economy continues to be structured by participatory institutions and credit offerings, much understanding of economic life focuses primarily upon that which can be appropriated and quantified. Economic science is grounded on 'evidence', where evidence is understood in terms of data rather than in terms of trust.

Modern economic thought, life, and practice, therefore, offer a paradigmatic example of a category error: a substitution of goods of appropriation for goods of offering. In practice, the theological dimensions of economic life remain present in the form of credit, however much one endeavours to reduce credit to a form of economic exchange. While the theological, philosophical, and historical discussions in the previous volume may draw our attention to such neglected dimensions, they cannot show by themselves how this mechanism for the extension of trust inevitably leads to the misplacement of trust. To see what is really at stake here, we need to explore the structure and performance of this error in practice in the economy. If the apparent content of this volume is economic theory, dynamics, and finance, and if its apparent aim is to draw out the poor theology implicit within these, the actual subject matter remains within philosophy of religion. For the task is to discern how acting on the basis of a misplaced faith can fail to reconcile thinking with being.

This book is not intended to be a collection of opinions on theological and economic matters. Instead, concerned with offering fresh insights and perspectives, I have endeavoured to edit out my own views where they are simply in accordance with others, such as in shared concerns with liberation and ecofeminist theology or in broad agreement with contemporary British Green economics.[1] Likewise, I have downplayed the extent of my agreement with approaches to economic life grounded in Catholic social teaching which orders production and consumption around participation in the common good. Similarly, I have not sought to reproduce a political history of how the global economy has evolved since the 1929 crash.[2] What is presented here is deliberately partial and imbalanced; the emphasis is on offering rather than participation. This book does not seek to replace existing theology or economics, nor does it purport to be a definitive statement on their relations, but it seeks rather to offer additional value to certain theological and economic orientations. It is intended to offer a framework for ordering the possibilities of economic and theological creation – and, as such, it seeks to replace the ordering of human trust and obligation around the formalisations of debt.

Part II

MARKETS AND MONEY: DYNAMICS OF THOUGHT

Chapter 5

Alchemy: The Creation of Money

The contemporary economists Nobuhiro Kiyotaki and John Moore observed in a lecture in 2001 the close connection between religion and the role of money in economics:

> Money was the branch of the subject where people held views with religious fervour. In fact, money and religion have much in common. They both concern beliefs about eternity. The British put their faith in an infinite sequence: this pound note is a promise to pay the bearer on demand another pound note. Americans are more religious: on this dollar bill it says, 'In God We Trust'. In case God defaults, it is countersigned by Larry Summers.[1]

Perhaps the American option is a little more prudent: for faith in the value of money is essentially a faith that it will be accepted in exchange by someone else, who in turn has faith that it will be accepted in exchange. As Kiyotaki and Moore observe, if there were a known end point of history, the entire structure of beliefs would collapse back from the end – the last person to hold a British pound would not be able to spend it, and so would find it worthless, and, anticipating this, would not accept it in exchange, and so it would be worthless to the preceding person and so on. It seems more prudent to rely on God, or at least in the meantime, Larry Summers or Timothy Geithner. Money is essentially a matter of trust. Yet Kiyotaki and Moore's argument depends on perfect information about the future; in conditions of radical uncertainty, God may determine whether money will prove to have held value, but in the meantime it may be prudent to accept the value of money.

Lord Mervyn King, governor of the Bank of England 2003–2013, who himself oversaw the signing of a fair few British pounds by his chief cashier, was perhaps more cautious than the Americans of monetary idolatry: 'God may have created the universe, but we mortals created paper money and risky banks'.[2] Nevertheless, God is still mentioned, not necessarily to express religious belief, but to signify that trust is central to money and banks. King also quotes Confucius: 'Three things are necessary for government: weapons, food and trust. If a ruler cannot hold on to all three, he should give up weapons first and food next. Trust should be guarded to the end: without trust we cannot stand'.[3] If weapons, food, and trust signify the three spheres managed by politics, economics, and religion respectively, why does a central banker allude to a pre-modern valuation of religion as holding the highest priority in civilised life? How has central banking itself come to inherit the role of managing and guaranteeing that trust, thus speaking in the absence of God?

One might suspect that the declaration, 'In God We Trust', really means the opposite, 'In the dollar we trust', like the statement, 'I'm not an atheist, but . . .' which the hearer understands is an attempt to allay sensitivities prior to making a strikingly atheist statement. In the disavowal inscribed on the dollar, there is furthermore an attempt to harness the faith directed to God and attach its aura of confidence to money. For money enables people to carry their value, their claim on the goods and services produced in society, forward through time in conditions of uncertainty. King explains this clearly:

> Money is not principally a means of buying 'stuff' but a way of coping with an uncertain future. We do not know which new goods and services will exist in the future, nor what their relative prices will be. . . . Maintaining a reserve of purchasing power denominated in a monetary unit reduces the risk from placing one's eggs in the basket containing only contracts that can be written today.[4]

Yet the wider significance of King's book is that it is an inquiry into why the Bank of England had no model that could predict the global financial crisis of 2007–2008 – a matter for which he personally held considerable responsibility, being the chief economist from 1993 prior to becoming deputy governor and then governor. His answer offers a substantial challenge to any attempt to turn economics into a science based on mathematical models: 'in a world of radical uncertainty, where it is not possible to compute the "expected utility" of an action, there is no such thing as optimising behaviour'.[5] In regard to the future, people simply do not know and cannot express any preference. While there are some futures markets, many of the markets in which prices would move towards equilibrium simply cannot and do not exist. 'The market economy, therefore, cannot coordinate spending plans. There are too many missing markets. As a result, a market economy is not self-stabilising, leading to occasional sharp ups and downs in spending'.[6] King is quite emphatic on this point: 'Radical uncertainty drives a gaping hole through the idea of complete and competitive markets'.[7] An account of what would be involved in practice in 'rational expectations' is sufficient to show that it is nonsense, as the rarity of King's imagined dinner conversation at home reveals:

> Darling, I'm worried that domestic spending in the economy is too high, and that at some point real interest rates will have to rise and the trade deficit come down. At that point, domestic spending will fall and we'll be part of that adjustment. Perhaps we should adjust our own spending now to a new and more sustainable path.[8]

Instead, King has to return to a key insight of Keynes, which is that as a result of radical uncertainty a capitalist economy needs money and credit.[9] 'A capitalist economy is inherently a monetary economy, and, as we shall see, a monetary economy behaves very differently from the textbook description of a market economy, in which households and businesses produce and trade with each other'.[10] In the real world, money, banking, and financial markets evolve as ways of coping with an unpredictable future.[11] Yet where both Keynesian and neoclassical models of fluctuations in the economy are concerned with the economics of 'stuff', King appeals to the radical temporality and event-driven nature of economic life, the economics of 'stuff happens'.[12]

What might it mean to develop an economics of events instead of one of expectations? In addition to financial crises, one of the most significant economic events that happens in the economics of 'stuff happens' is the creation of money. For this is not a matter of costs but of mere words alone. Banks are the main source of money creation: 'They create deposits as a by-product of making loans to risky borrowers'.[13] Yet there are a variety of ways of conceiving this creation of money. The 'traditional view' depends on the 'economics of stuff', and starts with a deposit of commodity money, such as precious metals standardised as coins. The money multiplier model, as found in many finance textbooks, outlines this approach: if someone deposits $1000 with a bank, which could be in coins or notes, then the bank could retain 10% as a reserve to pay the depositor in case it is needed, and loan out $900 to another individual, who spends the sum with the result that the seller deposits the $900 in another bank, which, in turn, lends a further $810 and so on. The money deposited is effectively multiplied each time, since it is still in the account of each depositor, yet also in use elsewhere. By this process, with a reserve ratio of 10%, the money can be multiplied to a limit approaching $10,000.[14]

King's own explanation starts with a version of this model: gold bullion was deposited with goldsmiths for safe-keeping, and the goldsmiths would issue receipts, which could then be transferred to third parties in payment for goods and services.[15] The receipts functioned as paper money, backed by bullion. Yet where some histories write of enterprising goldsmiths issuing more receipts than they had gold deposited,[16] once they had observed that the notes were very infrequently exchanged for gold (as the gold was safer with the goldsmiths), King (never one to undermine trust in a banker) invokes a different model which dispenses with gold:

> As it became clear that most notes were not in fact immediately converted into bullion but were kept in circulation to finance transactions, merchants started to issue notes that were backed by assets other than gold, such as the value of loans made by the merchants to their customers. Provided the holders of the paper notes were content to carry on circulating them, the assets backing those notes could themselves be illiquid, that is, not suitable for conversion quickly or reliably into money.[17]

So did money creation arise when merchants copied the bankers? In fact, medieval continental bankers had long been involved in discounting bills of exchange – accepting receipts offered to merchants for goods in transit, assets that would take time to mature, and lending a reduced sum of coins in advance in return for the receipt, and so being in a position to claim the full value of goods later on. Moreover, given the prevalence of the use of deferred exchange in the English economy, there was no need for merchants to copy goldsmiths in issuing notes that were backed by promised assets – each written promise was already such a note. However, whatever the history,[18] this alternative account of money creation situates notes in relation to credit rather than in relation to coinage. The essence of money creation, on King's account, is maturity transformation or 'financial alchemy': that banks could take secure short-term deposits and transform them into long-term risky investments. While depositors could in principle call upon their deposits at any time, in practice they were content to leave their deposits in the bank, while the bank could use such deposits for long-term loans and investments. King refers to the process as one of 'alchemy' because there is no gold accessible behind the note or loan:

> By alchemy I mean the belief that all paper money can be turned into an intrinsically valuable commodity, such as gold, on demand and that money kept in banks can be taken out whenever depositors ask for it. The truth is that money, in all forms, depends on trust in its issuer.[19]

This declaration is a little confusing: it seems to refer to bullionism, or faith in the 'economics of stuff' as underpinning the value of money, as an illusion, while faith itself in the value of money ought to be retained. If this is the illusion King wants to bring to an end, then it is surprising that his book is not primarily a tract against bullionism; instead, it is targeted against irresponsible credit creation justified by free market ideology. On the other hand, he actually uses 'alchemy' for maturity transformation, the process of creating money by borrowing in the short-term to lend in the long-term. This process is inherently dangerous, since short-term liabilities have to be paid out before long-term assets mature. In the financial crisis, banks had issued long-term loans (or bought securitized assets) whose value could not be realised immediately, while they had funded themselves with short-term borrowing from money market funds. Such short-term debt has to be continually rolled over, but in the crisis, banks found that they could only borrow for shorter periods – one month instead of three, then only for a week, then only for a day. In October 2008, two major UK banks – the Royal Bank of Scotland and Halifax Bank of Scotland – found themselves unable to get to the end of the day without emergency funding from the Bank of England of £60 billion – required to prevent a collapse of the banking system.[20]

The major conceptual difference involved in regarding banking as essentially maturity transformation, borrowing short to lend long, instead of simply intermediation, taking deposits and to issue loans, is that the former approaches economic value in terms of an irreducible future time, the latter in terms of 'stuff'. The major practical difference is the possibility of financial crisis. For on the money multiplier model, all of the money that had been lent out, at whatever degree of leverage, should have been deposited in someone's bank account somewhere, and so should have been present as a reserve to guarantee the banking system as a whole, at the same degree of leverage. On this model, there is no possibility of financial crisis. The other crucial practical difference is that banks do not require deposits in advance, but actually create credit, money and purchasing power that did not previously exist.[21] Where King hesitates to make this explicit, the other person with direct overall responsibility for overseeing the response to the financial crisis in the UK, Lord Adair Turner, the Chairman of the UK Financial Services Authority at the time, is far less reticent: banks create deposits without needing to receive them in advance.

> They make loans to borrowers, crediting an asset on the banks' balance sheet; at the same time they put money in the borrowers' account, creating a bank liability. The loan is repayable at later date, but the money is immediately available. It is this 'maturity transformation' that creates effective purchasing power.[22]

This is a rather different account of 'maturity transformation' – prior borrowing is not required, for the loan appears as both a liability and an asset on the bank's balance sheet and so cancels itself out. Money is genuinely created by this process. One might question how this is possible, given that the loan can be immediately spent, with the bank obliged to pay out the newly created money. In fact, in an ideal market system, with an unlimited number of banks, any such fresh money creation could easily destabilise the bank, leading to bank runs. In practice, in the contemporary global economy, there are only twenty major banks, each somewhat similar in size – and while the vast majority of transactions result in transfers between these, the majority of transactions also take place within national economies between just a few of these at a time (or between other banks that hold accounts with these major banks). So if a major contemporary bank creates a liability for itself by issuing a loan (and this is how they have become major banks), that money will be deposited either with itself or with its neighbour. The vast majority of such transactions between neighbouring banks cancel out, since the fresh deposits resulting from the new loans can be used to fund these very same loans, leading only to a small difference – and this can be funded by interbank borrowing or go to money market funds. Turner summarises Knut Wicksell's account of this from his 1898 book *Interest and Prices*:

> For reasons of convenience and security, households and businesses hold almost all their money in bank deposits, and almost all payments involve transfers from one account to another, effected through the interbank clearing system. As a result, once bank money has been created by the extension of new credit, it is almost certain to remain in the banking system: very little is taken out and used in the form of notes and coins.[23]

The operation of banking and money creation cannot be described in terms of money multiplication or maturity transformation alone; as Wicksell saw so clearly, it also involves the clearing system. For banks fulfil the functions of recording assets and liabilities in the form of deposit accounts and overdrafts and 'reckoning' or the mutual cancellation of debts. As Turner notes, in the UK, 98% of the money in circulation is composed of retail and wholesale deposits, money created in this way – in other nations, the figure is a little lower.[24] This is almost a cashless economy, where the vast majority of transactions are conducted through the reckoning of debts and credits. As Wicksell explained, 'There is no real need for any money at all if a payment between two customers can be accomplished by simply transferring the appropriate sum of money *in the books of the bank*'.[25]

The philosophical significance of this economics of 'stuff happens' is that one person's paper asset is another person's liability. One person's purchasing power is another person's obligation. When it comes to expressing preferences and spending money, therefore, whatever one's preferences, there remains an overriding demand constituted by debt. It is the same as that reported by Daniel Defoe as the principal demand on an early modern tradesman.[26] In order to maintain one's credit (normally now constructed as a credit-rating), one is under an obligation to conduct oneself according to the principles of financial probity: to conduct oneself in such a way as to be able to meet obligations. Without such a credit score, one may not even be able to open a bank account, and so may be largely excluded from the economic process of exchange via credit and reckoning. As Turner makes abundantly clear, debt weighs upon each agent in the global economy. It makes little sense to call the repayment of principal and interest upon a loan a preference – it has become an obligation.

Where the neoclassical approach to borrowing regards it merely as a time-based preference – a wish to spend now, on a house or car or education, so that one might save later – this is to imagine economic life before time starts. It assumes the sovereignty of the individual consumer. It is to treat time as 'stuff', subject to supply and demand. Yet people are subject to the passage of time; time is not subject to people. Joan Robinson saw clearly how the reality of time destroys any notion of economic equilibrium:

> Once we admit that an economy exists in time, that history goes one way, from the irreversible past into the unknown future, the conception of equilibrium based on the mechanical analogy of a pendulum swinging to and fro in space becomes untenable. The whole of traditional economics needs to be thought out afresh.[27]

Once time starts to unfold, then promises hold sovereign power over individuals, credit becomes debt, and preferences become obligations. Now people have become the 'stuff', and recorded debts hold sovereignty. Borrowing might start out as a promise to pay, but when there is little option for participating in economic life other than by borrowing – and even spending money from one's own account involves transacting credits and debts – then there is no live option here. In short, the expression of preferences constitutes a limited proportion of economic life. The fulfilment of obligations is also a significant component. Financial alchemy turns trust into obligation, credit into debt. Given that economic life continues to be mediated by trust and obligation, then the management of trust and obligation – the sphere of the religious – remains paramount, as alluded to by many of the titles to which this discussion has referred.

Chapter 6

Moral Equilibrium

The motive for taking out loans, creating at once purchasing power and debt obligations, is usually the hope for bettering one's condition. Whereas early modern theorists of progress had written only of bettering society, Adam Smith, under the same motivation but in different circumstances, wrote about the desire for individuals to better themselves. For once money, rather than creditworthiness, is treated as a measure of wealth, then wealth is seen as an object of possession rather than an object of participation. Smith's writing, however, inherits a deep ambivalence about whether the good should be conceived as a virtue or as a possession. In *A Theory of Moral Sentiments*, Smith imagined a colourful story of the progress of the vice of ambition:

The poor man's son, whom heaven in its anger has visited with ambition, when he begins to look around him, admires the condition of the rich. He finds the cottage of his father too small for his accommodation, and fancies he should be lodged more at ease in a palace. He is displeased with being obliged to walk a-foot, or to endure the fatigue of riding on horseback. He sees his superiors carried about in machines, and imagines that in one of these he could travel with less inconveniency. He feels himself naturally indolent, and willing to serve himself with his own hands as little as possible; and judges, that a numerous retinue of servants would save him from a great deal of trouble. He thinks if he had attained all these, he would sit still contentedly, and be quiet, enjoying himself in the thought of the happiness and tranquillity of his situation. He is enchanted with the distant idea of this felicity. It appears in his fancy like the life of some superior rank of beings, and in order to arrive at it, he devotes himself for ever to the pursuit of wealth and greatness. To obtain the conveniences which these afford, he submits in the first year, nay in the first month of his application, to more fatigue of body and more uneasiness of mind than he could have suffered through the whole of his life from the want of them. He studies to distinguish himself in some laborious profession. With the most unrelenting industry he labours night and day to acquire talents superior to all his competitors. He endeavours to bring these talents into public view, and with equal assiduity solicits every opportunity of employment. For this purpose he makes his court to all mankind; he serves those whom he hates and is obsequious to those whom he despises. Through the whole of his life he pursues the idea of a certain artificial and elegant repose which he may never arrive at, for which he sacrifices a real tranquillity that is at all times in his power, and which, if in the extremity of old age he should at last attain to it, he will find to be in no respect preferable to the humble security and contentment which he had abandoned for it. It is then, in the last dregs of his life, his body wasted with toil and diseases, his mind galled and ruffled by the memory of a thousand injuries and disappointments which he imagines he has met with from the injustice of his enemies or from the perfidy and ingratitude of his friends, that he begins at last to find that wealth and greatness are mere trinkets of frivolous utility, no more adapted for procuring ease of body or tranquillity of mind than the tweezer-cases of the lover of toys; and like them too, more troublesome to the person who carries them about with him than all the advantages they can afford him are commodious. . . . In his heart he curses ambition, and vainly regrets the ease and the indolence of youth, pleasures which are fled for ever, and which he has foolishly sacrificed for what, when he has got it, can afford him no real satisfaction. In this miserable aspect does greatness appear to every man when reduced either by spleen or disease to observe with attention his own situation, and to consider what it is that is really wanting to his happiness. Power and riches appear then to be, what they are, enormous and operose machines contrived to produce a few trifling conveniences to the body, consisting of springs the most nice and delicate, which must be kept in order with the most anxious attention, and which in spite of all our care are ready every moment to burst into pieces, and to crush in their ruins their unfortunate possessor.[1]

Let us leave this sorry character for the moment with a single observation: at least he has been of service to others through his industry and ambition, even if not to himself. Yet what of the son who is born rich? Smith offers a complementary account of his circumstances:

It is to no purpose, that the proud and unfeeling landlord views his extensive fields, and without a thought for the wants of his brethren, in imagination consumes himself the whole harvest that grows upon them. The homely and vulgar proverb, that the eye is larger than the belly, never was more fully verified than with regard to him. The capacity of his stomach bears no proportion to the immensity of his desires, and will receive no more than that of the meanest peasant. The rest he is obliged to distribute among those, who prepare, in the nicest manner, that little which he himself makes use of, among those who fit up the palace in which this little is to be consumed, among those who provide and keep in order all the different baubles and trinkets, which are employed in the oeconomy of greatness; all of whom thus derive from his luxury and caprice, that share of the necessaries of life, which they would in vain have expected from his humanity or his justice. The produce of the soil maintains at all times nearly that number of inhabitants which it is capable of maintaining. The rich only select from the heap what is most precious and agreeable. They consume little more than the poor, and in spite of their natural selfishness and rapacity, though they mean only their own conveniency, though the sole end which they propose from the labours of all the thousands whom they employ, be the gratification of their own vain and insatiable desires, they divide with the poor the produce of all their improvements. They are led by an invisible hand to make nearly the same distribution of the necessaries of life, which would have been made, had the earth been divided into equal portions among all its inhabitants, and thus without intending it, without knowing it, advance the interest of the society, and afford means to the multiplication of the species. When Providence divided the earth among a few lordly masters, it neither forgot nor abandoned those who seemed to have been left out in the partition. These last too enjoy their share of all that it produces. In what constitutes the real happiness of human life, they are in no respect inferior to those who would seem so much above them. In ease of body and peace of mind, all the different ranks of life are nearly upon a level, and the beggar, who suns himself by the side of the highway, possesses that security which kings are fighting for.[2]

This is hardly the last word on class relations – one notices a striking absence of issues of power, debt, and scarcity here.[3] Yet Smith's storytelling is not designed to offer a comprehensive moral justification of the industrial and landholding classes, but rather to indicate that there are unintended consequences of human behaviour, even immoral behaviour. Just as self-deception and avarice drive industry, so also the love of status and luxury drive distribution. If it is only in a state of despondency that one grasps the futility of each vice, it is only in a state of elation that one can observe the true virtue that lies beneath that of wealth. What Smith had in mind by the 'invisible hand' is explained in the paragraph that lies between the preceding two narratives.

Our imagination, which in pain and sorrow seems to be confined and cooped up within our own persons, in times of ease and prosperity expands itself to every thing around us. We are then charmed with the beauty of that accommodation which reigns in the palaces and oeconomy of the great; and admire how everything is adapted to promote their ease, to prevent their wants, to gratify their wishes, and to amuse and entertain their most frivolous desires. If we consider the real satisfaction which all these things are capable of affording, by itself and separated from the beauty of that arrangement which is fitted to promote it, it will always appear in the highest degree contemptible and trifling. But we rarely view it in this abstract and philosophical light. We naturally confound it in our imagination with the order, the regular and harmonious movement of the system, the machine or oeconomy by means of which it is produced.[4]

What is most beautiful about utility, that which receives our highest approbation, is the system, machine, or economy.[5] Perhaps the invisible hand is
precious not only to those who receive its benefits through redistribution,
but above all to those who observe its effects and see the movement of the
system. In such a vision, the messiness of real life is concealed by the imagination of perfect machines instead of either Platonic forms or the happiness
of fellow-creatures:

> The perfection of the police,[6] the extension of trade and manufactures, are
> noble and magnificent objects. The contemplation of them pleases us, and we
> are interested in whatever can tend to advance them. They make part of the
> great system of government, and the wheels of the great political machine seem
> to move with more harmony and ease by means of them. We take pleasure in
> beholding the perfection of so beautiful and grand a system, and we are uneasy
> till we remove any obstruction that can in the least disturb or encumber the
> regularity of its motions.[7]

And yet there seem to be certain conditions for such a vision: it is not seen by
those preoccupied by their own vices of luxury or ambition. Yet neither is it
seen by the 'philosophical' or the despondent, those who see reality only in
isolation. It is only in ease and prosperity that imagination expands. It is as
though economic growth were a precondition for the perception of beauty –
and this is the true value of wealth.

Now, many of Smith's admirers and detractors have seen his theory of
market exchange either as an instantiation of the hand of providence, or else
as a secular replacement for it. Many have also applauded or lamented his
love of the systematic nature of the market as the fundamental innovation that
establishes economics as a science in independence from moral philosophy.
For if the system brings beneficial consequences out of immoral conduct,
then behaviour ought to be governed by its natural spring in self-interest and
judged on the systematic basis of its consequences, not merely according to
the virtues or the moral law. Yet Smith himself regarded the moral system
of Mandeville, which dispenses with the distinction between virtue and vice,
as 'wholly pernicious'.[8] It is less often noticed that even within Smith's economic system there are conditions that need to be fulfilled in order for its
operation to be beneficial. After all, it is only when the system is viewed with
the eyes of imagination that it is perceived as a thing of beauty; when viewed
with the eyes of responsibility, such systems consist of 'springs the most nice
and delicate, which must be kept in order with the most anxious attention, and
which in spite of all our care are ready every moment to burst into pieces, and
to crush in their ruins their unfortunate possessor'. Perhaps Smith's market
system differs from Newton's rotating planets in two crucial respects: it needs
continual care and tending, and it needs to be fed with energy. The system
itself is only beneficial when it is far from equilibrium.

This is evident, above all, in his discussion of the wages of labour. When a market economy is in a stationary state, however wealthy, then the market tends to reduce wages to subsistence level. For people, like all other animals, naturally multiply in proportion to their means of subsistence. There would be a constant scarcity of employment, and the labourers would be obliged to bid against one another in order to get it. Wages would be reduced to the 'lowest rate which is consistent with common humanity'.[9] Any surplus produced would be appropriated by the masters and the landowners in the form of profits and rent. Even in a 'civilized' society, the scantiness of subsistence sets limits to the further multiplication of the human species: while the poor tend to have many children, few of them survive into adulthood. Equilibrium between the supply and demand for labour is achieved by infant mortality.[10] This is not a situation that Smith finds to be equitable:

> Servants, labourers and workmen of different kinds, make up the far greater part of every great political society. But what improves the circumstances of the greater part can never be regarded as an inconveniency to the whole. No society can surely be flourishing and happy, of which the far greater part of the members are poor and miserable. It is but equity, besides, that they who feed, cloath and lodge the whole body of the people, should have such a share of the produce of their own labour as to be themselves tolerably well fed, cloathed and lodged.[11]

The situation is far worse, however, in a country where the funds available for the wages of labour are declining. Declining wages leads to declining demand, and as many businesses fail, many from other classes would join the labouring classes. The consequences of such an extreme competition for employment would be severe as wages are reduced to the most miserable level:

> Many would not be able to find employment even upon these hard terms, but would either starve, or be driven to seek a subsistence either by begging, or by the perpetration of perhaps the greatest enormities. Want, famine and mortality would immediately prevail in that class, and from thence extend themselves to all the superior classes, till the number of inhabitants in the country was reduced to what could easily be maintained by the revenue and stock which remained in it, and which had escaped either the tyranny or calamity which had destroyed the rest.[12]

If the 'invisible hand' of providence operates solely through market forces, then these are its effects: infant mortality, penury, mendicancy, and crime.

While the condition of the greater number of people, the labouring poor, is hard in a stationary state and miserable in a declining state, it is best in an economy that is growing. Here, increasing profits lead to increasing investments, and so increasing demand for labour. Wages rise and with a delayed effect the population grows as workers become more capable of providing for their families. Smith even expects workers who are paid by piecework to be more highly motivated to work, and to work for longer hours, when their wages are high. A further effect is that an owner who employs a greater number of labourers can increase the division of labour and is motivated to find the best machinery for these more specific tasks, meaning that such machinery is more likely to be invented. The result is a growth in both population and productivity, leading to greater profits overall.[13] Smith effectively identifies economic growth as a positive feedback effect, a postponement of equilibrium. Only in such circumstances does a market economy produce a beneficial effect. Since Smith has observed that the extremely poor tend to have far more children than the wealthy, it does not take too much of a leap to imagine that as general prosperity grows and the population multiplies, its rate of multiplication would decline along with infant mortality. Even as the rate of profit tends to decline towards a stationary state, it might be a far more prosperous state for all if population growth has stabilised. Labourers would effectively become tradespersons and would no longer be regarded as commodities.

So how is this market utopia to be achieved? I have suggested that there are two external conditions for realisation of the beauty of the market system: continual care and tending, and feeding with energy. Smith adds another. The root of rising prosperity, on Smith's account, is the increase in productivity made possible by the division of labour.[14] This improves dexterity and skill, saves time, and is even a condition for the invention of machinery for specialised tasks.[15] Yet what enables the division of labour is the capacity to exchange: it is the market that increases productivity. Even though a market economy might produce harsh results in a stationary or declining economy, by its very nature, it tends to facilitate economic growth. For this reason, the introduction and extension of market relations of exchange contributes to economic growth by facilitating the division of labour. Nevertheless, this extension and intensification of market relations does not simply occur by itself: care of the market consists in removing the obstacles to free trade, but also in planning the division of labour. Smith's entire effort in the *The Wealth of Nations* is to encourage this care for the source of wealth, market exchange. The free market is to be cultivated for the sake of relieving poverty. Like any other machine, it cannot run by itself.[16]

At the same time, any growing structure has to be fed with energy. This energy, of course, is expressed through human labour, but since Smith treats the quantity of labour itself as subject to supply and demand, it is internal to the market structure. While Smith rejects the Physiocratic notion that the land is the source of all wealth, he still inherits from them the notion that the basic product that enables labour is food:

> As men, like all other animals, naturally multiply in proportion to the means
> of their subsistence, food is always, more or less, in demand. It can always

purchase or command a greater or smaller quantity of labour, and somebody can always be found who is willing to do something, in order to obtain it.[17]

The price of labour, for Smith, is regulated by both the demand for labour and the 'price of the necessaries and conveniences of life'.[18] This is, however, rather inconvenient for any attempt to construct a consistent theory of the market system, for the price of food and the price of labour can hardly be considered to be entirely independent variables. The price of food depends on the price of labour, the costs of planting, tending, harvesting, storing, and distributing it, while the price of labour depends on the costs of the necessaries of life, the price of food. There is no equilibrium to be found here. Market fluctuations simply modify a customary price. The market only seems to be an autonomous, self-regulating system when commodities answer to preferences, not to needs for the conditions of existence. Some, in order to maintain the fantasy of the imaginary machine, might even go so far as to deny the reality of such needs.

David Ricardo may have sought to rectify this problem by formulating a labour theory of value correlated to the marginal productivity of land, but in doing so, he abstracted from what was essential in Smith's optimistic system: that the market functions as a dissipative structure, far from equilibrium, fed by a supply of energy and subject to continual tending and care so as to increase productivity. For only when a market grows can it be morally justified. The stationary state is dismal.[19] The gain in analytic clarity achieved by Ricardo's equilibrium model, and its subsequent improvement by the marginalists who substituted utility for labour as the unit of value, is at the expense of a connection to reality. What is lost in the system of perfect competition is crucial: the exogenous elements to the market, whether the supply of energy, the supply of money, or the supply of care and credit. What is also lost is any objective conception of value: efficiency and preference became the only measures of success, and any boundary between value creation and value extraction became invisible.[20] For while Smith integrated the supply of population into the market with its forces of supply and demand, he at least indicated how an escape from such subjection to necessity might be possible. The market, in Smith, is not a brute, objective mechanism but a tool to be chosen by moral philosophy. Smith constructed his system on the basis of the moral distinction between production and rent-seeking. While Smith's model of the market was itself somewhat abstract and should certainly not be applied retrospectively to societies where distribution was not entirely governed by self-interested exchange, it did at least speak of an abstraction that could grow and realise itself in the real world, increasing prosperity for many. Whether such a model bears much relation to contemporary economic reality dominated by large corporations, governments, financial institutions, and advertising campaigns is quite another matter.

Chapter 7

Choice

Yesterday, while shopping, I noticed by the checkout an eye-catching device: an illuminated transparent column filled with water containing five or six cheap, colourful, and rather gaudy plastic fish. Remarkably, each fish was maintained at a different height in the tube, and although some would gradually rise, owing to being caught up in a stream of bubbles released at the base of the column, others would slowly fall, having slipped out of the upward current. Overall, though, the fish spent most of their time close to equilibrium and were distributed throughout the height of the tube. I was certainly not intending to make a purchase, until one of these gaudy fish seemed to whisper to me of Thorstein Veblen's description of the conception of human beings as maximisers of utility:

> The hedonistic conception of man is that of a lightning calculator of pleasures and pains, who oscillates like a homogeneous globule of desire of happiness under the impulse of stimuli that shift him about the area, but leave him intact. He has neither antecedent nor consequent. He is an isolated, definitive human datum, in stable equilibrium except for the buffets of the impinging forces that displace him in one direction or another. Self-imposed in elemental space, he spins symmetrically about his own spiritual axis until the parallelogram of forces bears down upon him, where upon he follows the line of the resultant. When the force of the impact is spent, he comes to rest, a self-contained globule of desire as before. Spiritually, the hedonistic man is not a prime mover. He is not the seat of a process of living, except in the sense that he is subject to a series of permutations enforced upon him by circumstances external and alien to him.[1]

Now I was stumped: Would it maximise my utility to make a purchase of these gaudy fish for the sake of offering a physical exemplification of a conception of human behaviour? Would it fulfil my preference for exemplification at the cost of my preference for keeping my home and office free from such clutter? How could I decide between such different preferences? What scale could I weigh them upon? They are quite incommensurable. My economic confusion is in fact far more grave: even in my research activity, I cannot estimate in advance whether the benefits to be obtained for my own work from reading a book will be worth the expenditure of the time devoted to it, requiring the sacrifice of other reading and writing opportunities. Each act of reading a book is an act of faith, just as is every endeavour to commit words to speech or writing. I make a very poor hedonist, a poor rational economic agent. While the gaudy fish seem to know how to respond to shifting signals in the form of bubbles, I have no idea how to respond to shifting signals in the form of tastes, rumours, prices, and ideas. Perhaps like many others, I fall rather short of *homo oeconomicus*. It was this very uncertainty which made up my mind: I kept the money.

However, I do not aspire to behave like a plastic fish, and only do so under conditions of uncertainty. The six fundamental motives for human behaviour discussed by Adam Smith in his *Theory of Moral Sentiments* strike me as far more admirable, even if somewhat incomplete: self-love; sympathy; the desire to be free; a sense of propriety; the habit of labour; and, of course, the 'propensity to truck, barter and exchange'. Smith even treated the latter motive as a characteristic that distinguishes humans from animals, plastic or otherwise: 'Nobody ever saw a dog make a fair and deliberate exchange of one bone for another with another dog. Nobody ever saw one animal by its gestures and natural cries signify to another, this is mine, that yours; I am willing to give this for that'.[2] Yet when it comes to humans expressing preference in exchange, we are sometimes as helpless as dogs. For how can we possibly compute from the multitude of signals to be found in prices, rumours, and news announcements which course of action will fulfil our own preferences – even if we were aware of what these preferences might be? And even if we are not aware, and only reveal our preferences in acts of exchange, how can we be sure that such decisions bear any consistent relation with either the information received or the preferences expressed?

One fundamental problem in constituting economics as a science, based on consistent and deterministic laws of objective market forces, is that of how to make appeal to human subjectivity. Economic theory is caught in a dilemma in its treatment of human agency. On the one hand, it assumes that human beings are autonomous rational actors intent on maximising their own self-interests and exercising free choice; on the other hand, it attempts to determine the laws that govern actual behaviour as though people behave like fully determined particles.[3] For while there is much rhetorical appeal to choice in economics, the exercise of choice tends to be eliminated from analyses and models. While real choice means that an individual could always have acted otherwise, under such conditions there could be no determinism, prediction, or science. In economic theories, there is almost always one preferred or rational course of action – and the theory only applies to reality if this course of action is actually followed.[4]

What is especially striking here is that human subjectivity itself becomes an essential component of objective market forces. The basis of any notion of a market mechanism is that the balance of market forces, including such factors as supply and demand, is measured by its resolution in terms of a price, which then impacts upon the exercise of human preferences. If the price is too high, then consumers will look elsewhere; if it is too low, then vendors will raise it to increase their profits. Overall, the price is expected to approach towards equilibrium. However, this does place a considerable burden upon consumers who have to calculate how to respond to price signals. Perhaps it is not so hard to bear such a burden in a relatively expensive restaurant – while the finest foods and wines on the menu might be preferable, their cost places them out of reach for most, and a decision of what to order can usually be attained through some compromise. Even so, one often suspects that one might have received greater satisfaction from ordering another item on the menu, as often the satisfaction anticipated differs from the satisfaction received, and the actual choice taken is often arbitrary, shaped more by imagination than experience. Yet when the choice is extended to spending the same sum in a restaurant or at the theatre or on a gift for a grandchild or investing it in some scheme with an uncertain rate of return and an uncertain degree of risk or donating it to one of a variety of worthy charities, then expressed preferences can hardly be assumed to be either determinate or consistent – for there is no longer any consistent scale upon which such heterogeneous choices can be compared. In practice, the burden of choice is even more challenging to bear for participants in financial markets, who have no better super-computer for resolving the complex equations of global market forces than do economists, and so struggle to make consistent predictions. Even if they employ algorithms to determine definite responses of buying and selling to particular news stories and price signals, people still switch inconsistently between such algorithms as they make variable and inconsistent rates of profit and loss. But the main point is that the human subject itself lacks a determinate algorithm to guide its behaviour, so preference functions are always incomplete. No eye has ever seen or hand has ever touched a preference function, not even the eye or hand of a consumer. As Alfred Marshall emphasised, 'It cannot be too much insisted that to measure directly, or *per* se, either desires or the satisfaction which results from their fulfilment is impossible, if not inconceivable'.[5] If this much is true for economists, then it is also true for rational actors and consumers. One cannot know how others will behave. One cannot even compare one's own different satisfactions at different times. And in weighing up a purchase, one cannot estimate precisely how much satisfaction it will give as the satisfaction remains in future, and is still to be achieved. Joan Robinson exposed the essential problem here: 'Utility is a metaphysical concept of impregnable circularity: *utility* is the quality in commodities that makes individuals want to buy them, and the fact that individuals want to buy them commodities shows that they have *utility*'.[6] If, in response to Robinson's challenge, Paul Samuelson and his followers substituted the empirical notion of revealed preferences, shown in actual purchases, for the metaphysical notion of utility, it was to the advantage of the economist at the expense of the consumer. How can a consumer know his or her revealed preferences in order to reveal them? The individual has no privileged way of surveying the relative balance of their preferences, given certain perceived costs and benefits other than their own actual behaviour. How can I follow my actual behaviour when I am faced with the responsibility of making a decision? While specific conceptions of utility might guide behaviour in the market, a preference function cannot – it cannot do the complex calculations involved. Neither can rational expectations if one does not know what to expect. There is a gaping hole in the theory of consistent market behaviour.

One may attempt to fill this hole by the law of large numbers, through which individual divergences cancel each other out. This is the approach recommended by Marshall: 'if we take averages sufficiently broad to cause the personal peculiarities of individuals to counter-balance one another, the money which people of equal incomes will give to obtain a benefit or avoid an injury is a good measure of the benefit or injury'.[7] Yet now the problem is compounded by the lack of independent variables. If a price is to approach equilibrium, then it will do so through a succession of bids and offers until agreement is reached. Yet each bid and offer price is determined by keeping an eye on the prices in closely associated markets, where an alternative purchase might turn out to be preferable. Of course, the prices in these related markets are also determined by a similar set of sellers and buyers making bids and offers – and often, an overlapping set. Prices between markets are not independent. Moreover, in the markets for positional goods, such as designer brands, the price is one of the main indicators of how much an item is to be preferred. Under such circumstances, the offer price is not independent of demand. Once one allows for conversation between market participants apart from the exchange of prices and atoms of information, then market behaviour becomes a social process that is not mediated by transactions alone. Preferences are no longer consistently ordered or transitive.[8] Economics needs replacing by social theory.[9]

Veblen discloses what reality lacks that the utilitarian model of the consumer presupposes: the power to measure pleasures and pains; the power to calculate future pleasures and pains; and how they might result from present

choices. In reality, by contrast, one encounters the power to act under heterogeneous motives, the power to remember the past and anticipate the future,
the power to act in concert with others, the power to imagine and initiate a
novel course of action, the power to live. In short, what is missing from a
preference function is humanity itself. As John Milbank and Adrian Pabst
have identified, what is missing here is the constitutive role of participation
in the construction of value:

> Trivial material goods or things that are *merely* the election of my passing fancy
> (which is all that liberalism and neo-classical economics can recognise in terms
> of valid desire) are subject to the reverse lure of boredom and lose their sig-
> nificance and so economic value over time. But that is not true of *symbolically*
> valuable objects, like your grandmother's ring, or of *relational goods* whether
> enjoyed along with other people or other natural realities.[10]

Such considerations might tempt one to dispense with ideological uses of
marginalist economics from Jevons onwards, and dismiss, with Pope Francis,
'certain economic theories which today scarcely anybody dares defend'.[11] In
its place, one might recover a humanist and social account of the economy, in
which commerce is a matter of human cooperation more than it is a matter of
human competition.[12] These are promising lines of exploration. However, it is
not the purpose of this discussion to contribute to the critique of marginalist
economic theory.[13] The main criticisms are widely known: some concern the
differences between the model and the reality itself. Many of the assumptions necessary for markets to be competitive are utterly unrealistic: that there
exists a complete set of markets, that prices are always public, that buyers and
sellers behave competitively and know what is in their interests, that workers
can be easily separated from their responsibilities for and dependencies upon
others, and that some kind of equilibrium is always achieved. Such criticisms
need not be fatal, for models are intended to be simplifications and can be
complicated to take account of such factors. Other criticisms are moral: defining value in terms of price counts every event as positive. Hegel's vengeful
arsonist, whom we encountered in the introduction, contributes to GDP by
stimulating the demand for rebuilding. Marginal preference theory leaves
no scope for any distinction between value creation and value extraction,[14]
no account of exploitation or unearned income, no real difference between
preference and need, no moral care for matters of life and death: what you get
is, by definition, what you are worth. Once preference is made the standard
of value, those preferences which are ignorant of their destructive effects
on others are evaluated simply by how much money they earn and spend.
The market fails as a moral system for regulating just outcomes because
most interactions in life, which spread like wildfire, take place outside of the

marketplace and are not specified in contracts: the world is largely composed of 'externalities'. We have all the other arts and sciences to describe how things work outside of market relations. That the theory of competitive markets has ever been extended from a useful model in certain circumstances to a moral ideal is a celebration of moral ignorance. As with Hegel's arsonist, our preferences are often largely ignorant of their conditions and consequences; these conditions and consequences are largely unrepresented in a market price – they do not have money to spend in proportion to their significance. In practice, advocating unrestricted liberty within the market is advocating unrestricted liberty to exploit others' misfortunes, dependencies, and needs. Such ideology is beneath further discussion here.

Notwithstanding such criticisms, there are many circumstances in which the theory of competitive markets does seem to approximate to reality. Many useful conclusions can be drawn from the 'laws' of supply and demand. The crucial question, then, is under what conditions does human behaviour become consistent and predictable, a mere response to external forces? When does our behaviour start to resemble the deterministic motion of a plastic fish floating in a current of bubbles? What are the conditions of possibility of an economic science?

Chapter 8

Money as Moral Measure

Alfred Marshall, in his *Principles of Economics* (first edition 1890) – the textbook that was most widely used in the first half of the twentieth century – while acknowledging the variety of high motives that might affect an individual's conduct in business made a revealing admission:

> But, for all that, the steadiest motive to ordinary business work is the desire for the pay which is the material reward of work. The pay may be on its way to be spent selfishly or unselfishly, for noble or base ends; and here the variety of human nature comes into play. But the motive is supplied by a definite amount of money; and it is this definite and exact money measurement of the steadiest motives in business life, which has enabled economics far to outrun every other branch of the study of man. . . . An opening is made for the methods and tests of science as soon as the force of a person's motives – *not* the motives themselves – can be approximately measured by the sum of money, which he will just give up in order to secure a desired satisfaction; or again by the sum which is just required to induce him to undergo a certain fatigue.[1]

Precision in measurement, in quantification, is that which sets economics apart. Marshall is well aware that there are many goods, many objects of desires, which cannot be exchanged and measured, but he restricts economic goods to those which are both goods of appropriation, being one person's property or another's, and are directly capable of money measure.[2] Of course, money is never a perfect measure of human motives, 'and it is not even a tolerably good measure unless careful account is taken of the general conditions under which it works, and especially of the riches or poverty of those whose action is under discussion'.[3] Yet since most actions which are motivated by a sense of duty or love of neighbour cannot be measured, economics will have to make do with those that can be so measured.[4] Even though, as Marshall explains, purely business relations assume honesty and good faith, pleasure and pride in work, and express the desire to earn approval,[5] economists 'deal with a man who is largely influenced by egoistic motives in his business life'; they are concerned with 'those aspects of life in which the action of motive is so regular that it can be predicted, and the estimate of the motor-forces can be verified by results'.[6] Yet 'the desire to make money does not itself necessarily proceed from motives of a low order, even when it is to be spent on oneself. Money is a means towards ends, and if the ends are noble, the desire for the means is not ignoble'.[7]

The admission is twofold: on the one hand, economics does in fact measure values in terms of money, whatever its endeavours to postulate an underlying value, whether conceived in terms of labour costs, utility, revealed preference, or anything else. After all, such preferences are only revealed in actions aimed at acquiring or spending money. There is no other widely used unit of comparison, even if money, rather like the price of gold, is a rather elastic and imprecise ruler. On the other hand, economics is also restricted to measuring values in terms of money, and thus in terms of the 'egoistic' component of human behaviour, even when the acquisition and spending of money is driven by higher motives. Such higher motives are not denied; they simply disappear from analysis. They do not belong to quantification and thus to exact science, even if they belong in reality.[8] The result is that the economic description of human behaviour only seems to allow for the motives of self-interest in determining actual economic conduct in the regular behaviour of large numbers of people, for other motives are inexact. Collective social motives, such as imitation, participation, fear, and even the collective aggression of war, are simply eliminated from the inquiry, whether or not they have an effect on how people handle money. For the very fact that economics is restricted to goods of appropriation reduces the human motivations studied to those that seek to appropriate. The very fact that economics is restricted to those goods of appropriation that can be measured by money reduces human motivations to those that seek to appropriate through exchange involving money. It is as though the human person is bisected to extract a thin layer to be placed on a microscope slide – the self-interested individual – and then recombined through the law of large numbers to reconstruct a composite individual – the market – determined entirely by self-interested behaviour. Mariana Mazzucato explains the circular reasoning here:

> Incomes are justified by the production of something which is of value. But how do we measure value? By whether it earns income. You earn income because you are productive and you are productive because you earn income. So with a wave of the wand, the concept of *unearned income* vanishes.[9]

Now, our question is not whether this offers a legitimate perspective on human economic life of producing, exchanging, consuming, and borrowing as a whole, which it clearly does not, but under what conditions it might approximate to a description of economic behaviour. Here are two possible conditions: a first is when people believe that they are morally justified in acting primarily in their own self-interests, or even better, when they believe that through acting in their own self-interests, they are best contributing to the welfare of others; a second is when they are under an obligation to act in their own self-interests, such as when their obligation to the wider society is quantified in the form of a debt. Belief and debt are features of human life that endure through time; they cannot be reduced to expectations.

In the first case, belief in economic theory is a vital component in the behaviour that might make it approximate to the truth. In particular, beliefs that free and efficient markets maximise production through the division of labour and the invention of machinery (from Smith and Ricardo), that they effect an optimal distribution of goods and services to preferences (from Vilfredo Pareto), and that all goods and services offered on the market will be utilised, including labour (from Say's law), offer a fine apologetic for exercising justice through self-interest. Of course, economic behaviour guided by such beliefs does not make these particular beliefs true in practice – it is a simple matter of observation that all developed economies have achieved their position through protectionism rather than through free trade[10] that deregulated markets produce increasing inequality[11] and that there are serious problems of involuntary unemployment throughout the global economy.[12] These deductive 'laws', based on highly simplifying assumptions, do not have to be true in reality to be believed; they simply have to be desirable for those who are encouraged to pursue their own self-interests. Critique achieves little for those whose desire for either wealth or for precision is stronger than their desire for truth; and if critique is blithely ignored on account of deduction from an inapplicable model, it is tempting to blithely ignore those who ignore it. Yet the apparent instantiation of *homo oeconomicus* in reality is made possible, in part, by economic theory, for this figure was largely absent from former cultures and times – not that people in former times lacked selfishness, avarice, and ambition, but they lacked a belief structure that could reassure them that their vices in themselves were public benefits; they lacked a society organised largely around a market.

The canonical statement of the necessity for self-interest in economic life is Adam Smith's famous account of the means by which he (or his mother) sought his dinner:

In civilised society [man] has stands at all times in need of the cooperation and assistance of great multitudes, while his whole life is scarce sufficient to gain the friendship of a few persons. In almost every other race of animals each individual, when it is grown up to maturity, is entirely independent, and in its natural state has occasion for the assistance of no other living creature. But man has almost constant occasion for the help of his brethren, and it is in vain for him to expect it from their benevolence only. He will be more likely to prevail if he can interest their self-love in his favour, and show them that it is for their own advantage to do for him what he requires of them. Whoever offers to another a bargain of any kind, proposes to do this. Give me that which I want, and you shall have this which you want, is the meaning of every such offer; and it is in this manner that we obtain from one another the far greater part of those good offices which we stand in need of. It is not from the benevolence of the butcher, the brewer, or the baker that we expect our dinner, but from their regard to their own interest. We address ourselves, not to their humanity but to their self-love, and never talk to them of our own necessities but of their advantages.[13]

While this passage has been commented on endlessly, a few brief observations may still be relevant here. In the first place, it should perhaps be repeated that such a description may have been true for Edinburgh in the eighteenth century, but was not necessarily so for Ireland in the seventeenth, if much of the population did not engage in trade. Many societies have existed in which exchange was minimal, and redistribution could be effected by mutuality in a small-scale society, or patronage in a larger one. Moreover, given Craig Muldrew's historical work on seventeenth-century England, it is likely that religious and social motivations would have been an explicit part of any such lengthy acts of persuasion merely a century before Smith, let alone in other societies.[14] Unless exchange takes place with money, there is no direct way of comparing goods, and so no way of consistently formulating and pursuing self-interest. Yet the cooperation and assistance of great multitudes of strangers requires a more extendable means of persuasion, and the pervasiveness of monetary exchange is both a condition for and an effect of the division of labour. Only when persuasion takes the form of an offer of money does it become exclusively concerned with self-interest.

In the second place, then, we address ourselves to the butcher, the brewer, and the baker through the offer of money. Money offers a single scale of values in relation to which any advantages may be measured, calculated, and planned. For the consumer who is confused about the order of their preferences, money itself is to be preferred, as it is the means by which later preferences may be realised. Yet this effect, as André Gorz has noted, goes beyond anxiety over preferences and choices to address anxiety over morals. Money offers moral certainty: the measures of efficiency and 'value for money' offer a means by which the more can be preferred to the less. As Gorz puts it:

> Quantitative measurement as a substitute for rational value judgement confers supreme moral security and intellectual comfort: the Good becomes measurable

and calculable; decisions and moral judgements can follow from the implemen-
tation of a procedure of impersonal, objective, quantifying calculation and individual subjects do not have to shoulder the burden anxiously and uncertainly.
'It is virtuous to earn money'. . .

   Capitalism has been the expression of economic rationality finally set free of
all restraint. It was the art of calculation, as developed by science, applied to the
definition of the rules of conduct. It raised the quest for efficiency to the level of
an 'exact science' and thus cleared the factors of moral or aesthetic criteria from
the field of decision-making. Thus rationalized, economic activity could hence-
forth organize human behaviour and relationships 'objectively', leaving the
subjectivity of decision-makers out of account and making it impossible to raise
a moral challenge on them. It was no longer a question of good or evil but only
of correct calculation. 'Economic science', insofar as it guided decision-making
and behaviour, relieved people of responsibility for their acts. They became 'servants of capital' in which economic rationality was embodied. *They no longer*
had to accept responsibility for their own decisions since these were no longer
attributable to them in person but were the result of a rigorously impersonal
calculation procedure in which individual intentions had (apparently) no place.[15]

It is not only the division of labour and the availability and usage of money
which are preconditions for this moral apologetic but also the existence of
economic science as such that contributes to the credibility of this morality –
even if such economic science, as we have seen in the case of Marshall,
selects only the self-interested aspect of humanity for study.

   In the third place, we might observe that Smith's choice of his dinner as
an object of negotiation, while following directly from the discussion of the
ways in which dogs seek attention when they wish to be fed, is not entirely
arbitrary. For the butcher, brewer, and baker trade in consumption goods,
things which, if consumed by Smith himself, could not also be consumed
by the dogs in the street. These perishable consumption goods have to be
either consumed, exchanged, given away, or else they go to waste. In this
respect, they offer a simple moral choice between self-interest and altruism. As such, they are a rhetorical device for reducing moral motivations
down to this simple alternative – while self-interest and sympathy are much
more deeply intertwined in the *Theory of Moral Sentiments*, here they are
presented in stark opposition for rhetorical purposes. By contrast, when it
comes to working for the common good, no such alternative between self-
interest and altruism needs to be invoked. Yet more than that, they offer a
paradigm for the consideration of economic activity as primarily motivated
by consumption: 'Consumption is the sole end and purpose of all production;
and the interest of the producer ought to be attended to only so far as it may
be necessary for promoting that of the consumer'.[16] This is the 'economics
of stuff' – it is primarily concerned with the experience of consumption, not

with the experience of work. It can, therefore, only be directly concerned with individual interests.

In each of these ways, then, Smith and his successors enhance a view of economic life that is apparently solely concerned with self-interest. This is hardly a matter of 'science', but it is a matter of morality, of rules to guide conduct. If one believes in such a 'science', then one is acquitted from all prior social obligations and moral justifications. But in no sense does it mean that one behaves like a particle subject to external forces, or a plastic fish, for behaviour is governed by belief, and not by force. It is as though the economic agent participates in a game, where the objective is to 'maximise utility', and the measure of one's success in doing so is simply the money that one has spent. For, to repeat, the satisfaction of utility cannot be directly measured or compared, not even by the consumer. Neither, therefore, can it be estimated in advance by that consumer. Even after consumption, the consumer is in little better position to determine whether money spent on an expensive car would have been better allocated towards a grandchild's deposit for a house purchase or money spent on an expensive vacation would have been better spent on an educational course or spiritual retreat. The art of allocating personal consumption is not included in textbooks of micro-economics – *therefore*, such textbooks show no real interest in consumption as the 'sole end and purpose of all production'. The responsibility for living well is left entirely as a matter for the consumer. Of course, a condition for living well might be that of having money to spend, to make one's demands effective, and microeconomics is concerned with the conduct that is effective in acquiring money. But money, if not even a 'tolerably good measure' of the strength of human motives, is an extraordinarily poor measure of self-love. It can so easily be misspent. The act of persuasion upon the butcher, brewer, and baker is, first of all, an appeal to each of them to measure their self-love in terms of money. It is an entreaty to them to think first of all of the means. It is an entreaty to them to delimit their ends to those that can be measured in terms of money and acquired by money.

It is often claimed, of course, that while economics is the science of the means, ethics is concerned with the ends. Economics can be considered as purely descriptive, as a positive science rather than a normative one. Yet our question is this: Under what conditions do human beings try to behave as if they were in the ideal model of a market under perfect competition? When do they seek to maximise their self-interest through acquiring money, whether through wages, rents, profits, or interest? When are their free choices identical to the outcomes that would arise from the impersonal determination of market forces? When does human freedom start to resemble necessity? This dichotomy between freedom and necessity can be resolved when supposedly impersonal laws governing behaviour become explicit reasons for free action.

Yet how have so many butchers, brewers, and bakers been so effectively persuaded to take a market view of economic life and count their interests in terms of money? Here, at last, we find a deterministic process: such a moral choice is self-reinforcing. If one counts one's self-interest in terms of money, then one values, above all else, an unspecified future claim on the market. The acquisition of money becomes the condition for prosperity and influence. Those who are not 'rational actors', in the specific sense of measuring and seeking their interests in terms of money, will not remain significant actors for long. Only those with prosperity and influence, who are often subject to emulation, can use their money to contribute towards the reconstruction of social life in the image of the ideal market.[17] Only those with money can make economic science come true. Economics is a guide to moral conduct long before it approaches being a science.

What gets lost in this process is any consideration of ends.[18] Economic growth is substituted for other measures of welfare so that what is measured is simply how much money is spent. The means is substituted for the end.[19] What counts is power in the market, not the wise or moral determination of ends – these have comparatively less effective ways of spreading their influence through society, such as religions. On this matter, where it becomes a matter of money or calculation alone, it is no longer even a question of self-interest, of fulfilment in consumption. Only the money counts. It does not matter how one spends the money; it simply matters that it is spent. And the complete inversion of means and ends, where acquisition of means, whether of power or of money, has become as end in itself, has been described by Weil as 'the very essence of all evil in society'.[20] Why invoke such a theological term for what appears to be, at most, a moral or a political matter?

Chapter 9

Money as Theology

The pursuit of profit is not the only dimension of faith in the market. While self-interest might appear to be directly in conflict with the common good, its complementarity is also sometimes acknowledged. Take the paradox described by Robert H. Nelson:

> The market is based on the idea of the individual pursuit of self-interest. At the same time, however, a market system will work best if there is a clear limit to self-interest. The pursuit of self-interest should not extend to the various forms of opportunism, such as cheating, lying, and other types of deception, misrepresentation, and corruption found within the marketplace. . . . Another key consideration is that property rights, contracts and other legal arrangements should be fairly and consistently enforced. In short, the market must exist within an institutional and civic-value context that transcends individual self-interest and supports and encourages actions that have a wider benefit for the common good.[1]

The mechanics of rational self-interest must be set within the wider context of human integrity and trust. For this, as Joan Robinson explains, it is the honesty of other people that is necessary for one's own comfort, whereas the truly rational course of action for the individual would be to act as an opportunistic free rider.[2] Since a market cannot function if all seek to be free riders, it is impossible to generate a market purely from the pursuit of profit. The generation of wealth results not from narrow self-interest but from a communal sense of trust. Francis Fukuyama has celebrated the role of trust inherent in society as a fundamental feature of economic wellbeing, where 'reciprocity, mutual obligation, duty toward community and trust' are based on habit rather than rational calculation.[3] Indeed, if social capital is fostered through religion and tradition, then the greatest utility maximisers are not the most rational ones.[4] Religion may even make a significant contribution to the creation of wealth.[5] In other words, there are at least two heterogeneous dynamics in the construction of market relations: playing the game to win and upholding the rules. These require differing frameworks for thought.

In general, modern thought has been divided between two kinds of explanation based on a distinction between two kinds of power: there is the power achieved through physical work, defined in terms of mechanics, but resulting from the action of fundamental physical forces, such as gravity, electromagnetism, and nuclear bonds; there is also the power of the human will, evident in speech, action, and persuasion. While history tends to explain the world in terms of narrative, intention, and purpose – as if will were the fundamental substance of reality, the ultimate ground of explanation, as if the realities in the world exist because they are intended, whether or not by a creator God – economics tends to explain the world in terms of the mechanical effect of market forces – as if the motive of self-interest (measured by money) were the fundamental substance of reality, the ultimate ground of explanation, as if the realities in the world exist because they are purchased. While these two approaches have often clashed, there is an underlying complementarity throughout modern science. Ever since Newton linked astronomy and mechanics by imagining the moon initially at rest, and then observing that the movement by which the moon would fall towards the earth is identical to the movement by which it in fact declines from its inertial tangent to its orbit, scientific explanation has proceeded by isolating independent variables to determine dependent variables. This depends on an act of decision. Whether in physical theory, in the laboratory, in the technological artefact or in economics, the creation of a closed system depends on an act of will. Closed systems are not out there to be discovered. The mechanical is embedded within the purposive, but likewise, the purposive only operates in and through the mechanical. This entire modern division of the world between means and ends depends on the complementarity of the two, despite attempts to reduce the world entirely to means, in the forms of mechanics and natural selection, or attempts to reduce the world entirely to ends, in the form of theology.

As argued in the previous section, economic science can approximate to reality by acts of will, such as political acts of constructing and maintaining market systems,[6] and moral acts of the pursuit of money within the boundaries of honest conduct, avoiding lying, theft, and free-riding. For such moral concerns extend one's estimation of self-interest over a lifespan, instead of responding to immediate and instantaneous forces. In any case, such economic conduct is an expression of the sovereign will, and if this will is guided by a belief system, the primary significance of which is to be found in its effects rather than in its correspondence to reality, then such a belief system is best described as an ideology, 'for they know not what they do'.[7] It makes little difference that a subjective faith in the power and justice of the market is promoted by economists and politicians in the manner of priests, as maintained by Robert Nelson.[8] Such a faith is an ideology; its resemblance to religion is analogical.

Now, I have suggested in the previous volume that there is another mode of 'thinking economically', one that has nothing to do with either instrumental or purposive causes. More fundamental in determining human conduct is another mode of thinking: it concerns what we count as significant, how we direct our attention, what becomes visible to us, what we record, and what we trust. In short, the reality we experience results from the way in which we invest credit. In some circumstances, credit can become creative, a self-fulfilling prophecy – such as when entrusting an individual with responsibility leads to them living up to that responsibility or when investing in a new economic venture leads to the creation of a profitable enterprise. In other circumstances, the investment of credit can have unintended consequences. Even the market itself is one formulation of a law of unintended consequences, where the pursuit of self-interest serves the public good through acts of exchange. It may also, however, have other unintended consequences.

Let us start with a consideration of a person in debt. While a person considering taking out a debt may be in a position to weigh up costs and benefits, apportioning their preference for spending now and saving later on, a person in debt no longer has this freedom. Once the money borrowed has been spent, the debt is irreversible. While a person without debts is free to make whatever promises they please, a person in debt is subordinate to the record of their promise. To take an extreme case: suppose one borrows a sum of money secured against collateral such as a house; changing market conditions may cause the house to fall in value, while the debt maintains its original price. In negative equity, the debtor loses their freedom to sell and repay the debt. Yet even in the converse case of a rise in prices, there remains an enduring obligation to repay debts. If maintaining one's credit, one's ability to borrow, is essential for participation in market activities, then the obligation to repay the debt is an acute one. Such a debtor has to acquire money, whether through wages, rents, profits, or interest, for debts have to be repaid in the form of money. The debtor is under an obligation to view all possible modes of conduct in relation to the quantity of money they might yield – and, if sufficiently desperate, the temptation to cheat, steal, or extort must be great.[9] After all, Aquinas said that it is not theft if a starving man steals a loaf of bread,[10] and debtors, under sufficient pressure, may be at risk of becoming the starving poor.

There is at least some resemblance between such a debtor and Marshall's economist, who only values goods and services in terms of the money they might cost or yield. Debt, it would seem, offers a strong incentive for taking

the economic point of view.[11] While the debtor is under one kind of obligation, the economist is under another: the obligation to quantify, so that one
can calculate profit and loss. Notice here that insofar as these are obligations, questions of self-interest, which while apparently prominent for the
tradesperson, the entrepreneur, or the speculator, are not the primary concern
of either the debtor or the economist. Yet insofar as the tradesperson, the
entrepreneur, and the speculator only consider their self-interest in terms of
profit and loss, then their preferences are irrelevant: they aim to maximise the
acquisition of money. This has rather curious consequences.

In what sense is the utility-maximising individual rational, if such a person
is unable to measure utility? How can one have rational freedom without
knowledge, where there is only the guess, the impulse, and the hunch? How
do people determine their preferences, except through the limitations of
what they pay attention to, and what they take as real? Each of the previous
mentioned social types adopt the only measure that can substitute for desire,
satisfaction, utility, obligation, and knowledge: money. The only way of comparing preferences and their marginal costs and benefits is on a single quantitative scale the scale of money. The only way of revealing such preferences
is to purchase with money. The real economic calculus does not take place in
the soul and has little relation to self-interest: it takes place in account books.
Where economic theory replaces an individual with a preference-function –
as Pareto put it, 'The individual can disappear, provided that he leaves us with
this photograph of his tastes'[12] – in reality even the tastes can disappear, since
all share a preference for money. The economic system becomes determined
to the extent that each agent seeks to maximise their acquisition of money.
Of course, money, once acquired, can no longer be acquired by the same
person. It can no longer yield any profit. It may as well be spent, or at least,
lent or carefully invested. Yet in the final analysis, the economic imperative
is neither to maximise consumption through spending nor to maximise profit
through investment, but to count as significant only the money. Where Smith
supposed that the division of labour gives rise to markets, now we find that it
is money that gives rise to both markets and the division of labour.

Why is money so significant? On the one hand, money is a unit of
account – it is a means of measuring the strength of motives, the value of
values. On the other hand, money is a means of exchange: it converts preferences into effective demands. As Marx put it,

> If I have no money for travel, I have no *need* – that is, no real and realisable
> need – to travel. If I have the *vocation* for study but no money for it, I have *no*
> vocation for study – that is, no *effective*, no *true* vocation. On the other hand,
> if I have really *no* vocation for study but have the will and money for it, I have
> an *effective* vocation for it. *Money* as the external, universal *medium* and *faculty*

(not springing from man as man or from human society as society) for turning an *image into reality* and *reality into a mere image*, transforms the *real essential powers of man and nature* into what are merely abstract notions and therefore *imperfections* and tormenting chimeras, just as it transforms *real imperfections and chimeras* – essential powers which are really impotent, which exist only in the imagination of the individual – into *real essential powers* and *faculties*.[13]

Insofar as people, whether debtors, economists, tradespeople, entrepreneurs, bankers, or speculators, regard only the money, then they only respond to needs, vocations, or obligations insofar as these are expressed in terms of money. The real world, if not illuminated by money, is left in the shadows, while the imaginary world of wishes becomes real. The result of market economics is a world where needs are denied, but it is also a world reconstructed out of images, imperfections, and tormenting chimeras. This almost magical power of money to turn image into reality is the source of endless fascination. In the preference for money, one finds much more than a preference for consumption later rather than consumption now, and much more than a liquid security against uncertainty: the semi-divine power of creation, the power of turning an image, however impractical, useless, and wasteful, into reality itself. Indeed, since preferences are only revealed to the extent that they are backed up by money as effective demand, and more money enables one to make one's demands more effective, the most powerful and effective preferences will, over the long term, be those that aim at profit.[14] The economy, as is widely known, is driven by the profit motive. Profits are earned in the form of money – nothing is more liquid, more exchangeable, more valuable than money. Whatever one's own insubstantial chimeras or substantial values, money has to be acquired first if those images and values are to be acknowledged by those who count – that is, by those who only count money.

Money is the supreme value because it is both the perspective through which the world is measured and valued, in terms of prices, and the means through which the world is reconstructed, through purchase. Since it is the means of realising all other values, money posits itself as the supreme value. This is to say that money lies above the sphere of human liberty. Just as one who undertakes a debt has to live subsequently according to obligation, one who measures value in terms of money is only valued insofar as he or she has money to spend. It is a case of selling one's freedom. One purchases all that money has to offer – in terms of a power of quantification, a measure for preferences, and a means of realising images – and finds that, as a participant in a market society, one is obliged to work for money. If values are measured by money to be spent, they are measured only from the perspective of one who has money to spend, as if the consumer turns their image into reality through money. In fact, this realisation is effected through the work of others, who submit themselves to the capricious desires supported by money for the sake of acquiring money. Money might seem to promise liberty to those who acquire it, but it affects servitude for all who seek it. What is short-circuited in this process is the opportunity to measure preferences against reality itself, to determine which preferences should be realised. What is short-circuited is the need for moral growth; the consumer remains infantile. For insofar as those around one are primarily interested in the money on offer, then they are unlikely to challenge preferences with alternative perspectives. Most of all, there is little apart from some relics of former cultures to challenge the supreme preference for money itself. In short, money offers an image of liberty – the power to realise preferences – but it imposes servitude: the obligation to conduct life in order to seek money.

There is something quite distinct from an ideological process going on here. While ideologies have effects, they do not impose obligations. Unavowed interests that operate through money are not the determining factor here, even if they are often present. Better analogies are to be found in religion, but neither Feuerbachian projection nor 'fetishism' offer the most relevant conceptions here. A more appropriate account is to be found in Nietzsche's description of the debt owed by the present generation to their forebears:

> Within the original tribal association – we are talking about pre-history – the living generation always acknowledged a legal obligation towards the earlier generation, and in particular towards the earliest, which founded the tribe (and this was not just a sentimental tie: this latter could, with good reason, be denied altogether for the longest period of the human race). There is a prevailing conviction that the tribe *exists* only because of the sacrifices and deeds of the forefathers, – and that these have to be *paid back* with sacrifices and deeds: people recognize an *indebtedness* [*Schuld*], which continually increases because these ancestors continue to exist as mighty spirits, giving the tribe new advantages and lending it some of their power. . . . Following this line of thought, the *dread* of the ancestor and his power, the consciousness of debts towards him, increases inevitably, in direct proportion as the tribe itself becomes ever more victorious, independent, honoured and feared. And not the other way round!. . . If you think this sort of crude logic through to the end: it follows that through the hallucination of the growing dread itself, the ancestors of the *most powerful* tribes must have grown to an immense stature and must have been pushed into the obscurity of divine mystery and transcendence: – inevitably the ancestor is finally transfigured into a *god*. Perhaps we have here the actual origin of gods, an origin, then, in *fear!*[15]

Whether this is an accurate account of the origins of ancestor worship is beside the point. What Nietzsche describes is an intensifying Faustian bargain, where the more one offers sacrifices, the more one is rewarded, the stronger the presence of the power to which one is related. It is a logic of positive feedback, of increasing returns to investment, but one conducted in relation to one's conditions of existence. It is similar to the logic of commitment to a particular faith: by freely committing oneself to a particular religion, one discovers that one has certain obligations, previously present but unacknowledged, obligations that are specified in practice by the religious group itself. One might commit one's life to Christ, but one is obliged to obey the church; and the more devout one is, the greater the sense of obligation.

Marx analysed the religious logic of this human relation to money as the condition of social existence in his comments on James Mill:

> If a man himself alienates this mediating function he remains active only as a lost, dehumanized creature. The *relation* between things, human dealings with them, become the operations of a being beyond and above man. Through this *alien mediator* man gazes at his will, his activity, his relation to others as at a power independent of them and of himself – instead of man himself being the mediator for man. His slavery thus reaches a climax. It is obvious that this *mediator* must become a *veritable God* since the mediator is the *real* power over that with which he mediates me. His cult becomes an end in itself. Separated from this mediator, objects lose their worth. Thus they have value only in so far as they *represent* him, whereas it appeared at first that he had value only to the extent to which *he* represented *them*. This reversal of the original relationship is necessary.[16]

Religion offers an analogy for the human relationship to money when the latter expresses the 'economic point of view' – as a condition for a market mode of existence, it is not merely a perspective adopted, counting values in terms of money, but it is also an obligation imposed. If one does not count the money, one loses credit and the ability to be a significant presence in economic life. Only those who accept the Faustian bargain gain access to influence and power, as suggested by a reformulation of the temptation narrative:

> Again, Money took him to a very high mountain and showed him all the kingdoms of the world and their splendour, and said to him, 'To you I will give their glory and all this authority, for it has been given over to me, and I will give it to anyone I please. If you, then, choose to master me, it will all be yours'. Jesus said to him, 'Be gone, Money! For it is written, "Worship the Lord your God, and serve only him". One cannot serve God and Mammon'.[17]

In fact, the power offered is largely an illusion. Of course, the wealthy can use money to turn their 'images and tormenting chimeras' into reality. But largely, their wealth consists of what Smith described as 'springs the most nice and delicate, which must be kept in order with the most anxious attention, and which in spite of all our care are ready every moment to burst into pieces, and to crush in their ruins their unfortunate possessor'. The wealthy only remain so by becoming the servants of the money system. If they are paid a few luxuries along the way, perhaps at the cost of their moral development, this is small compensation for their labours as agents of the global financial system. For true power would involve an engagement with reality, but reality is in short supply for those who adopt the 'economic point of view'.

There is an illusion of objectivity. For insofar as reality is measured in terms of prices, it is measured in terms of the alternative things that could have been bought with the same sum of money. Reality is measured in terms of replacement or substitution. In other words, to count reality only in terms of prices is to count only the imagined replacement or substitution, not the reality itself. The imaginary world of monetary values is entirely overlaid upon the real world and substitutes itself completely for it. The prices produced by market forces are simply illusions produced by collective agreement – and competition, here, simply masks an underlying collusion in adhering to the rules of the same game. Since the value of things themselves is not in question, all real values are devalued, while monetary values offer their illusion of objectivity.

There is also an illusion of trust. Again, Marx saw clearly how the basis for trust within economic life is mistrust: 'the mistrustful reflection about whether to extend credit or not; the spying-out of the secrets in the private life of the borrower; the revelation of temporary difficulties so as to embarrass a competitor by undermining his credit, etc.'.[18] He illustrated this through the example of credit offered by the wealthy to the poor:

> the poor man's life, his talent and his labours serve the rich man as a *guarantee* that the money he has lent will be returned. This means, then, that the totality of the poor man's social virtues, the content of his life's activity, his very existence, represent for the rich man the repayment of his capital together with the usual interest. For the creditor the death of the poor man is the very worst thing that can happen. It means the death of his capital together with the interest. We should reflect on the immorality implicit in the *evaluation* of a man in terms of *money*, such as we find in the credit system. It is self-evident that over and above these moral guarantees the creditor also has the guarantee provided by the force of law and varying degrees of other *real* guarantees at his disposal.[19]

Once credit is measured in terms of money, as an expectation of an ability to pay, then trust is replaced by mistrust. This is especially true when credit is loaned against the collateral of asset values. For investment assets, whether land, property, rare commodities, or financial assets are priced by what others might be willing to pay for them. This, in turn, is estimated by expectations of a future rise in price or anticipated rate of return – in other words, by the money that they might yield. Instead of money representing the value of assets, assets represent a certain value of money. Under such conditions of distrust, 'wealth' – which we have noted should be considered in terms of goods of appropriation, goods of participation, and goods of offering – is not counted at all. Only money is counted, the money that substitutes itself entirely for reality.

Once money becomes the supreme principal of theoretical knowledge, as the measure of prices, of practical conduct, as the goal to be sought and as the principle of mutual trust, as the embodiment of wealth, then this perspective of evaluation is not chosen but imposes itself as the 'real world', as an illusion of reality itself. For one can no longer appeal to anything outside the closed money system to effect any kind of critique, once knowledge, morality, and trust themselves are regulated by money. Locked into the darkness of his own making, *homo oeconomicus* lacks any authentic relation to his conditions of existence, whether in physical reality, in social reality, or in the reality that ought to underlie religion, the true basis for trust. He is set on a path towards self-destruction. For it is no longer humanity that lives in him, but another. As Marx explained:

> Money has not been transcended in man within the credit system, but man himself is transformed into *money*, or, in other words, money is *incarnate* in him. Human individuality, human *morality*, have become both articles of commerce and the *material* which money inhabits. The substance, the body clothing the *spirit of money* is not money, paper, but instead it is my personal existence, my flesh and blood, my social worth and status. Credit no longer actualizes money-values in actual money but in human flesh and human hearts.[20]

This is the theology of money. It is the underlying cause of why people only count money and why human behaviour approximates to the dynamics of the market.

Chapter 10

Sin

The recent theologian Wolfhart Pannenberg, in summing up Protestant conceptions of sin, explained that 'sin precedes all human acts as a power that dwells in us, that possesses us like our own subjectivity as it overpowers us'.[1] People engage in sin because they are deceived, 'All of us sin because we think we can attain a full and true life thereby'.[2] To sin is to be deceived about the true nature of wealth. For human choices, economic or otherwise, are limited by the things present to consciousness, yet we struggle to bring everything to consciousness so as to make it an object of choice. As Pannenberg puts it:

> All that we can choose is the way in which we will be ourselves, at least within limits, and mostly indirectly by way of the objects and activities to which we devote ourselves, and always in admixture with illusions because we never have ourselves before us as objects, except partially.[3]

Sin is considered here according to three different dimensions: sin is a matter of devotion to certain ends and activities – it is not the ends and activities as such which are the problem so much as the devotion itself an act of constituting oneself. If this act of self-constitution is shaped by certain illusions, then, as Kierkegaard saw, the project of constituting oneself will fail.[4] A second dimension, then, is the deception: here Pannenberg echoes the Platonic tradition, as found in Augustine, that people naturally desire the good, but fall into error insofar as they do not understand what that good is. A third dimension, however, is the power of sin: the way it substitutes itself for human subjectivity, making determinate choices on behalf of human beings. In this radical Pauline conception of sin, it is no longer a question of people choosing to worship idols; even if they once had a choice, they have one no longer. Such a sin may even be inherited, for it is no longer a matter of individual choice – in order to cooperate with those around one, one has to adopt, to some degree, the same illusions, the complementary activities, the same perspectives on what counts as significant. Yet the origin of sin under this conception is more Platonic than Augustinian. The Augustinian conception starts out with pride, putting oneself in the place of God, and so blocking out the rays of illumination from God with the consequence that, even if one does later desire to repent, one no longer knows which way to turn towards the good. Instead, this radical conception of sin fits better with Plato's analogy of the cave: it is as though one turns to worship a different source of light, or at least, one elects to see shadows only in the light of the fire, and for this, one has to enter the darkness of a cave – and, lest one get distracted by the action behind one's head, one is constrained only to look forward at the shadowy images on the wall. These shadows are lifeless: they might move, but they do not interact. And if one is really clever, one might perhaps hypothesise a model that governs their interaction. If this image is more apt, then what are the chains? Weil saw them clearly: 'The chain in the Cavern is *Time* – To look at one thing only at a time'.[5]

To place an entry in an account book is to look at only one thing at a time, a single transaction; it is also not to regard the transaction itself, but only its thinnest of representations, its pale shadow, its valuation in terms of money. The entire complexity of human interactions is reduced to a single quantity, whether asset or liability, credit or debt. The entire complexity of future interactions is reduced to a degree of risk. This is what it means to look at one thing only at a time. And if such an analysis promises a multitude of benefits, an elaborate if static image of the economy, it also comes with a hidden cost: the cost of one's soul, one's sight, one's virtue, and one's sensibility. It is as Paul wrote,

> But sin, seizing an opportunity in the commandment [now the command to count only the money], produced in me all kinds of covetousness. Apart from the law [of accounting] sin lies dead. I was once alive apart from the law, but when the commandment came, sin revived and I died, and the very commandment that promised life proved to be death to me. For sin, seizing an opportunity in the commandment, deceived me and through it killed me. (Rom 7.8–11)

The theology of money, its power to incarnate itself in human flesh and blood, has only one outcome: 'It is no longer I that live, but money that lives in me'. This is sin.

Few Christian theologians have gone so far as to identify money with the power of sin. Among those who have is the former Anglican bishop Peter Selby:

> For as is only to be expected of a god – and Our Lord identified money as a god – money has its own 'spiritual reading', its own demands for time and energy, and a constant thirst for sacrifices. Like all gods, it seeks the constant increase of its

territory, so that it determines more and more of the life choices we make. Like all gods, and unlike the Father of Jesus Christ, it produces its included ones and its excluded ones, in this case the haves and have-nots, and claims to determine human worth by its own simple standard. We may imagine all the while that we live in a confusing world in which we all have to determine our own ethical basis for living; in fact there is a far graver reality which is the constraining of our choices by the 'objective standard' of financial value that presses upon us from all sides.[6]

Part III

EXPLOITATION AND CONSTRAINT: DYNAMICS OF CONDUCT

The previous part concluded that money is like the fire of Plato's cave: it has become the source of illumination that gives orientation to human knowledge, practical conduct, and trust. As such, it leaves in obscurity those dimensions of economic life which do not involve payment. Money, created as debt, is the log in the contemporary human eye when life is counted only in terms of money. In this part, our aim is to pull back the 'veil of money' to expose real effects of economic practices on society, ecology, and spirituality. While human life is still lived in relation to natural necessities, social obligations, and cultivated values, money offers an order or framework for orienting human relations to nature, to others, and to time, respectively, by preference, estrangement, and debt. Such a framework is commonly imagined as a market, an exchange of goods and services facilitated by money. Now the market is a system of circulation: it produces neither land nor natural necessity, neither labour nor human capacities, neither time nor value. It does, however, promote a certain kind of relation to these: land or natural necessities become objects of appropriation; goods and services become objects of substitution; and time and value become objects of anticipation. Only by these means can the real world enter into the marketplace. In spending money, one makes a claim upon what is produced in society, decides between options, and anticipates the outcomes of courses of action.

As a moral ideal for promoting freedom, equality, and justice, the concept of the market is severely lacking because it obscures the non-reciprocal relations upon which any market is founded: in reality, invoking a market promotes constraint, inequality, and unearned income. As a model of economic life, the concept of the market provides a simple approximation only in certain circumstances: when people believe in the logic of the market or they are constrained to act as if they do so by debt. Nevertheless, the idea of money has a strange kind of necessity: once adopted, not only does it provide a systematic framework for accounting what is significant, but it also has a tendency to promote and advance this framework of thinking itself. Most significantly, it is an idea that tends to realise itself in concrete practices of exchange, institutions, laws, customs, systems of accounting, and associated bodies of knowledge. The creative power of money reorganises the human world itself, and with it, the physical environment. The world is prepared for exchange by enclosure and appropriation, by organisation, technology, and the expenditure of energy, and by anticipating future value as if it could already be counted as present. These are material processes of *abstraction and extraction* – just as the data of empirical knowledge are prepared by processes of appropriation of quantities, substitution of variables for determinate realities, and anticipation of results, so also must the natural, social, and cultural worlds be prepared by material processes.

Market exchange cannot exist without appropriation, substitution, and anticipation. In other words, what is normally imagined simply as an exchange of commodities should be understood as mental relations to the real world conducted through appropriation, substitution, and anticipation. Real commodities – baskets of tomatoes, barrels of oil, haircuts, and advertising campaigns – may be physical entities or events, but they are already abstract as well as physical insofar as they are prepared for market exchange: physical processes of separation enable their consideration as isolated entities. In imagination, one is concerned with a thing by itself, whether its substance, use, or exchange value – the thing is imagined as an object of human mastery. The marketplace is imagined as the site of human freedom, where freedom is exercised by appropriation, substitution, and anticipation. Yet in reality, there is no escape from natural constraint, social obligation, nor cultivated value: the market ideal of freedom offers a very poor image of economic reality since so many other processes are also at work. Nevertheless, following Adam Smith, the market has been imagined and adopted as a primary catalyst of growth on the grounds that it promotes human freedom and maximises human productive capacities. Such images of exchange depend on treating money as if it were a commodity, like gold and silver, at once a passive instrument of exchange, unit of account, and store of value. If, by contrast, money is treated as a token of credit, then it possesses other functions: it extends trust, orders values, and gives a reason for appropriation. It offers a system that subsumes human subjectivity.[1] In other words, prior to market exchange, as conditions of its possibility, one finds appropriation of socially produced wealth, substitution of means of profit in place of fulfilling natural necessities, and anticipation enabled by the distinctive spiritual reality of debt.

It is time to explore these overlooked dimensions of markets and money in order to move beyond imagining the world in terms of commodities and exchange. In effect, one may crudely divide contemporary economic life into a three-tier system. One tier consists in the given yet humanly constructed reality: at this level, there are markets and money, yet there are also reconstructed landscapes, reordered societies, and human aspirations. The acts of exchange which coordinate such reconstruction and extraction rest in practice on a second ontological level, the ideas and thoughts in which we participate: these include acts of appropriation, substitution, and anticipation, the dynamics of which will be considered here. Finally, the orientation of such participatory acts underlying economic life is determined by the ordering of credit. The dynamics of this third tier, the organisation credit through exchange by means of banking, will be considered subsequently. There we will see how the actual operations of banking result in disequilibrium dynamics rather than market tendencies to restore equilibrium.

There are two philosophical shifts to be enacted here. A first is familiar: economic life has to be re-embedded not only in ecological life but also in political life as its condition of possibility. Our interest, here, is not in all the material practices, juridical arrangements, and knowledge constructions enacted by imperial command to prepare the world for the marketplace, nor the political ordering of markets as such. Rather than discussing the rich and extensive literature which charts the recent political history of markets,[2] however, I have chosen to focus on how shared acts of cognition – as such necessarily political – detach economic life from political and ecological awareness. The episodes of thought which focus our attention will come from a heterodox tradition of French economic philosophers – Pierre-Joseph Proudhon, Simone Weil, and André Gorz. The purpose of this part is to construct an overview of nature and dynamics of appropriation, substitution, and anticipation, as well as introduce the dynamics of the debt system. For these are practices of cognition imposed upon the mind by the debt-money system. The aim is to show that the debt system, quite unlike an ideal market even while operating in and through a real market, produces incompatible and conflicting constraints.

This is to prepare for the second shift in the final part of this book, one which is far less familiar: the politics of markets has to be re-embedded within institutional life as its condition of inner necessity. One shifts from the level of perspectives to the level of the ordering of trust. People constitute money and markets through words and thoughts, acts and assumptions, which themselves emerge from within the institutionalised lives that they lead. The institutions of finance are the conditions of possibility and machinic necessity of the contemporary economic reality which is typically imagined as free market capitalism. This ordering of economic life takes place through credit. Since widespread market exchange is enabled in practice by bank credit, one may situate Adam Smith's vision of the productive potential of the market, realising opportunities afforded by the division of labour, as a successor to Potter's alchemical scheme of credit (as discussed in *Credit and Faith*). For a bank money is at once capital and a means of exchange. It enables the growth dynamics of a system for organising credit as well as enabling the growth dynamics of exchange and a division of labour. Since it was created through exchange, this miraculous system for the generation of growth does come at a cost: money is created as debt. Money is at once credit, purchasing power, and debt. It expresses opportunity, means, and obligation. Each of these dimensions has its own effects on the dynamics of economic life. While past economics has concentrated on the dynamics of the market and more recent approaches concentrate on generating quantitative data and models, some more heterodox theory explores the dynamics of credit and debt – such approaches, largely developed in the wake of Keynes, will be discussed in part IV.

Chapter 11

Appropriation

> If all our institutions are based on an error in calculation, does it not follow that
> these institutions are so many deceptions? And if the whole social structure is
> built on this absolute impossibility of property, is it not true that the govern-
> ment under which we live is a chimera and our present society a utopia?[1]

Pierre-Joseph Proudhon was among the most trenchant critics of capitalism.
In line with the scholastic insight that usury is theft because it takes advantage of another person's need, he extended such reflections to all unearned
income, whether from rent, dividends, interest, capital appreciation, or any
other source. In each case, it is a matter of claiming a portion of the wealth
produced by others: as he famously stated in his 1840 book, *What Is Property?*, property is theft. Now, property in itself is a complex notion with a
wide range of historical variations: in the case of land, it involves a range
of such rights as to enter, pass through, occupy, use the fruits of, exclude
others from, build on, pass on to inheritors, or sell a designated portion of
land.[2] In the case of a regulated technological object such as a car, it involves
a complex set of rights, liberties, and duties.[3] Proudhon was not opposed
to possession, nor to the natural increase of grain or cattle due to careful
farming, nor even to the sale of such if considered as products of labour.
By property, he meant the 'right of increase claimed by the proprietor over
anything which he has marked as his own'.[4] Essentially, he endeavoured to
distinguish between a real, productive economy, composed of matters of fact,
and a series of property claims, composed of matters of right. Such a distinction, so easy in imagination, is harder to maintain in practice when one tries
to conform rights to facts. For Proudhon, the tenant farmer who labours in the
fields is entitled to the full value of their product; the landlord who claims the
right of rent imposes their right by force. The assertion that property is theft

81

has a dual force: in the first place, claims to property are appropriated and maintained by force; in the second, the very assertion of the absolute right of private property already requires a certain overriding of that right, a seizure of income from another's property. For Proudhon, the conception of property undermines itself. One example of this self-undermining of property is taxation: the state, in order to maintain the power to defend private property, has to levy a compulsory charge – it takes from the 'right of increase'. To have private property without its infringement is impossible – and its infringement, of course, is theft. Proudhon argued that property is impossible. If the right is argued on the basis of equality, because it is a right held in common, then property undermines equality insofar as it involves the right to transfer, sell, give, or abandon, resulting in the concentration of property in the hands of the few. If the right is argued on the basis of occupation, as a means to subsistence, then this right undermines itself, since property must be reallocated arbitrarily after each birth and death.[5] Nevertheless, notwithstanding its impossibility as an absolute right, we still have societies organised around private property.

Proudhon's arguments are instructive because he endeavoured to reach behind existing institutions, in his case property, to attain a natural phenomenon, possession. In this respect, he endeavoured to engage in a naturalist philosophy, like Feuerbach and many others, escaping the constraints of human convention. Many of his economic arguments intended to demonstrate that private property is impossible depended on two questionable assumptions derived from Physiocratic economics: that values can be counted purely in terms of what is produced without taking into account either preferences or money; and that 'a man's labour is worth no more than his consumption'.[6] As such, he had no conception of a surplus product, nor of the rentier or capitalist as one who extracts that surplus. Proudhon is largely remembered as a political thinker rather than as an economic one. Nevertheless, Proudhon grappled with a perennial problem in modern thought, that of reaching beyond our institutions, concepts, and words to grasp reality as it is. The classical economists grappled with the same epistemological problem: How might one reach behind the 'veil of money' to the reality of value? Proudhon himself observed and mocked this problem in the work of Jean-Baptiste Say, who claimed that value (being based on preference) is as variable as opinion:

> Now political economy is the science of values, of this production, distribution, exchange and consumption, so that if exchangeable value cannot be absolutely determined, how is political economy possible? How can it be a science? How can two economists look each other in the face without laughing?[7]

Such epistemological problems arise because any act of knowledge is already an act of appropriation. To know the reality of nature or the reality of value claims a metaphysical knowledge of things-in-themselves.

Nevertheless, Proudhon's considerations of property do shed some light on appropriation and what is appropriated. He offers the basis for a general theory of appropriation as exploitation.[8] By inquiring into the nature of property, and the right by which it is established, he asked: by what right does a proprietor, whether of landed estates or paper assets, make any claim on the produce available? On this problem, Proudhon quoted Jean-Jacques Rousseau:

> The rich have vainly said, 'It is I who have built this wall, I who have earned this land by my labour'. 'Who gave these orders?' we may reply, 'and by what right do you demand payment from us for labour which we did not impose upon you?'.[9]

For the right claimed to land on the basis of occupancy is one thing, but to lend out that land and charge rent is quite another. What, exactly, is being compensated here? One may acquire property through purchase, but that presupposes a prior right to claim and sell property. What is the basis for this original right?

Instead of treating property as an original distribution of land, like many political economists, Proudhon started instead with society. Let us take his account of a person's ownmost property, their talent:

> Talent is a creation of society rather than a gift of nature; it is an accumulated capital of which the recipient is only the guardian. Without society, without the education and powerful assistance which it gives, the finest nature would be inferior to the most ordinary capacities even in the areas where it ought to shine. The more extensive a person's knowledge, the more fertile his imagination, and the more versatile his talent, the more costly has his education been, the more brilliant and numerous his teachers and models, and the greater his debt. The labourer produces from the time he leaves his cradle until he enters his grave, but the fruits of art and science are late and rare, so that often the tree dies before the fruit ripens. Society, in cultivating talent, makes a sacrifice to hope.[10]

In other words, property, whether as talent or as improved land, is produced by credit. Proudhon lamented the equivocation which identifies property as right with property as characteristic or endowment – evident whenever one claims a characteristic as a right for which one should be paid. He did not believe that talent should be rewarded, for it is the product of society, not the product of the owner. He made a comparable judgement about property in land: 'Who is entitled to the rent of the land? The producer of the land, no doubt. But who made the land? God. Therefore, proprietor, retire'.[11] Even if a landlord has improved the land, this is largely through the labour of others. Proudhon concluded that 'all capital, whether material or mental, is the result of collective labour and so is collective property'.[12]

Instead of imagining a primordial distribution of property, then, Proudhon imagined a primordial distribution of ability. He observed that humans may be differentiated from animals – among whom members of the same species have similar capacities – by the markedly different endowment of human abilities. The result is mutual dependence – expressed in exchange and a division of labour:

> Man continually exchanges with man ideas and feelings, products and services. Everything learned and performed in society is necessary to him; but of this immense quantity of products and ideas, what each has to produce and acquire for himself is but an atom in the sun. Man is man only through society, which is supported, for its part, by the balance and harmony of the powers which compose it.[13]

Within this framework of mutual dependence, only the proprietor sets himself outside of society by demanding something for nothing:

> The force of things, the necessity of our consumption, the laws of production, and the mathematical principle of exchange combine to associate us. There is only one exception to this rule, that of the proprietor, who, producing by his right of increase, is not associated with anyone and consequently is not obliged to share his product with anyone, just as no one has to share with him.[14]

While possession and use might be part of productive association, to claim the right of private property is to set oneself outside of society, against society, by asking others to work in one's own place. A proprietor who claims to be offering the use of land or capital for the sake of the common good is simply an unfaithful guardian who denies receipt of the deposit.[15] What Proudhon indicated is a theory of exploitation: the labourer is exploited insofar as he or she creates the means of production – the fenced land, or the tools of labour – for someone else and not for themselves. Of course, the labourer is paid a daily wage. But the reality is that the capitalist has employed many labourers. While wages increase arithmetically in proportion to the number of labourers, production grows geometrically through the division of labour:

> For he [the capitalist] had paid nothing for that immense power which results from the union and harmony of labourers and the convergence and simultaneity of their efforts. Two hundred grenadiers set the obelisk of Luxor on its base in a few hours; do you imagine that one man could have accomplished the task in two hundred days? Yet according to the calculation of the capitalist, the amount of wages paid would have been the same. Well, a desert to prepare for cultivation, a house to build, a factory to run – these are all obelisks to erect, mountains to move. The smallest fortune, the slightest establishment, the beginning of the lowest industry all demand the combination of so many different kinds of labour and skill that one man could not possibly execute them all.[16]

Instead of appropriating the surplus labour time, as in Marx, in this analysis, the capitalist appropriates the social contribution to production.[17] In this respect, it is society itself that is exploited by the capitalist.[18] Yet the individual labourer is also exploited in another respect. For while the labourer is supported for the duration of his employment, he does nothing to guarantee his future support. In collective production of the means of production, the capitalist gains a promise of independence and security for the future, while the worker simply gains wages for today. Tomorrow, he or she may no longer be needed, and will lack the means of production. Even if the wages contain an additional component beyond subsistence costs to put aside for the future, they do not directly compensate the worker for capital, the means of production that has itself been produced.

There are two dimensions to this account of exploitation: the social dimension, in terms of increased productivity, and the temporal dimension, in terms of preparation for the future. A capitalist who has prepared for the future, who has appropriated the social contribution, has received their property in the past. Yet these relations to past and future are set aside, while only the present right of increase is counted. In this respect, on Proudhon's account, exploitation implies the reduction of relations to past and future to rights which can be counted only in the present, such as a present claim to rent or interest or a quantity of labour time that is measurable as a wage. This is how the proprietor denies receipt of the gift, and then feels entitled to make a claim on society. The proprietor in fact sets themselves outside of society insofar as they impose an arithmetic division of property, building an effective wall of 'right' around it, and claiming a portion as their own. Society itself, on Proudhon's account, does not admit of such arithmetic division, since its essence is found only in the enhanced power of mutual combination. This then is the fundamental illusion in exploitation: to treat productive power, which only exists in combination, as something which admits of division and so can be counted, measured, bounded and claimed as private property. For, in truth, neither land nor labour nor capital are productive by themselves, but only in combination.[19] The fences erected around private property offer an illusion of independence; in reality, the productive force of capital depends upon society.

Like the classical economists, Proudhon protested against unearned rent for falling short of justice in exchange. In this respect, he appealed to a market among equals against a primary claim to land by status or force. Of course, the essential question is whether an extensive market is possible without prior acts of enclosure and appropriation.[20] For without some kind of enclosure, even simply of one's talents, there would simply be nothing to sell. Perhaps Proudhon should have been arguing that the market is impossible. Nevertheless, he did clarify how economic rent, whether from land or from interest, leads towards disequilibrium. In the dismal case of depression, Proudhon turned the difference between arithmetic division and geometric growth back against Thomas Malthus: before trying to check the reproduction of workers, it is the right of property to increase exponentially through rent or interest that should be checked.[21] For this right to claim rent is the cause of poverty. One of his arguments (slightly modified) explores a scenario of economic stagnation: suppose that a landlord extracts rents at the monopoly rate, leaving a mere subsistence income for the collective of tenants whose productive capacity depends on the combination of their labour power. Then, as a result of a poor harvest or accident, one of the tenants dies. The estate is capable of the same product as before, and so the same overall rent is still expected by the proprietor. Without a new worker, the remaining workers have to contribute more rent per capita, but they will produce less overall because of the missing worker – and so they each receive below the subsistence rate until another of their number dies, intensifying the situation still further. Eventually, perhaps, an 'enlightened' landlord might reduce the rent to the monopoly rate again – until the next poor harvest and death. Proudhon's point is that there will always be an excess population when rent is extracted, even when the land is under-utilised. The right to increase of private property amounts to removal of the means of subsistence; property is murder.[22]

For the positive case of economic growth, Proudhon offered another argument. Suppose a landowner, who charges rent at 5% of the value of the estate, reinvests that sum each year in the purchase of further productive land. By Proudhon's calculations, a sum of 100 francs, invested at 5% for 600 years, would amount to over 107 million million francs, more than twenty times the value of the terrestrial globe.[23] Perhaps the value of land might increase in the meantime as a result of competition between landowners – but so would the relative price of other goods and the inequality between workers and landowners. Pauperisation is again the direct result of the right of property to claim an increase, as the landowners progressively appropriate all possible property. Property is theft. Again, the root of exploitation is the difference between arithmetic and geometric growth, where in this case, the proprietor claims the geometric portion: while production might increase fourfold, tenfold or even a hundredfold, compound interest increases exponentially. The right of property to increase is therefore unsustainable.

Proudhon was among the first in modern times to point out that economic growth leads to increasing inequality and the depletion of resources. The ultimate outcome would be economic collapse, impoverishing the rentiers as well as all others. Of course, in an economic collapse, the measures of wealth are those which fall, including incomes, assets, and prices – businesses may no longer be viable, even though the same labour, technology, and resources are present as before. What is lost is social cooperation as a condition for the production of wealth. For those who appeal to a natural, productive economy, what is lost is merely fictitious wealth; nevertheless, such fictions have real effects via trust.

Weil, commenting on Proudhon in Depression era 1937, went so far as to suggest that total economic collapses cannot occur. 'An economic system is not like a building, and economic ills are not like falling masonry'.[24] What may happen, by contrast, is a change of political regime: even then, the new political regime inherits precisely the same economic conditions as its predecessor, and, unlike its predecessor, it may somehow manage to survive under those conditions – no economic conditions are impossible to live with economically, even if stagnation leads to the starvation of the population. The rise in inequality and the threat of starvation may or may not provoke political change, but the overall economic conditions, including methods and levels of production and circuits of distribution, are not immediately ameliorated by that change. One might hesitate here: the social embodiment of wealth in contracts, businesses, and employment may vanish overnight – her point was not that matters cannot worsen, but no political revolution can immediately make them better. Her main point, however, is that a purely financial equilibrium – balancing income and expenditure (at the level of circulation) – can be no substitute for a real economic equilibrium (at the level of production and consumption), for the former is compatible with growing inequality. For capital invested at 3% will multiply a hundredfold in two centuries. It is mathematically impossible for a society based upon money and loans at interest to succeed in maintaining its debts over the long term – the automatic result would be that all resources would pass into the hands of a few people. Weil, then, leaves us with an apparently insuperable dilemma:

> The payment of debts is necessary for social order. The non-payment of debts is quite equally necessary for social order. For centuries humanity has oscillated, serenely unaware, between these two contradictory necessities. Unfortunately, the second of them violates a great many seemingly legitimate interests and it has difficulty in securing recognition without disturbance and a measure of violence.[25]

There are, of course, ways of reducing overall debt: inflation, devaluation, and default. Yet even these can be deferred: debts can be perpetually refinanced, as has occurred with national debts and currencies issued by central banks.

In the centuries since the Financial Revolution in England, it is notable that property has not yet entirely passed into the hands of the few. Given that Proudhon identified such strong tendencies towards disequilibrium, it is worth remarking the tendencies which operate in the other direction towards broadening the distribution of wealth. There is direct redistribution of wealth, whether through taxes and welfare or through philanthropy and aid; inheritance taxes especially affect the distribution of landed estates. There is social sharing of wealth, whether through public goods and infrastructure, or through sharing of knowledge and techniques. There are the dynamics of the market itself, identified by Smith, whereby the wealthy redistribute money by spending for others to provide their goods and services, so distributing purchasing power. There is the extension of wealth-creating activities, whether extensively across lands and through the creation of new markets or intensively through increases of productivity. Perhaps most significantly, there is the reconstruction of landscapes and societies to yield sources of cheap fuel, food, resources, and labour, turning people from subsistence to market-oriented production: with a wide variety of kinds of property, many can become rentiers. There are also the destructive effects of war, for although a few can get rich in wartime, the overall destruction of accumulated wealth tends to equalise the fortunes of the majority. There is credit and investment: for extracting interest by creating the means of production is entirely unlike buying agricultural land to extract rent from those who work it. Finally, there are the dynamics of debt-funded asset appreciation, to be described in chapter 14. The relative prominence of differing dynamics working toward equilibrium or disequilibrium will depend on local conditions, regulations, and values. Nevertheless, each of these depends on property, which is appropriation of the productive power inherent in society. The key question is not who owns property, but whether its productive power is invested and distributed once more in society.

The extension of markets, whether they concentrate or distribute wealth, involves an extension of acts of appropriation. If the limits to markets are not always found in social inequality, they may be understood more broadly as appropriation of nature, involving substitution and appropriation of the future, involving anticipation. On these issues, Weil may guide us beyond Proudhon in order to find the sources of incompatible demands.

Chapter 12

Substitution

> The long-foreseen moment has arrived when capitalism is on the point of seeing its development arrested by impassable barriers. In whatever way we interpret the phenomenon of accumulation, it is clear that capitalism stands essentially for economic expansion and that capitalist expansion has now nearly reached the point where it will be halted by the actual limits of the earth's surface.[1]

Weil opened her critique of Marxism, *Oppression and Liberty*, with an announcement of the limits to economic growth – limits she expected to be reached in about two generations. Yet beyond external, planetary limits, she also conceived of internal limits to the increase in production. She divided the causes of increased productivity into three kinds: the rationalisation of labour in space; the rationalisation of labour in time; and the utilisation of natural sources of energy. The first factor is based on mass production and exchange: the concentration, division, and coordination of labour. Instead of expecting ever-increasing returns to scale, she expected this effect of mass production to be counterbalanced by increasing overheads – the more complex the system of production, the more people that are required to coordinate and oversee it. Those who work within an organisation in management, administration, accounting, legal services, marketing, and public relations start to grow in numbers to outweigh those whose primary work is in production. Similarly, those who work outside productive firms in retail, banking, finance, and consultancy, together with those who provide services for this vast cadre of professionals, constitute an enormous overhead on the whole process of production. This process was to be accelerated when finance became an autonomous sphere, detached from production. The result 'leaves an ever wider and wider margin for waste and brings about an accelerated, and no doubt, to a certain extent parasitic, increase'.[2] After a certain threshold, progress is transformed into regression for the system consumes more than it produces.

Another cause of the increase of productivity, the coordination of effort in time, is achieved by technological advance: first the use of tools, then the mechanisation of processes, and finally automation – entrusting a machine with a combination of varied operations. Automation can, in theory, develop indefinitely. Nevertheless, Weil still envisaged limits: for in automation, the variety of operations has to be defined and limited beforehand. If conditions change, then the machines will need adapting, repairing, or replacing, resulting in a certain overhead of human labour. As change accelerates, it is difficult to be certain about whether productivity gains will always outweigh overheads, but Weil expected that, at higher levels of technical efficiency, the advantages from new developments would start to diminish in comparison to the drawbacks. But there is a further limit: machines require raw materials that themselves require the costs of mining. While Weil noted the human costs in blood of mining iron, coal, and potassium, the costs of human sacrifice have rarely constituted a limit – more relevant today with vastly improved extraction technologies are the overall amounts of cheaply extractable mineral deposits. There are very limited deposits of silver, tin, zinc, lead, copper, sulphur, and fluorspar remaining.[3] At some threshold, the costs of extraction become greater than the gains of extending technology.

The crucial procedure for increasing productivity, however, is utilisation of natural sources of energy.[4] Energy, as the capacity to do work, is pure quantifiability; as such, it is also unlimited convertibility or substitutability. What money is to markets, energy is to physics: a principle of measure, comparison, and substitution. As a result of its indifferent utility, its unlimited substitutability, its transportability, and its universal use in nearly all processes of production and consumption, the market for energy could in principle behave rather like an ideal model of a market – except, of course, for political interference.[5] This does not, however, mean that energy extraction has unlimited potential; markets are also subject to physical interference from resource depletion.[6] Just because we do not know what new sources of energy may become available does not mean that we can be confident of unlimited progress in this direction, for it costs labour to obtain that energy. Yet in the case of fossil fuels, the cheaper deposits are utilised first, and then costs of prospecting and extraction rise. 'It may even happen, at the worst, that the utilization of a natural source of energy involves more labour than the human expenditure of energy one is seeking to replace'.[7] Weil clearly understood the economic concept, before its time, of energy return on energy invested.[8] It does not matter if foolish people are willing to invest in novel forms of energy production that cost more in fossil fuel energy than they produce overall; such activity only accelerates the approach of limits to economic growth. Overall, though, Weil's fundamental concern is this:

> an unlimited increase in productivity . . . is what everybody assumes, both among capitalists and socialists, without the smallest preliminary study of the question; it is enough that the productivity of human effort should have increased in an unheard-of manner for the last three centuries for it to be expected that this increase will continue at the same rate. Our so-called scientific culture has given us this fatal habit of generalizing, of arbitrarily extrapolating, instead of studying the conditions of a given phenomenon and the limits implied by them.[9]

Extrapolation ignores limits by invoking substitution. In modern resource economics, it is possible to envisage the sustainable production of a finite resource only if the continually diminishing rate of production can be compensated in other ways.[10] This might involve a relatively high degree of substitutability between capital and production, so that more and more can be done with less and less (although, one might add, that approaching the limit, the degree of substitutability would have to increase to an unlimited extent, so that something can be done with almost nothing). This might involve a sufficiently large rate of technical progress so that previously unextractable resources can be extracted at the same rate as before (although, one might add that difficult to extract resources are still finite, and technological progress is unlikely to be infinite). This might involve some kind of permanent back-stop technology, such as renewable energy, that becomes more economically viable as prices rise (although, one might add, that even renewable energy production requires resources other than energy from the sun such as minerals, and so is not unlimited). In other words, extrapolation of growth depends upon the assumption of an infinite power of substitution, whether of capital, technology, or alternative resources. This assumption relates far more to the conditions of an ideal model of a market, where the value of a thing consists in its price, in other words, in a comparison of what might be substituted for it, than it does to real life on a finite planet. Such ideal market economics is mere dogma – one does not make a science out of the superficial effect of resemblance achieved by the use of equations, models, and the gathering of data. Real science, Weil insists, involves finding the conditions of a phenomenon and the limits implied by them.

Economic production can be conceived as a linear process involving extraction of resources, transport of materials, production of commodities, delivery and consumption of goods and services, with the production of material waste at each stage of the process. The condition of possibility for this linear process is the wider environment. In this wider environment, there is continual change, and here many linear processes occur, such as increases in some populations and decreases in others. While some linear processes are very long-term, such as heat radiation from the sun, organic linear processes usually have much shorter timescales, since they tend to either exhaust the resources that made them possible or pollute their environments. Sustainable processes are embedded in wider circular structures, whereby the waste of one process is the resource for another, and so on. Evolutionary processes involve continual adaptation to changing conditions. Within this context, many civilisations have come and gone because they were unsustainable.[11] It remains to be seen whether human civilisation as a whole can be an enduring evolutionary process – this depends on adaptation to continually changing conditions. The crucial issue for contemporary economic life is whether the substitution of resources and technologies is alone sufficient to achieve adaptation, or whether the entire system of the concentration, division, and coordination of production has to undergo radical changes.[12]

The effects that the current industrial system of production has on its wider environment are well understood: they contribute to a changing climate; sea level rises; shortages of fresh water; deforestation; desertification; soil degradation; accumulation of toxic and non-toxic waste; depletion of minerals and fossil fuels; the pollution of air, freshwater, seawater, and soil; interruption of ocean circulation; species invasions; disease epidemics; loss of biodiversity; ecosystem collapses; natural disasters; food insecurity; mass immigration; and conflict and war.[13] Each of these 'externalities' involves complex interactions between a range of factors outside of processes of production. In other words, the concentration, division, and coordination of production processes are not the prerogative of humanity alone. Nature itself consists in organic and ecological processes of production that cannot be broken up into isolated resources and placed onto a linear and anthropocentric production process without disrupting existing networks and conditions of existence. To attempt to address environmental problems through mitigation and adaptation via abstractive and linear patterns of thinking is highly likely to exacerbate the problem. There are very limited possibilities for substitution for a stable climate; for cities built at sea level; for fresh water, forests, and fertile land; for spaces clear of waste; for available minerals and fossil fuels; for clean air; for consistent ocean circulation, species stability, health, biodiversity, functioning ecosystems; for the absence of natural disasters; for food availability; for population stability; and for peace. Attempts to mitigate and adapt might amount to the enclosure of islands of stability amid oceans of chaos but can rarely replenish entire systems of complex interactions. As the German economist Elmar Altvater put it immediately after the fall of the Soviet bloc:

> The ecological problem arises from the fact that eco-networks cannot survive if they are broken up through various uses of natural resources. But markets base themselves upon the commodity-form, which rests in turn upon isolated private

property that requires fencing or other kinds of division. Abstraction is inevitably made from systemic interconnections of a social or ecological character.[14]

The isolation of independent variables in science and economics, the extraction of resources, the mechanisation and automation of production, like the appropriation of private property, depend upon abstraction and division. Ecological health depends upon connection.

There is something deeply irrational about such linear thinking: it does not proportion attention to what matters, to the varied conditions of existence. For example, in the harvesting of natural forests for timber or their clear-cutting for agriculture, only a tiny proportion of the material cleared is of any interest for usage. The rest is waste. Such production of waste is conceptual as well as physical. As Altvater explains:

> Of the immense variety of organic and inorganic natural materials and species of life, the industrial system takes an interest in comparatively few: minerals, mass agricultural products, and above all energy. Unexploitable species have no value: plants are weeds, unusable trees are jungle, animals are pests and materials are dross.[15]

In other words, linear thinking affects a devaluation of values. Substitution invokes its own criteria of success by excluding in advance any other recognition of value.

Chapter 13

Anticipation

Wealth has an intrinsically social dimension in the concentration, division, and coordination of labour. Any attempt to appropriate this power of increase by means of private appropriation is a form of estrangement, a way of cutting oneself off from valuing this productive power. Similarly, wealth also has an intrinsically environmental dimension in the provision of resources and the processing of pollutants. Any attempt to substitute for non-linear processes is a form of uprooting, a way of cutting oneself off from the conditions of existence. Now Weil also believed that wealth has an intrinsically spiritual dimension:

> To be rooted is perhaps the most important and least recognized need of the human soul. It is one of the hardest to define. A human being has roots by virtue of his real, active and natural participation in the life of a community which preserves in living shape certain particular treasures of the past and certain particular expectations of the future. This participation is a natural one, in the sense that it is automatically brought about by place, conditions of birth, profession and social surroundings. Every human being needs to have multiple roots. It is necessary for him to draw wellnigh the whole of his moral, intellectual and spiritual life by way of the environment of which he forms a natural part.[1]

Such spiritual wealth is intimately connected to the need for honour. Honour, in Weil's thought, is a good of offering: one only lives an honourable life by offering honour. And yet honour is a vital need of the human soul:

> This need is fully satisfied where each of the social organisms to which a human being belongs allows him to share in a noble tradition enshrined in its past history and given public acknowledgement.

For example, for the need of honour to be satisfied in professional life, every profession requires to have some association really capable of keeping alive the memory of all the store of nobility, heroism, probity, generosity, and genius spent in the exercise of that profession.

All oppression creates a famine in regard to the need of honour, for the noble traditions possessed by those suffering oppression go unrecognized, through lack of social prestige.[2]

In this way, writing in London in 1943 during the occupation of France, Weil formulated a further dimension of oppression and exploitation: uprooting. Uprooting is the loss of institutions, traditions, and expectations. For insofar as previous generations have conducted their lives according to the vision of the legacy they might leave to subsequent ones, such a legacy consists in far more than accumulated asset values: it consists in stable institutions, goods of participation, living traditions, and a culture of performance of excellence. Of course, few might wish to be entirely bound by the expectations of their forebears, for changing circumstances require adaptation, and moreover, traditions only truly live when they are inwardly appropriated and creatively performed. Yet to simply squander the wealth of spiritual resources available from the past through the pursuit of narrowly defined objectives, whether through capitalist rationalisation or socialist revolution, is to impoverish both one's own generation and all that follow. For participating in a living tradition is entirely different from analysing a dead text. The loss of a living relation to the past is such that one no longer comprehends what it meant for that past to live. The result of uprooting is that one has little conception of what one has lost – and little conception of what one might still lose by further uprooting. Uprooting is progressive: those who are uprooted uproot others. Just as there are dangers of climate or biodiversity crises wiping out human habitats, and economic crises wiping out human subsistence, there is also the danger of a spiritual crisis of uprooting, wiping out meaningful aspiration and evaluation. In the latter case, one would not even notice that it has happened as one slowly endeavours to rebuild the meaningful world piece by piece, even if it perpetually falls apart once more.

While military conquest is the principal cause of uprooting, Weil also saw two others. One is education, producing a culture removed from the world in a 'stove-pipe' atmosphere, broken up by specialisation and directed strongly towards technical science, entirely deprived of contact with this world or a world beyond.[3] The other cause of uprooting is money:

Money destroys human roots wherever it is able to penetrate, by turning desire for gain into the sole motive. It easily manages to outweigh all other motives, because the effort it demands of the mind is so very much less. Nothing is *so* clear *and so* simple as a row of figures.[4]

While money might satisfy the human need that Adam Smith identified for sympathy and approbation, it lacks specific qualities, and therefore cannot truly satisfy the need for honour identified by Weil in the form of participating in a tradition of excellence and virtue.

Insofar as modernisation involves processes of rationalisation, the reordering of social institutions and practices of production and education, as well as the reordering of the environment, then one of the costs is to the human soul: it is participation in a tradition of virtue. While such changes are expected to bring progress, such progress is rarely assessed in terms of excellence and virtue. Weil was suspicious of much that counts for progress:

> It would be useless to turn one's back on the past in order simply to concentrate on the future. It is a dangerous illusion to think that such a thing is even possible. The opposition of future to past or past to future is absurd. The future brings us nothing, gives us nothing; it is we who in order to build it have to give it everything, our very life. But to be able to give, one has to possess; and we possess no other life, no other living sap, than the treasures stored up by the past and digested, assimilated and created afresh by us. Of all the human soul's needs, none is more vital than this one of the past . . .
>
> For several centuries now, men of the white race have everywhere destroyed the past, stupidly, blindly, both at home and abroad. If in certain respects there has been, nevertheless, real progress during this period, it is not because of this frenzy, but in spite of it, under the impulse of what little of the past remained alive.
>
> The past once destroyed never returns. The destruction of the past is perhaps the greatest of all crimes.[5]

For what is lost in this process is the capacity to pay attention to what matters. What is lost is the capacity to evaluate. Unless one is confronted by an urgent crisis, forcing one to restore attention to what now seems to be decisive, then the ability to pay attention to what matters is dependent on records of past credit – these offer external validation of practices of attention as embodied in a living tradition. Without this, one merely lurches from crisis to crisis, from urgent demand to urgent demand, in an entirely fragmented spiritual existence. For what the human soul requires, above all else, is a principle of synthesis, a source for the evaluation of values, a way of integrating reality, and all that matters as a whole.[6] Nevertheless, each means of integrating reality into an interconnected whole is liable to direct attention to some matters at the expense of others.

Integrating reality in thought is itself dependent on integrating reality in practice. Participation in a living tradition is a condition for integrating free human beings with each other in society through trust. While each individual may endeavour to appropriate and express that tradition in his or her own way, such different individuals are capable of trusting each other to the extent that they perceive each other as motivated by the same source. Once uprooted, this basis for credit is lost, and other bases for unity need to be sought. Weil was sceptical about these alternatives. One condition for unity is common emotion, as in a mass movement or uprising: 'At certain moments in history, a great rush of wind sweeps over the masses; their breath, their words, their movements are merged together. Then nothing is able to resist them. The mighty know in their turn, at last, what it is to feel alone and defenceless; and they tremble'.[7] The problem with such moments is that they have no enduring relation to past and future; they cannot last. They may be sufficient to suspend all action, and even unseat the ruling regime; but unless the group is sufficiently small, they cannot offer a new basis for cooperation, coordination, and trust. 'The mass dissolves once more into individuals, the memory of its victory fades, the erstwhile situation, or its equivalent, is gradually re-established; and although it may be that in the interval there has been a change of masters, it is always the same ones who have to obey'.[8] Another condition for unity is collective self-interest, formed around competitive goods, such as power, privilege, and consumption. In this way, the few can unite against the many, gaining all the advantages of concentration, division of tasks, and coordination. This is how the few are always able to dominate the many: 'precisely because they are few they form a whole. The others, precisely because they are too many, are one plus one plus one, and so on'.[9] Such cohesion can only be established in small groups.

In modern life, however, it has been possible to facilitate the concentration, division, and coordination of an unlimited number of people through a mixed combination: hierarchical units, as firms and enterprises, may be combined with free markets, enabling exchange, and sovereign states, enforcing the rule of law. The result is a coordination of human activity far beyond the understanding and attention of any one individual. In such a context, the individual is disempowered:

> In almost all fields, the individual, shut in within the bounds of a limited proficiency, finds himself or herself caught up in a whole which is beyond him, by which he must regulate all his activity, and whose functioning he is unable to understand. . . . The rationalized factory, where a man finds himself shorn, in the interests of a passive mechanism, of everything which makes for initiative, intelligence, knowledge, method, is as it were an image of our present-day society.[10]

Following Marx, it is as though reason and method are embodied in the machine or process, rather than in the individual operator. In place of a living tradition, which coordinates goods of offering and fosters goods of participation, one has a machine or procedure, serving a clearly defined objective. Specialisation – the result of the division of labour – implies the subordination of those who carry out a process to those who coordinate the process.

Yet both are subordinate to the process itself. While this is evident in all work
that consists in carrying out a procedure specified in advance – one may think
here of those formulaic conversations with people in call centres or even on
the doorstep – its essence is captured in Marx's famous remarks on machine
production:

> Not as with the instrument, which the worker animates and makes into his organ
> with his skill and strength, and whose handling therefore depends on his virtu-
> osity. Rather, it is the machine which possesses skill and strength in place of
> the worker, is itself the virtuoso, with a soul of its own in the mechanical laws
> acting through it; and it consumes coal, oil, etc., just as the worker consumes
> food, to keep up its perpetual motion. The worker's activity, reduced to a mere
> abstraction of activity, is determined and regulated on all sides by the move-
> ment of the machinery, and not the opposite. The science which compels the
> inanimate limbs of the machinery, by their construction, to act purposefully, as
> an automaton, does not exist in the worker's consciousness, but rather acts upon
> him through the machine as an alien power, as the power of the machine itself.[11]

As Marx comments, this process of the real subsumption of labour under
capital is not an extrinsic by-product of rationalisation; it is the essence of the
process of the formation of fixed capital itself. Weil simply follows Marx in
extending this insight beyond the factory to the entire process of the organisation of labour, whether within a firm or beyond it in the market and state.
Each agent has limited knowledge of the structures and forces that have a
bearing on his or her conduct, and even less ability to act directly upon them.

Machines, procedures, and institutions all involve a process of concrete
abstraction: it is not that such forms of capital think, but they contain and
transmit the legacy of those who designed them. Such capital is itself a
form of writing, a materialisation, and transmission of ideas. The difference
between dead capital and a living tradition, however, is that while the latter
only survives to the extent that it is inwardly appropriated and creatively
expressed, dead capital short-circuits the consciousness of the operator of
the machine. While this may have immensely valuable consequences, such
as saving time and attention so that it may be given to what matters, it can
also have serious drawbacks. As work becomes more specialised, capital is
accumulated, and activities are coordinated from without, it is no longer sufficient to rely upon the cooperative impulses of the worker. As André Gorz
has noted, the personal motivation, goodwill, capacities, and virtues of the
worker, while so significant for participation in civil society, are insufficient
to regulate conduct in a professional capacity. Rationalisation involves the
formal codification and regulation of the conduct, duties, and relationships
of both workers and professionals.[12] For in such a technical environment,
there is no role for ethical and political reason, which have been developed to

regulate personal conduct in relation to participation in a common good, nor for religious reason, which has been developed to regulate personal conduct in relation to goods of offering. These prove to be radically incompetent in the new situation: they do not offer specific guidance on the technical conduct to be followed. They fail to offer an appropriate motive.[13] Such may be taken as a fundamental reason for a dynamic of secularisation: traditional and religious thoughts struggle to find any purchase or relevance in everyday life. In many forms of work, one simply cannot comprehend how the common goodwill be achieved by one's own contribution – if, indeed, it contributes to the common good at all – and one simply cannot see how the common good might be enhanced by any particular modification of conduct. Past traditions are voluntarily abandoned because they seem inadequate for handling contemporary reality.

Yet just as workers require food, they also require motivation for work. Gorz explains the complete split between the consciousness of the worker and the requirements of the role: individuals are induced to function in a complementary manner, like parts of a machine, towards an end that is unknown to them only by the promise of a reward that is entirely independent of the process.[14] Since the worker's own functioning is heteronomous, their motivation has to be extrinsic and unrelated to the process of work: work becomes merely a means to a wage. The odd consequence of compensation, as Gorz notes, is that the objective of work becomes leisure: on the one hand, work has to be adapted to the rationality embedded in the machines, procedures, and organisation, where the worker disciplines herself to be more and more productive, more and more heteronomous; on the other hand, compensation is offered in monetary terms to be spent on consumer goods, entertainment, and leisure, promoting the hedonistic values of comfort, instant pleasure, and minimal effort. Where production is ascetic, consumption is hedonic. In neither case is there much opportunity for a life of participation or service. The price of rationalisation is that it divorces work from life: 'Learning how to work means unlearning how to find, or even to look for, a meaning to non-instrumental relations with the surrounding environment and with other people'.[15] There is little role for religious or philosophical reflection in the workplace:

> Work is a protective shell. 'It's all set up for you'. Questions about the meaning and goal of life are resolved in advance: since there is no room in a worker's life for anything other than working for money, money is the only possible goal. In the absence of time for living, money is the only compensation for lost time, for a life spoiled by work. Money symbolizes everything that the worker has not, is not, and cannot be because of the constraints of work. This is why work will never pay *enough*, but also why money earned by working was originally perceived as *being worth more* than the life one had to sacrifice for it.[16]

Gorz identifies here one of the most fundamental contradictions of capital-ism. On the one hand, production must be as efficient as possible; on the other hand, in order to maximise profits, consumption must be as profligate as possible. When it comes to working hours and the scarcity of employment, Gorz's analysis is so provocative as to require extensive quotation.

> *People must be prevented from choosing to limit their working hours so as to prevent them choosing to limit their desire to consume.* A growing number of wage earners must work and earn *beyond their felt needs*, so that a growing proportion of income may be spent on consumption determined by no need. For it is such optional, superfluous consumption which can be directed, shaped and manipulated according to the 'needs' of capital more than to individuals' needs. *It is to the extent that consumption frees itself from felt needs and exceeds them that it can serve production, that is, serve the 'needs' of capital.*
>
> . . . Such a system demands meeting felt needs *at the lowest cost* but, at the same time, *maximum expenditure* on consumption exceeding felt needs. It has nothing to gain from eliminating poverty and reducing inequality; for needs are limited and cannot assure an indefinite growth of production. Wants and the desire for the superfluous are, by contrast, potentially unlimited. Meeting unsat-isfied needs by transferring revenue from the rich to the poor thus runs counter to economic rationality as it expresses itself, totally unfettered, in capitalist rationality. For such a transfer would come down to increasing need-determined demand which seeks satisfaction *at the lowest cost*, at the expense of fashion- and fancy- led demand which lends itself to any and every extravagance.[17]

In all this, the fundamental motivation for human conduct is anticipation. The human mind closes itself off from the spiritual treasures transmitted from the past only by anticipating the future, whether this is a future of leisure, a future of consumption, or a future of profit. This effect reaches its highest intensity in undertaking debt, whether for consumption, for education, for investment, or for speculation. For in borrowing, one anticipates both the costs and the benefits, the money to be earned, and the pleasure or profits to be obtained. Anticipation is a way of appropriating the future, substituting present expectations for contingent possibilities. It is a commitment to one-self to keep the world out, to fence in one's future life, except insofar as the world can be rationalised to meet one's profit objectives. Such anticipation is a denial of creation.

In this sense, debt is not at all the converse of the conception of credit developed in part III of the previous volume. For the previous discussion introduced a conception of credit as a good of offering: it involves attention to what matters, discerning potential and offering such nutrients as will promote the growth of that potential. Such credit is entirely open to contingency and to failure. Such credit can even be achieved through the offer of money which, if the enterprise is successful, will later be repaid. In this respect it may operate through debt; but it is not at all the same activity because it involves a different relation to the future. Credit does not need to quantify its success in terms of money; money remains the means, not the end. Debt, by contrast, overwrites the future with a contractually defined 'need': an objective to fulfil, as well as an amount of money to be repaid. All other values become subordinate to this specified objective, along with the requirement to repay money. Most of all, the one in debt is inclined to sacrifice spiritual wealth for the sake of anticipation of the future. Debt is a colonisation of both the future and the past. But such a future is just a thin expectation; it has nothing of the thickness, the specificity, the variety of the past. It has nothing to feed us or teach us. It 'brings us nothing, gives us nothing; it is we who in order to build it have to give it everything, our very life'.

Chapter 14

Debt Dynamics and Inequality

Modern economic freedom involves three essential powers: a power to anticipate, to form rational expectations about the future; a power to substitute, to
make choices among available options; and a power to appropriate, to claim a
benefit or its increase as one's own. Such freedom regards the world from the
perspective of one with money to spend. In part II, we saw how the mechanism that functions as the basis of trust for human cooperation has migrated
from religion to money. The traditional functions of money as a store of value,
a unit of account, and a means of exchange each name an aspect of the ways
in which people can handle, measure, and access value. People have trust in
money to the extent that it enables them to preserve value under conditions of
uncertainty, to estimate value under conditions of heterogeneity, and to obtain
value under conditions of lack of trust. Only if people trust in money do they
gain any sense of independence. Only if people trust in money do their free
activities of appropriation, substitution, and anticipation make sense.

The preceding discussions of appropriation, substitution, and anticipation
have endeavoured to show the real limits to the exercise of such freedom. For
human life and productive capacities are entirely dependent upon the cooperation of others: even the person of independent means who spends money
realises his or her aims only through commanding the provision of goods and
services by others. The fulfilment of human needs is also entirely dependent
upon the cooperation of the nonhuman world, in the form of an inhabitable
environment and the availability of resources: the consumer fulfils his or her
preferences only through their provision by nature. Even the capacity to anticipate, to project into the future, is dependent upon a basis for trust through
which activities can be coordinated and predicted: the speculator has to rely
on evidence from the past. If the activities of appropriation, substitution, and
anticipation disrupt their own conditions of existence, then both the freedom

they presuppose and the reason which guides their conduct are grounded in illusion. A change in their conditions of possibility will disrupt any attempt to pursue 'rational' conduct.

The process of uprooting involves more than the subordination of the individual to economic and political imperatives. One still makes evaluations, but such evaluations are only effective insofar as they are in accordance with an automatic, machinic process. The presence of positive feedback dynamics, independent of any human will, in the evaluation of values can best be approached first by observing its operation in economic life. It is widely supposed that money is a passive instrument which serves free human evaluations. It is therefore deeply undermining if people discover that the institution in which they have placed so much trust – money itself, usually conceived as representing intrinsic value in the manner of coinage – should prove to have been replaced from outset of secular modernity by a rather different institution – banking. What is taken as a given turns out to be a collective construction. For, in the contemporary economy, it is very largely the operations of banks which offer a store for value, a means for counting and recording value, and a method of exchange. For the apparent independence of a person of means is in fact a complete dependence on the functions of the banking sector. In other words, freedom to anticipate, substitute, and appropriate is only effectively exercised if it is in accordance with the obligations of credit and debt ordered by the financial sector. To be 'rational', in this context, is no longer a matter of understanding reality; it is merely a matter of taking one's place within a wider institutional framework.

Money is a concrete abstraction: it is a token of value, a means of recording the social recognition of purchasing power. The replacement of coinage by paper notes demonstrates that it is by no means essential to the function of money that it should hold that value in its own substance as a given weight of valuable metal. What is more essential is that there should be a means of recording the social recognition of purchasing power. An economy mediated by banking can largely dispense with notes and coins altogether: all that is required is the technology of recording and transfer. What are recorded are credits and debts, assets and liabilities, not the accumulation of a substance of value.[1] For the first principle of modern money theory, that each financial asset corresponds exactly to a financial liability, is what enables the creation of purchasing power out of nothing.[2] In other words, each person's purchasing power corresponds to a liability, whether their own or that of another. In Wicksell's account of a pure banking economy, payment is effected not by the transfer of money but by the transfer of reserves between banks. In this model, further developed by Richard Werner, banks function as institutions for deposits, accountants of records, and agents of transfer.[3] The interdependence of banks within the clearing system enables most exchanges to cancel each other out, while the possibility of interbank lending allows any differences to be charged at an overnight rate. The 'reserves' transferred are no longer stocks of gold but balances held at another bank – either a foreign one, for international exchanges, or a central bank (or at the centre of the global economy, the Bank for International Settlements). 'Money' or purchasing power is created when a customer takes out a loan, and a bank adds that figure to a current account: at one stroke, the customer has an asset, the sum of money in the account, and a corresponding liability, the new debt. Simultaneously, the bank has an asset, the loan that is now on its books, and a corresponding liability, the sum of money in the current account to be spent. As a result of the interdependence of banks in the clearing system, this new sum of money will return once it is spent as a new deposit in another bank, or even the same one. It is as though the borrower has ultimately borrowed the money from the person who receives and deposits that sum. In this respect, as Wicksell noted, the 'supply of money' is furnished by the demand itself.[4] There is a destabilising positive feedback dynamic here.

It is important to notice that this 'demand for money' is not a demand for a store of value, a medium of exchange, or a unit of account, for these are already provided by the banking system. The demand is for debt, not simply money: it is demand for access to investment or consumption now in return for later repayment. It is such debt that becomes the means of exchange issued by the banks. As a result, there is no correlation between the overall provision of purchasing power in bank accounts and how much money an economy actually needs to store value and facilitate exchange. While it is useful to think of the medium of exchange as 'money', it is better understood in reality as debt. This has enormous effects on the dynamics of the economic system, for what is used in practice as money also has the property of debt. Instead of being a passive instrument of free usage, a debt involves an obligation to acquire purchasing power. Only certain usages of money can be anticipated as meeting such obligations.

While anyone can apply for a loan for any reason, banks effectively decide to whom the new credit will be issued and for what purposes.[5] It is both costly and risky for banks to lend to productive enterprises, since this involves a large amount of scrutiny of their viability and building an ongoing relationship with their managers. Even so, most start-up businesses eventually fail. By far the safer procedure is to lend against collateral, whether to speculators who purchase financial assets or to those who purchase property.[6] The result is a positive feedback effect between rising asset prices and increasing debt creation: property and financial assets are purchased because they are expected to rise in price. Insofar as the purchaser is permitted to borrow to support that belief, they are able to offer a good price for the asset. Since many purchasers borrow to purchase assets, the prices of assets rise. Since the prices of assets rise, they offer good collateral for the lenders. Since the lenders have good collateral, they are willing to lend in higher proportions. Since others observe prices rising, they also endeavour to enter the market by borrowing, so that even though there may be limits to loan-to-value ratios, there is still no limit for the demand for borrowing for asset prices that rise in value. In other words, the supply of credit for speculative purposes creates its own demand.[7] Instead of lending being limited by saving, as in ideal models which treat it as the transfer of wealth from investors to borrowers, and instead of lending being limited by supply and demand, as in the ideal model of a market system, the demand for credit creates its own supply.[8]

Such disequilibrium economics produces its own inequalities. Let us take the hypothetical example of a buy-to-let property speculator who puts down a £50k deposit on a house worth £200k and lets it out at a rate of rent sufficient to cover mortgage interest and maintenance costs. After a few years, the house increases in value to £300k, whereupon it is sold to a family that will live in it. The bank has gained the full value of the interest payments. The speculator returns the borrowed £150k to the bank, which cancels out the financial assets and liabilities originally created. Yet the speculator retains a profit of £100k, tripling the size of the initial investment. Where has this new purchasing power come from? Most immediately, it has come from the new homeowner – the wealth gained by the speculator consists in the mortgage debt owed by the purchaser. Imagine that the new homeowner has also put down a deposit of £50k and has taken out a new mortgage of £250k. The profit that the speculator has gained is provided directly by the new homeowner's debt – and while this sum is advanced by a bank, the new homeowner will spend years paying off that debt, instead, perhaps, of saving into a pension plan. Speculative wealth is appropriated at the expense of another's debt; freedom, here, corresponds to another's constraint. In effect, the new homeowner is constrained to become a speculator, in turn, gambling that property prices will continue to rise, and hoping that by downsizing in retirement a pension can be released from the equity in the home. At the same time, the general rise in house prices places such properties beyond the reach of first-time buyers, so that properties are bought instead by buy-to-let speculators who can afford the deposit. The entire process involves the transfer of wealth from those who buy later to those who buy sooner, from the younger generation to the older, like a pyramid scheme. It also involves a transfer of wealth from those who cannot afford to buy property, who pay rent to landlords, to the lending institutions such as banks in the form of mortgage interest.[9]

However, this is not the full story. For the economic effects are far more general. On the one hand, those homeowners who do not consider selling their house, but find that its nominal price is rising, feel a 'wealth effect' – they are inclined to spend more money, whether from savings or from equity release on their property, so contributing to consumption demand. Likewise, the successful speculators are also inclined to increase their spending alongside their future speculative investments. This rise in the consumption demand, facilitated by rising asset prices and rising borrowing, then contributes to rising production – even though such production might take place in another country which does not have increasing levels of debt (albeit leaving a balance of payments deficit). As a result, there is increasing prosperity throughout the entire economic system – except that much of this increased consumption from discretionary spending is for positional or luxury goods, not for basic necessities. Such a growing economy leaves little for those who are stuck in low-wage employment, or who have no employment at all. There is very little scope for such individuals to join in the cycle of growth.[10]

Such credit creation, leading to an increase in the 'money supply', produces inflation – primarily in asset prices and positional goods. For the notion of a single rate of inflation based on a basket of goods is a rather arbitrary construct – money may have an exchange rate and interest rate, but it has no price – since price changes are very different for different assets and commodities. At the same time, since each new unit of purchasing power corresponds to a new unit of debt, this debt has a deflationary effect – those in debt reduce expenditure on other items in order to repay their debt, and the debt they repay is simply cancelled. Since purchasing power is extracted from those with lower incomes by those involved in finance, effective demand for basic necessities barely increases while there is increasing demand for speculative assets and luxury goods.

Of course, the positive spiral of asset and debt-based 'wealth' creation can and does, at times, move into reverse – this occurrence is now well understood.[11] A blockage at any stage of the spiral can lead to a reverse movement. For example, in the 2007 US sub-prime crisis, the rates of profits for lenders had been so remarkable and consistent that there was a higher demand for borrowers than there was supply of reliable borrowers. As a result, the conditions for mortgage lending were relaxed in order to attract a wider range of borrowers. Given that such loans were securitised and sold on, slicing and dicing individual mortgages into complex packages in order to distribute risk, this seemed like a safe procedure. In 2007, a combination of the ending of 'teaser' interest rates, inflation in the prices of basic necessities such as fuel, and a general rise in interest rates following hikes in the Federal Reserve rate led to an increase in rates of default. The subsequent dynamic was already described back in 2005 by Werner: if a few more speculative borrowers default, there appear bad debts in the banking system, leading to risk aversion and a reduction in credit offered. The outcome is that demand for speculative assets decreases since credit is harder to obtain, leading to a fall in prices, reducing the nominal wealth of all owners in property. Falling asset prices lead to a general loss in confidence, an increase in bankruptcies, and the threat of a deflationary spiral. With a loss in spending power, there is a general reduction in spending, and the productive economy also suffers, with rising unemployment and decreasing demand.[12] The enduring result, as Adair Turner makes clear, is a 'debt overhang': if asset prices fall in value, they no longer provide sufficient collateral for the loans that have been issued. For while asset prices vary with demand, debts to be paid remain fixed at the price of the amount originally borrowed. When individuals move to pay off their debts, the economic downturn leads to increases in welfare payments and decreases in tax receipts, leading to an increase in government borrowing. Debt continues to increase faster than GDP.[13] If government spending is then restricted by austerity measures, those who have previously benefited most from government spending, the most vulnerable, are those who feel the effects. The end result of such an adjustment, as in the case of debt-driven growth, is that purchasing power is transferred from the poor to the rich.[14] The cycle of debt-fuelled growth can then begin again – and even if nominal GDP increases due to the activities of the rich, this may conceal an economy that for the majority is continuing to stagnate.

Overall, then, the supply of purchasing power is unlimited, so long as the banks advance their lending 'together and in step'.[15] When this purchasing power is invested in a finite supply of assets, the result is growing inequality. While nominal GDP can continue to grow overall, the resources and wealth of the proportion of the population without significant investment assets can shrink at the same time. There is no intrinsic limit to such growth in inequality – even in a world of finite resources, nominal GDP can continue to grow, while a shrinking proportion of the population hold an ever-increasing proportion of global assets. Speculative bubbles tend to be pricked by state agencies, such as through a change in regulation or a rise in underlying interest rates. For infinite growth is incompatible with finite resources. To extend this brief overview of disequilibrium economics, it will be necessary to consider the dynamics of deflationary collapse.

Chapter 15

Constraints

There is some vague resemblance between prophecies of impending ecological catastrophe and biblical visions of apocalypse, such as 'pestilence and mourning and famine' and 'being burned with fire' (Rev. 18.8). One prophecy, however, simply describes the destruction of demand.

> And the merchants of the earth weep and mourn for her [Babylon], since no one buys their cargo anymore, cargo of gold, silver, jewels and pearls, fine linen, purple, silk and scarlet, all kinds of scented wood, all articles of ivory, all articles of costly wood, bronze, iron, and marble, cinnamon, spice, incense, myrrh, frankincense, wine, olive oil, choice flour and wheat, cattle and sheep, horses and chariots, and human bodies and souls. (Revelation 18.11–13)

Far from the earth running short of resources or luxury goods, what is striking here is the sudden destruction of purchasing power. The power of sorcery or alchemy is brought to an end:

> The merchants of these wares, who gained wealth from her, will stand far off, in fear of her torment, weeping and mourning aloud,
>
> > 'Alas, alas, the great city
> > clothed in fine linen,
> > in purple and scarlet,
> > adorned with gold,
> > with jewels, and with pearls!
> > For in one hour all this wealth has been laid waste!'
>
> And all shipmasters and seafarers, sailors and all whose trade is on the sea, stood far off and cried out as they saw the smoke of her burning,
>
> > 'What city was like the great city?'

And they threw dust on their heads, as they wept and mourned, crying out,

'Alas, alas, the great city,
where all who had ships at sea grew rich by her wealth!
For in one hour she has been laid waste'. (Revelation 18.15–19)

Whether the biblical apocalypse reflects a memory or a prophecy of the collapse of a centre of merchant civilisation, the global effect it describes is a destruction of demand. Indeed, this image may be more relevant to the effects of constraints on growth than apocalyptic images of ecological destruction.

Among the many environmental constraints on economic growth, the most prominent and urgent would seem to include these: the loss of biodiversity; depletion of sources of fresh water such as glaciers and aquifers; global heating, intimately related to most of the other constraints; and the depletion of fossil fuel supplies, especially oil. Since our concern here is with the disequilibrium effects of the physical limits to substitution, the discussion will concentrate purely upon oil as representative of the whole – while recognising that, although some similar disequilibrium dynamics might arise from each physical constraint to growth, there are also likely to be quite notable differences.

The debate over the phenomenon of 'peak oil' – a global limit to conventional oil production – rose to prominence in the early twenty-first century as a result of the campaigning work of retired geologists such as Colin Campbell.[1] The nature of oil production is that a well, once drilled, will gush out at high pressure first, before gradually reducing in output. Under conventional extraction techniques, about half the reservoir of oil in each well would not be extracted at all. Cheap and accessible sources of oil are utilised first, before turning to more expensive sources. Campbell's forecast was for conventional cheap oil production to peak globally around 2005, just as it had peaked in the United States in 1971. The difference between increasing global demand and diminishing supply would be made up at first by unconventional sources of oil and improved extraction techniques, after which costs would rise. Campbell insisted that improved extraction techniques might be able to accelerate the rate of production, but would then deplete overall reserves more quickly, so compensating for any increase in extractable oil. He was also aware of the paradox identified by Stanley Jevons when exploring a similar situation – the implications of the limits to accessible deposits of coal in Britain over a century beforehand: to attempt to reduce consumption, whether through foregoing it or improving efficiency of usage, results in a fall in price, and thus in an increase in demand. Such effects largely cancel out. In the early 2000s, Campbell predicted, at some stage in the near future, a sharp rise in the price of oil resulting in recession or 'demand destruction', followed by successive booms and busts. These predictions were confirmed in 2007 by the sudden rise in oil prices to $147 per barrel, followed by a sharp slump and a rebound. Sceptics of 'peak oil', who were generally economists, insisted to the contrary that each rise in prices could open up new sources of oil that had been previously too expensive to extract, as well as improved extraction technologies, so that the world need never run out of oil.

There are many important considerations to bear in mind in this debate. A first is the empirical question of how large the new sources of oil might be that are facilitated by each doubling in the price of oil – if these newly accessible reservoirs are successively smaller than the previous set, then prices might have to rise indefinitely to obtain an equivalent supply. A second is the overall energy return on energy invested for each new source of unconventional oil – the absolute limit would be reached here when it costs more conventional oil overall to extract, refine, and transport a source of unconventional oil.[2] The remaining oil would then stay in the ground. A third is the relationship between oil consumed and climate change, such that limiting atmospheric carbon dioxide requires limiting the overall global production of oil. Yet perhaps the most immediate concern is a fourth: the interaction between rising oil prices and an economy driven by debt and asset price speculation. Here oil price constraints affect possible anticipations of the future.

The retired reinsurance actuary Gail Tverberg has updated the analysis of 'peak oil' by making the connection between oil prices and economic performance. Citing studies that show a close correlation between global economic growth and oil production, as well as others that show most recent recessions preceded by oil price shocks, Tverberg attributes limits to oil production to rising inequality.[3] For the oil price is a component of the price of most commodities – every calorie of food consumed in the developed world has ten or twenty calories of fossil fuels invested in it for fertiliser, pesticides, farming technology, storage, and transportation. Rising oil prices therefore lead to rising inflation, including rising food prices. An oil price spike results in a reduction in discretionary spending, leading into recession and demand destruction. As a result of recession, the overall effect of oil supply limits is therefore a drop in price and an apparent oil supply glut. The consequence is counter-intuitive: as one approaches the limits of production, just when one might expect oil to be scarce, it once again appears to be more abundant. For oil production cannot respond immediately to market signals since the timescale for projects is a matter of several years – even those highly indebted oil production companies that go bankrupt continue to produce oil during bankruptcy in order to repay their creditors – so production can outstrip demand. Of course, given time, this glut of cheap oil can gradually fuel an economic recovery until the next brief price spike and recession. The key question is the level of the oil price that triggers recession. On Tverberg's analysis, the price will never rise sufficiently for the oil that is expensive to extract to be accessed.[4] Indeed, as cheap oil diminishes, there comes a time when the price at which oil can be successfully extracted is higher than the price at which an oil price shock causes recession, leading to a shrinking economy and delimiting oil production to the cheapest of sources. Tverberg therefore employs the image of demand destruction from Revelation 18 as exemplary for the future collapse of the oil economy.

It would seem that Tverberg's vision has not yet been fully realised. At the time of writing, while the price of crude oil recently settled into a new, lower band, this was not the result of demand destruction since oil consumption reaches ever new peaks. The recent glut resulted from higher rates of production, itself an outcome of additional investment at a time when prices were consistently high. Since there remains a considerable time lag between investment and production, the recent period of low investment due to lower prices is likely to lead to a future shortfall in production, and a future brief price spike, followed by another recession – a smaller price spike and fall occurred in 2018, without an accompanying recession. There are, of course, a multitude of other factors in play, including the overall debt burden within the global economy itself. In the meantime, oil consumption continues to rise to ever-higher levels. Demand destruction, which occurred between 2007 and 2009, was short-lived. At any rate, Tverberg's analysis offers some vision of the likely outcome of resource constraints in general – a brief spike in prices, followed by demand destruction and a period in which there seems to be glut of cheap resources on the market – as though resource constraints had no connection with limits to economic growth. Under such circumstances, it is very hard to demonstrate the key role of environmental factors in setting limits to economic growth. Nevertheless, the lack of recognition does not mean that economic life is not subject to insuperable constraints. Such constraints make the task of financial governance impossible.

This analysis can be taken as illustrative of the kinds of constraints that are found within debt finance itself. The overall purposes of banking and finance in economic life are threefold: to facilitate economic growth through making profits; to redistribute purchasing power to those who can make the most efficient and effective use of it; and to ensure stability by maintaining the value of money and enhancing credit. In each of these respects, the banking and financial systems operate under incompatible constraints which require separate discussion. In respect of growth, the economy is at once both constrained to grow and constrained to deplete resources. The constraint towards growth results from interest on debt; yet this constraint does not show up on balance sheets. For in the creation of money as debt, an equal and opposite asset and liability are created for both the customer and the bank. Each of these cancels out to zero. Where, then, is the constraint? There is, of course, one obvious asymmetry: since the customer spends in the short-term and borrows over the long-term, such a borrower pays interest to the bank. Why is there an asymmetry of power? On the one hand, the borrower bears the primary risk, since, for example, if she invests in property which subsequently falls in value, she is still required to repay the debt in full. On the other hand, the borrower also pays a rate of interest to compensate the bank for its share of risk. Of course, the borrower may also take the upside if the property rises in value, as well as gaining the benefits of use of the property. Yet these are temporary and delimited effects, while the compounding of interest continues indefinitely. The reason for the difference in power is that while the customer is an individual who participates in economic life with other separate individuals through market exchange, the bank is part of the privileged clearing system, where transactions are 'reckoned' or cancelled out, each benefiting from acting in consort. This exercise of collective power might seem to be fair compensation for allowing the customer use of the asset purchased, yet it does have system-wide effects. It places a constraint of continuing growth upon the economy, even if this is merely a growth in asset values. The creation of money as debt inaugurates a perpetual disequilibrium which requires an increasing money creation as debt.

This is a somewhat complex dynamic which requires further discussion. The debt, once it is repaid, is cancelled, and with it the purchasing power that had been created – in this respect, there is no demand for growth. Yet interest has to be repaid with freshly created purchasing power. It is possible to imagine that this interest is a sum of 'money' which, once received by the bank, will later either be issued as a further loan or used to purchase a capital asset in order to maintain its loan to capital ratio. Now this picture of money circulating once more is a little deceptive: we are concerned here with accounting records, not with coins. What circulates was first created as a debt. There is a demand in the economic system as a whole for the creation of economic value to grow in proportion to the rate of interest upon such debts. Of course, this demand could be met by an increase in the frequency by which each unit of existing debt is used to make interest payments; if this were the case, then there would be no overall demand for debt to grow. In practice, however, the data for the past four decades show the rate of money creation, which is almost equivalent to the total debt, increases far faster than economic growth.[5] There is no demand to increase the frequency of interest payments, for such 'money' tends to accumulate and lie idle in the accounts of those who benefit from the unequal system. Large corporations hold vast cash reserves, and even financial speculators who trade on margin need to hold a large proportion of their wealth in cash so that they can benefit from unforeseen opportunities or insure themselves against margin calls. While it is possible for money to circulate faster than ever before, this does not mean that it will necessarily do so. Instead, it is up to the debtors to transmit the force of this demand for more and more money, whether they do this through sale of their resources, through speculation in asset prices, or through earning an income. The sale of resources does not tend to make subsequent sales more frequent. However, debtors can have a macroeconomic effect by offering more money to purchase assets, increasing asset values, and so raising the demand for them, or by increasing production, making more available for purchase. The net result is an increase in debt in the system, an increase in overall interest paid, and, since this 'money' does not necessarily circulate in wider circuits but in narrower ones, an increase in inequality. Overall, the macroeconomic effect of the creation of money as debt is an increased demand for money for the sake of paying interest. To facilitate this systemic demand for increasing debt, more and more dimensions of human society, environmental resources and the human spirit have to be subordinated to the task of making profits. It is this process of increasing colonisation of the planet, the social world and the human spirit that runs up against external constraints.

Once the population as a whole gains access to increasing purchasing power, this is spent on increasing consumption. Even apparently non-material consumption is supported by an ever-greater throughput of material resources at a global level. The demand for growth inherent within the financial system, which is based on interest and profit, runs up against the limits of colonisation and appropriation. Yet this is by no means the end of the growth demand, which can continue even as the economy shrinks and cannibalises itself, transferring resources from poor to rich. If the economy is constrained to grow and constrained to deplete resources, then it will continue to do both, even after reaching its limits – the resources it will deplete will be the wealth created by previous generations and enjoyed by a moderately broad section of the population.[6]

A second domain for the clash of conflicting constraints lies in the area of distribution. Market mechanisms produce inequality as a result of the competition between those who succeed and those who fail. In addition, the accumulation of capital through selling manufactured commodities at above cost price leads to a further concentration of resources. Both of these facilitate the dynamics of inequality that result from debt. The result of rising inequality is that significant proportions of the population can no longer afford to buy the commodities available in the market. This is a problem of under-consumption or over-production: if less people can afford goods and services, there is a limit to economic growth in that it is no longer possible to make profits through production. On the one hand, a free market, capitalist or debt-based economy has to produce increasing inequality; on the other, it cannot profit in conditions of inequality.

The most effective means for redistribution is probably high taxation and high welfare payments. For money only holds purchasing power insofar as it circulates; if it circulates in ever-tighter circuits, then it will undermine its own conditions of existence. This is encountered in cities where rents are too high and wages too low for service workers to live. The purchasing power of money undermines itself when it is not distributed in the broadest of economic circuits. However, such a redistribution is naturally unpopular with the wealthy and powerful who prefer to believe that the market rewards the 'creators of wealth' for their superior contributions. To compensate for this deficiency, other means have been found, such as funding consumption through credit. While low pay and high rates of debt do motivate a workforce to long hours of high productivity, they only increase the tendency towards increasing inequality in the long run. Some temporary stability may be offered, by contrast, by the wealth effect of rising asset prices: the middle classes, who benefit from the rising value of property, may maintain the overall size of the economy as a whole for much longer. Even this effect is temporary, for the younger generation of the middle classes is excluded from the wealth of the older generation by a combination of rising property prices, low pay, and large debts for education. Inheritances can be used up through the provision of pensions and care in old age. As a result, an increasing proportion of the middle class are pushed down into the precarious classes, while rising asset prices benefit a smaller and smaller circle. The economy is caught between incompatible constraints: it has to increase inequality through competition, profit and debt; it also has to expand the circulation of purchasing power to prevent itself from shrinking.

A third area of incompatible constraints concerns the free movement of capital.[7] For insofar as there exists a market for capital investment, then corporations and governments are in competition to attract credit. Conditions have to be set in order to attract capital, and foremost among such conditions is enabling a free market in capital, so that capital can appropriate, substitute, and anticipate as it pleases. The cost for setting unfavourable conditions is 'capital flight', which results in high rates of interest. In an economy structured by debt, the creditors rule: the bond market can dictate government policy. Such policies have to be constructed according to whatever fanciful notions of free market economics have been prominent in the education of those who work for large financial institutions that invest in bonds. Yet more significantly, such policies have to be constructed according to the demand for meeting debt repayments in preference to ensuring the welfare of the population. Since capital is mobile, however, it is only interested in short-term profit at the expense of long-term stability. If economic policies compromise the future creditworthiness of a nation, then so be it – that will be a problem for future holders of government bonds, not for the current generation who are quite willing to profit at the expense of their successors – just as they would if selling an asset which they correctly believe has peaked in value. Insofar as governments, like banks, borrow in the short-term to invest in the long-term, their intentions are at odds with their investors who invest in the short-term to profit in the long-term. Capital has to be free to move in order to be attracted; capital has to be retained in the long-term in order to be invested. These are incompatible constraints.

To summarise, the logic of appropriation is subject to incompatible constraints: appropriation must increase exponentially; yet appropriation has insuperable limits. For both of these constraints to be fulfilled, once limits are reached, the economy turns cannibalistic, consuming its own wealth. The market logic of competition and substitution is also subject to incompatible constraints: inequality must increase progressively; yet inequality depletes the wealth of those from whom wealth is extracted. As time progresses, those who benefit from exploitation have no other resource but to substitute each other for those who were previously exploited. Competition, no longer balanced with cooperation, turns into naked conflict. The logic of anticipation is also subject to incompatible constraints: short-term interests are prioritised above all else, yet, as time advances, short-term interests cannot be met unless long-term interests are served. In each of these respects, the debt-based economy devours itself. The overall result is demand destruction. The prospects seem extremely grim: demand destruction can be easily accelerated by political unrest, mass immigration, conflict, and war. An ultimate result is a complete loss of faith in economic salvation: 'Every kingdom divided against itself is laid waste, and no city or house divided against itself will stand. If Satan casts out Satan, he is divided against himself; how then will his kingdom stand?' (Matt. 12.25–6).

Chapter 16

Preliminary Conclusion

Economic life consists in a wide variety of material practices: preparing the ground or location for work; constructing tools and machines; extracting or gathering resources, fuel, food and basic necessities; educating workers; organising and assembling a system of production; motivating workers and setting them to work; distributing or exchanging products; production, consumption, and waste disposal; and, above all, communication. Much communication takes the form of reporting such matters as what, how, how much, and why. Yet economic life is also oriented by communication which institutes beliefs and behaviour: statements of intention, promises, contracts, and debts, for example. Where material practices underwrite the words which merely report, trust underwrites the words which promise. Where words that report may be assessed and trusted according to their accuracy or truth, words that promise may be assessed and trusted according to their success in realisation. Yet in both cases, it is one thing to assess the trustworthiness of the words, quite another to assess the trustworthiness of the realities reported or successes promised. For the latter is a question that may be framed not as one of truth but of value. It raises a vital philosophical question: How do you speak words which communicate value? What is worth saying? What is saying worth?

The neglect of such matters raises an acute danger: both speech and material practices, for all their success, can become worthless. Both thought and work can become disoriented. Activities can be directed towards the destruction of what is valuable or the extraction of what is valuable from others rather than towards the production of what is valuable, the recognition of values, or the provision of values to others. Anxiety before such dangers can lead to mistrust undermining cooperation; mistrust itself fosters disorientation. To allay such anxieties, one can at least start by taking what others value as

116

a way of orienting one's own thought towards value. Yet others rarely speak about what they value and why these matters are valuable; they are more inclined to report experiences and intentions. Moreover, even when people do speak about what they value, their words may be mistrusted for they participate in other social dynamics than mere reporting. Since values are what is valued, they have a currency: speech about value may be motivated more by maintaining the esteem of oneself and others than by reporting thoughtful evaluation. Given such anxiety and mistrust, then, it is safer to turn from what people say to what people do: what they spend their money on. For spending money is an expression of evaluation, and that something can command a price offers some evidence that it is widely valued. Money spent is evidence of other possibilities foregone; the product or service bought has been valued more highly than any of these other such possibilities.

Now the sacrifice of other possibilities is by no means evidence that such other possibilities should be sacrificed. The disorientation of people, their subjection to a variety of incompatible influences and forces, entails that their behaviour may often amount to the destruction of what is valuable or the extraction of what is valuable from others. Assessing their preferences by the money they spend amounts to valuing their confusion and disorientation as much as their insight. Yet, worse than this, assessing values by means of money delimits evaluation to those goods and services which can be bought and sold. Those valuable entities that only exist insofar as they are shared, such as ideas, institutions, and bonds of affection, are devalued and neglected. Those valuable experiences that only exist insofar as they are spent, shared, or offered, such as time, care, attention, and love, are treated as merely private matters. As a result, evaluation is reduced to success or impact: gaining recognition from others in a competitive economy of attention, becoming an influencer, or at least gaining money. One hardly dares to speak any more of what one values; one speaks rather of what one promises or one's successes, or one merely reports what has happened. For values without the backing of recognition and money may be distrusted: they are divisive.

Entities that can be bought and sold are those that can easily be handled, controlled, measured, mastered, and manipulated, whether by hands or minds. Moreover, for a determinate price to be agreed, such entities need to be quantified and counted in some way. Quantification brings entities before the mind for the sake of management, modification, or assessment. Insofar as reality is quantifiable, it is subject to some degree of mastery by the mind. Nevertheless, quantification only brings one aspect of reality before the mind. Those aspects that can neither be measured, compared, nor mastered – such as cultural values and experiences – are left out of account. This may facilitate an illusion of mastery, but it hardly contributes towards enriching cultural values and experiences.

Now, alongside any disorders of thought, there are also processes of real subsumption of the world under quantifiable categories. The world is reconstructed in order to yield flows of energy, food, resources, and labour. Insofar as the effort involved in this reconstruction – the energy, food, resources, and labour expended – can be compared to what is yielded and found to be less, then such reconstruction is profitable from the perspective of those who make such a comparison. The exchange may not be profitable for those who carry out the tasks – their wellbeing, livelihood, and health may be staked or expended in the process. Likewise, those who bear the costs of the aftermath and the waste produced may not find the outcome profitable. Yet these may not be party to the exchange. Real subsumption takes place outside of the market, while within the market only quantified flows of goods, services, preferences, and profits find representation. Prior to any commodity exchange, the world is appropriated to yield some kind of flow or rate of profit: it is squeezed like a lemon until the juice runs. For in the mind that appropriates the world, other possibilities may always be substituted for that which is exhausted, decayed, or broken. Any consideration of offering honour or value is forestalled by the more urgent task of anticipating a rate of profit. By means of appropriation, substitution, and anticipation, the mind cauterises itself against the reality of value. The truth about the words such a mind speaks, whether its words are reports or promises, is staged elsewhere than in their content. Truth is to be found in their conditions and their consequences, in the experiences they give and the possibilities they offer, in the orientations they give to conduct and in the values they honour, neglect, or disdain.

This disconnection between thinking and being indicates a failure of understanding and, alongside this, a failure of the mind to master its circumstances. The mind knows not what it says or does. In reality, conditions and consequences, experiences and possibilities, orientations and values come together to set the direction of the mind and determine the kinds of words it must speak. For the entire social and economic system is set up with such complexity that it exceeds the understanding of any one individual. The rationality and order in which an individual dwells is quite different from the rationality and order that gives shape to their speech and action. Just as a worker can become a functionary serving the rationality of a machine, so also does the individual become a functionary, a cog in an apparent market system, or a wheel in an all-encompassing social machine. The speech and action uttered might be regular, reliable, automatic, and predictable – at least in respect of form, even if the illusion of freedom can be manifest in the content. One can express any values one wishes so long as, in order to be socially effective, one expresses them in the appropriate form. Yet these are merely arbitrary assertions, for only the form itself is persuasive. I may not trust your words, if my experience of reality is too delimited to offer any grounds for understanding, but I can trust your money, or I can trust all the social processes of validation and accountability which have filtered what you say until only a repetitive set of quantifications, substitutions, clichés, and promises remain. Above all, such words lack both interest and trustworthiness. They neither offer nor demand credit.

Now, it is perhaps misguided to assume that people are mere functionaries of an ordered system which they do not understand. For, where understanding is lacking, disorder can reign. In particular, short circuits in the constitution of preferences can lead to wild fluctuations in evaluation, trust, and credit. Once evaluation is uprooted from any sense for what matters, trust can be lightly invested in whatever offers a mere promise of value. In particular, speculative bubbles in asset prices inflated by credit and debt-deflationary crises triggered by mistrust are instances within economic life of the wider life of the mind. In such short circuits, one witnesses a purely machinic, autonomous structure inflating the mind with trust and distrust. This is not as one might expect. Once the highest values are devalued, once the mind is uprooted from that which matters, it would appear that the mind is liberated to assert its own values, offer its own credit, and invest its own trust. In reality, nothing could be further from the truth, for without any grounding in understanding reality, the mind lacks any will of its own. It can only express wishes. The trust that it invests, far from being a donation of value, rests on seeking after value, for wishes hold no power to convert imagination into reality. For that, one requires trust and cooperation from others; for that, one requires recognition in the form of money. Feeling one's own impotence, seeking honour is substituted for offering honour, and seeking honour requires submission to values encountered without. Speculative bubbles and crashes dramatize the inability to assess values which arise when life is measured primarily by quantities.

Positive feedbacks of trust and distrust lead to a life of disorder. Nevertheless, even when the mind parts company from reality, reality still impacts upon the mind. There are limits set to such a disordered existence. These limits are experienced in the form of mutually incompatible constraints. An economy founded on debt rather than value is at once constrained to grow and to deplete its conditions of existence. An economy founded on the accumulation of capital rather than its distribution is constrained at once to increase inequality by concentrating effective purchasing power and undermine the possibilities for profit by destroying demand. An economy founded on attracting investment rather than offering it has to allow capital freedom to move in the short-term, while relying on its presence over the long-term. Should such dilemmas prove insoluble, then reality sets limits to the existence of disordered minds and lives.

Part IV

FINANCE AND SALVATION: DYNAMICS OF FAITH

The previous part concluded that economic life, in a debt-based economy, is subject to conflicting constraints: it is compelled towards growth, yet it has external limits; it increases inequality, yet it turns the wealthy against each other; it advances short-term interests, yet it undermines long-term prospects. Debts must be repaid, yet some debts must default. These conflicting constraints need not be thought of as economic contradictions heralding the end of capitalism. On the contrary, when economic life falls short of the freedom, equality, justice, and stability of an ideal market, it offers all the more reason to intensify efforts to create such a market. When debt obligations predominate over market exchange, the most obvious response is to save. In times of uncertainty the demand for money and markets grows ever stronger. Where markets seem to fail, finance can claim to offer salvation through the creation of credit. In part IV, we explore finance as a mechanism for attracting and ordering trust.

Chapter 17

Saving: The Spirit of Finance

Someone in the crowd said to him, 'Teacher, tell my brother to divide the family inheritance with me'. But he said to him, 'Friend, who set me to be a judge or arbitrator over you?' And he said to them, 'Take care! Be on your guard against all kinds of greed; for one's life does not consist in the abundance of one's possessions'. Then he told them a parable: 'The land of a rich man produced abundantly. And he thought to himself, 'What should I do, for I have no place to store my crops?' Then he said, 'I will do this: I will pull down my barns and build larger ones, and there I will store all my grain and my goods. And I will say to my soul, Soul, you have ample goods laid up for many years; relax, eat, drink, be merry'. But God said to him, 'You fool! This very night your life is being demanded of you. And the things you have prepared, whose will they be?' So it is with those who store up treasures for themselves but are not rich toward God. (Luke 12.13–21)

This gospel narrative seems to offend against two of the most fundamental ethical principles bearing on economic life: the principle of just distribution of property, in that the petitioner's apparently legitimate claim is rebuffed by a moral lecture on greed, and the principle of prudent precaution or saving for the future. In speaking of his future enjoyment the fool has got ahead of himself – a privilege here reserved for God, for God takes his advance, over-stepping the boundaries of time by requiring the fool's life 'this very night' and yet after he has completed his planned preparations. This divine advance of judgement directly opposes the principle of deferral in saving for later. Now, Jesus has not been the only economic thinker to disparage saving for the future. Indeed, Jesus' teaching was echoed by John Maynard Keynes in his mockery of the 'purposive man' who:

is always trying to secure a spurious and delusive immortality for his acts by pushing his interest in them forward into time. He does not love his cat, but his cat's kittens; nor, in truth, the kittens, but only the kittens' kittens, and so on forward for ever to the end of catdom. For him jam is not jam unless it is a case of jam tomorrow and never jam today.[1]

Keynes objected to the principle behind 'pulling down barns': the sacrifice of the present for the sake of the future.[2] Unless the future can be conceived as concretely as the present, it cannot strictly be compared to it. Lacking any accurate predictions or knowledge of remote consequences, it is unwise 'to destroy a beneficent institution for the sake of a supposed millennium in the comparatively remote future'.[3] This is the specific charge which he lays against the political economists' 'religion' of laissez-faire: it does not count the present costs in the competitive struggle for survival, but only the future benefits of the final distribution which is assumed to be permanent.[4]

Keynes noted how, under conditions of uncertainty, there is a human tendency to prefer the abstract over the concrete, the indefinite over the definite: when comparing concrete goods against abstract money of equal worth, it is largely money that weighs heavily on the scales. 'The sanctification of saving tends dangerously on the side of abstract money. The growth of individual wealth does the same'.[5] If capitalism is founded on the preference for abstract possibility over actual enjoyment,[6] Keynes seems to have viewed it as a temporary madness rooted in the love of money which will one day be recognised for what it is, 'a somewhat disgusting morbidity, one of those semi-criminal, semi-pathological propensities which one hands over with a shudder to the specialists in mental disease'.[7] Yet a few years earlier he had argued that the main justification for the inequality of wealth distribution in capitalism was that instead of the rich spending their wealth on their own enjoyments, they largely invested it to the advantage of the whole community.

> The duty of 'saving' became nine-tenths of virtue and the growth of the cake the object of true religion. Saving was for old age or for your children; but this was only in theory – the virtue of the cake was that it was never to be consumed, neither by you nor by your children after you.[8]

When the propensity to save is manifest as a propensity to invest, it becomes the source of prosperity, the reason for offering credit. On this account, such a madness offers salvation.

As Keynes' thought developed, he seems to have distinguished between two kinds of maladies in the 'love of money'. The essential characteristic of capitalism, saving for investment for the sake of profit, seemed to him to be a comparatively mild vice, one that could eventually be resolved by its very success: as capital accumulates and there is more wealth to invest relative to productive possibilities, its ability to yield a profit drops towards zero, leading to the 'euthanasia of the rentier'.[9] The more serious malady that Keynes diagnosed was the propensity to save at the expense of both consumption and investment, the famous 'liquidity-preference'. There is always an alternative to the ownership of real capital assets – the ownership of money and debts. For capitalists do not desire an asset as such, but only its prospective yield – that is to say, what is desired is 'wealth' as such, a potentiality for consuming an unspecified article at an unspecified time.[10] This love of money is socially destructive primarily at the macroeconomic level. For if money is a scarce resource that exists in the banking system, then it is impossible for all individuals to simultaneously save at once. The collective effect defeats the intention to save.[11] Instead, money saved is withheld from circulation, reducing both consumption and investment. There is a lack of effective demand.[12] Keynes praised Thomas Malthus in his insistence against Ricardo that even the unproductive consumption of the wealthy stimulates effective demand.[13]

In this respect, one may perhaps discern a third sense of 'saving' in Keynes' thought: capitalism saves us from itself. The capitalists may bring economic salvation to the world by the combination of their investment and luxury consumption, by simultaneously gathering into barns and being merry. Yet our saviours cannot save themselves. For as they invest and profit, then at the macroeconomic level, the result of their accumulation at compound interest is that there is more capital to be invested than there are opportunities for profit. As expectations of profit fall, so also does new investment, leading eventually towards a stable state. This is a prime example of private vices leading to public benefits: in the euthanasia of the rentier, the capitalists sacrifice their very existence as capitalists for the sake of the common good, albeit in a grand collective gesture entirely beyond their intentions. The difference from the pre-capitalist period, however, is that this stable state of production and population is at a far higher standard of living than before. With productive capacities highly developed, Keynes imagined that humanity will have 'largely solved the economic problem'. For the struggle for subsistence, formerly the most pressing problem of the human race, would then be solved. Capitalism offers salvation from economic need in and through the process of destroying itself. The ultimate consequence is that humanity is restored to contemplation of the lilies of the field who toil not:

> I see us free, therefore, to return to some of the most sure and certain principles of religion and traditional virtue – that avarice is a vice, that the exaction of usury is a misdemeanour, and the love of money is detestable, that those who walk most truly in the paths of virtue and sane wisdom take least thought for the morrow. We shall once more value ends above means and prefer the good to the useful.[14]

Of course, this is all somewhat ironic: for until the end the capitalism, we must pretend to ourselves that fair is foul and foul is fair: 'Avarice and usury and precaution must be our gods for a little longer still. For only they can lead us out of the tunnel of economic necessity into daylight'.[15]

This vision of economic salvation through the power of sin is rather unconvincing for reasons given in the previous part. Indeed, Keynes himself offers the conceptual basis in the very same essay for thinking otherwise. He distinguishes between absolute needs, which he expects to be fulfilled through continued economic growth, and relative needs, insatiable desires to feel superior to one's fellows.[16] He thus only offers salvation from absolute needs not relative ones – and these latter may continue to determine the distribution of wealth, including perhaps whether absolute needs are fulfilled at all. While the rate of profit from productive investment might fall to zero, the rate of appropriation of the wealth of others need not until all others are impoverished. Since the desire for wealth in the abstract is so insatiable, and since such abstract wealth can only amount to a prospective yield and can only be held as a claim or debt, then one person's wealth is another person's poverty. Keynes himself exposed the difference between the individual and the aggregate, since for every buyer there is a seller – all choices have aggregate effects. Yet his approach is confined to the 'economics of stuff', treating saving as an accumulation of property rather than as an accumulation of power over others. For saving is either a matter of accumulating money and purchasing power, a claim on future goods and services, or else a matter of accumulating assets, others' debts, or their future profits. In saving, one person's relative wealth may be another's relative poverty. As a result, one may see that saving has aggregate effects beyond that of a liquidity crisis: it subjects the future lives of others to acquiring money.

There is, however, a deeper problem: under certain circumstances, the financial system can create the abstract yet liquid assets which provide a means of storing wealth. The financial system can produce its own opportunities for profit, absorbing any excess capital in futures and derivatives.[17] This is evident, in its simplest form, in the creation of money. At one level, one can consider the demand for money as part of a market: when money is scarce, people pay more in commodities or interest rates to hold this costly good. In Keynes' theory, while individuals are free to change the amount of money they hold, this does make a difference to the incomes of others: the total sum of money held has to add up to the cash which the banking system has created. In this way, he offers a formulation of the problem of freedom and necessity in terms of ownership of money: individuals are free to hold it in whatever quantity they please, and yet the total they hold in aggregate is already given. Keynes endeavoured to solve this problem of harmonising individual freedom with economic constraint by making the habitual suggestion of economists that a market mechanism would reconcile individual freedom with social necessity – incomes and prices would change until the amount of money individuals choose to hold has come to equality with the amount created in the banking system.[18] This is nonsense. The problem, here, is that the signals point away from equilibrium: if money were in short supply, then it would be held for longer, so intensifying the shortage. If money were in excess over preferences, it would be spent more readily, so increasing the frequency of transactions or 'velocity' of money and intensifying the excess. Money itself has aggregate effects. Therefore, in the case of already-created money, there can be no market equilibrium between supply and demand set by the interest rate. For money is not merely a scarce commodity; it is also a means of exchange, and the act of exchange, the use of money, modifies its availability on the market. There is always a shortage or an excess of money, and this shortage or excess has to be modulated by means external to the market such as the creation of credit. At another level, then, the demand for credit is a demand for the creation of money. Here, the scarcity of money is down to political restrictions on the rate, manner, and purposes of creation of credit. Even the deregulated creation of credit for any purpose whatsoever remains a political choice. There is, however, a third level: the amount of money that individuals, corporations, and public bodies collectively choose to hold is already identically equal to the amount created in the banking system; it can never deviate nor be subject to market forces tending to return to equilibrium. Someone has to hold the money; it is inelastic to supply and demand. While money is usually conceived as a stock transferred from creditors to debtors via the intermediary of the banking system, the creation of money as credit involves pairs of matching assets and liabilities for both the borrower and the bank. Given a perennial shortage of money, a new sense of salvation may now be understood: the banking and financial system may offer salvation by offering debts as transferrable stores of wealth. The limits to this process are set by the levels of risk. Since money is not merely a commodity, being also a means of exchange and a unit of account, its price is not limited by preference. Those who choose to sell assets, goods, or services, agreeing an acceptable price paid in money, will have to hold cash, whatever their preference, until they have found a subsequent purchase or investment, at which point, the cash will be held by someone else. In this respect, individuals do not simply choose how much money they hold.[19] How long they hold that money depends in part on circumstances. If the holding of money has an aggregate effect, it is not simply that of market supply and demand. The aggregate effect of banking and finance, by which money is held and invested, is different from the aggregate effect of the market, and has to be considered separately.

When it comes to coordinating individual freedom with social necessity, it will be vital to distinguish three layers in the ontological structure of economic life. There is the market, concerned with the distribution of goods of appropriation and consumption, which tends towards equilibrium through changes in prices and in quantities of supply and demand. There is the state and political life, concerned with maintenance of goods of participation, which operates through formulating and imposing a general will as a framework for the interaction of individual wills. There is also the banking, insurance, and financial system, concerned with saving and investment, which facilitates the orientation of trust. Any complete model of economic life has to take account of each of these domains on their own terms. In the case of finance, our concern in this part, finance creates a market through processes which do not consist in exchange. The misrecognition of its own nature by imagining an ideal market is constitutive of its very possibility. Our question is whether this ritual performance that creates what it presupposes offers any genuine salvation.[20]

The idea that Keynes omits from his general theory is that the amount of money created in the banking system, and therefore that people will have to hold, is determined by the amount of debt that people's animal spirits encourage them to undertake in the face of risk. In addition to a 'liquidity-preference' which might manifest itself in the time of crisis, there is a 'debt-preference' that manifests itself in times of optimism. The outcome, two generations after Keynes, is that the 'economic problem' is far from solved. For in practice the 'liquidity preference' is exercised less by storing coins under a mattress than by holding a claim on another's debt.

The important point, here, is that alongside the fallacies of composition that beset any attempt to understand economic life from the perspective of the individual, there are also fallacies of temporal expectation. There is the fallacy of salvation through procrastination. 'I just need to borrow a little more, then I can make enough to pay off all my debts and be free' – this is a debtor's desperate theology. It involves postponing settlement, deferring the moment when the debt will have proven to be part of a completed exchange. It is encountered in the creation of new financial products as new forms of saving. It is echoed by Keynes' judgements on the prospects of capitalism – just another two generations of avarice, and then people will be free to return to religion. It is echoed by Adam Smith's narrative of the ambitious poor man. It is also echoed by the rich fool's interior dialogue: 'I just need to tear down my barns and build new ones, and then I can relax, eat, drink and be merry'. The fallacy consists in treating as an imaginary exchange what is in fact a strategy of deferral.

There is also the fallacy of unnecessary accumulation, as in the rich fool's accumulation of his harvest which he will never use. This is echoed in Marx's account of the accumulation of productive capacity for which there will be no future, whether this is due to excess productive capacity, technological obsolescence, or lack of effective demand due to a lowering of wages.[21] There is finally the fallacy of conceiving the future on the basis of the present. The reason why God calls the prudent rich man a fool in the parable is because he talks to himself, imagining how in the future he will address his own soul. The fundamental distinction to be discovered here lies between two kinds of saving: that of a proprietor, who claims the increase, and that of a steward, whose work is an offering. The rich fool exemplifies how a proprietor offers himself to the future – by comforting himself with expectations of realising his prospective yield.[22] The alternative is to talk to others. If the rich fool had distributed his excess harvest to those in need, he would have earned the yield of their gratitude – and perhaps, in some circumstances, a good reputation with others can be a more effective investment than storing in barns. For investment to function as credit, it requires distribution rather than saving. Søren Kierkegaard explained a fundamental dialectic at work here:

> Wealth and abundance come hypocritically in sheep's clothing under the guise of safeguarding against cares and then themselves become the object of care, become *the care*. They safeguard a person against cares just as well as the wolf assigned to look after the sheep safeguards these against – the wolf.[23]

The work of a steward, by contrast with a proprietor, is offered to others in an entirely different conception of salvation: salvation is something that is only given or received. As Paul said: 'I have become all things to all people, that I might by all means save some' (1 Cor. 9.22). Or, in a comment that discloses a similar intention, 'He saved others; he cannot save himself' (Mark 15.31)

In our explorations of finance, it will be important to pay attention to the roles of both kinds of fallacies – the neglect of aggregative common goods and the neglect of temporal goods of offering. Taking these into account, finance is constituted by an ethical obligation to perfect the market and a faith in offering liquidity. Far from merely facilitating the production of goods and services in the 'real' economy, finance enables saving through 'fictitious capital' in forms which can be appropriated such as derivatives, forms which require participation such as clearing, and forms which enact faith such as deficit spending.

Chapter 18

Perfect Markets: The Duty
of Finance

Let us turn, then, to the ethics of finance which makes a market possible. It is difficult to imagine Socrates walking barefoot among the Twitter feeds of our modern financial markets, whether in New York, London, Shanghai, or Tokyo, and saying to anyone he happened to meet:

> Good Sir, you are an Athenian, a citizen of the greatest city with the greatest reputation for both wisdom and power; are you not ashamed of your eagerness to possess as much wealth, reputation and honours as possible, while you do not care for nor give thought to wisdom or truth, or the best possible state of your soul?[1]

For this is the concern of ethics. Now if anyone were to respond that he or she does care, and has indeed spent an entire career fulfilling duties and obligations, defending liberty and rights; dealing with fairness, honesty, and integrity; and has even taken courses on trading psychology as self-control – as indeed many of those employed in the finance sector could respond – Socrates would not let them go but would question and examine them, and if they fail the test, Socrates would reproach them because they attach 'little importance to the most important things and greater importance to inferior things'.[2]

The philosophical issue when it comes to the ethics of finance is not a matter of instructing finance professionals on how to apply concerns about obligations, rights, fairness, and self-control in their own professional lives. As a leading contemporary commentator on ethics in finance, John Boatright, says, 'an understanding of ethics and the ability to engage in ethical reasoning is part of human development; it is something that everyone learns by growing up in a culture'.[3] The Socratic question is whether this application of cultural values constitutes ethics; it is the question of whether dominant cultural assumptions in finance about justice are truly just.

Now, Socrates' dialectical questioning was intended to provoke in its recipients a sense of personal crisis: they did not know what they thought they knew. Yet such questioning was only possible on the basis of a pre-existing cultural crisis. For in a secure culture, no one asks the question, 'How should I live?', because the answers are clearly given, whether in the demands of one's lord and master, in the customs and obligations of one's tradition, or in both: in service of one's God – or one's employer. Perhaps only in fifth-century democratic Athens, one of the first societies constructed around trade following the recent invention of stamped coinage, was there sufficient freedom for self-determination and sufficient opportunity to care, not just for others but for one's self and the state of one's soul.[4] For such liberty, stripped of external validation, provokes both opportunity and anxiety: What is truly just? Ethics begins with crisis.

While the recent influence of finance has been sufficient to provoke a cultural crisis,[5] a more individual crisis might be felt keenly by finance professionals whenever opportunities present themselves to make a little extra at the expense of another. For the nature of financial wealth is that it is private property: one person's gain is another's loss; one person's asset is another's liability. As such, the temptations of finance can evoke the harshest judgements of conscience. Rarely spoken aloud, one has to turn as far afield from finance as Søren Kierkegaard to hear conscience expressed directly:

> Every earthly or worldly good is in itself selfish, begrudging; its possession is begrudging or is envy and in one way or another must make others poorer – what I have someone else cannot have; the more I have, the less someone else must have. . . . Furthermore, all the time and energy, all the mental solicitude and concern that is applied to acquiring or possessing earthly goods is self-ish, begrudging, or the person who is occupied in this way is selfish, at every moment has no thought for others; at every such moment he is selfishly work-ing for himself or selfishly for a few others, but not equally for himself and for everyone else.[6]

Nevertheless, such pangs of moral conscience might not be felt too keenly, for they are dulled by some among our economists who still occasionally don the garb of moral philosophers when required, informing us that a magnificent solution has been found to this perennial problem: the institution of the perfect market. For anyone who participates in market transactions does so voluntarily, and so stands to benefit; therefore, market transactions are always good for all. Since markets balance supply and demand, they avoid wastage and maximise efficiency; therefore, they ensure the most efficient use of resources and maximise welfare. Finally, extending market relations expands the sphere of liberty and private ownership of property, enabling people to fulfil their own preferences.[7] In each of these respects, the perfect market enacts justice by definition: it makes self-interest conform to the general welfare.[8] Not only does the ideal of a perfect market offer a solution to balancing care of self and care of others, and not only does it relieve the free agent of ethical anxiety, but it also offers a direction and a goal. There is a moral imperative to create and extend market justice. As even Keynes might have responded to Socrates: 'Are you not ashamed of your eagerness to possess as much individual virtue as possible, while you do not give a thought to the general welfare, or the best possible state of the market?'

For to perfect the market, as opposed to caring for one's soul, is to find redemption from conscience. It is to build a fence against extraneous social obligations. It is to invoke the power of social combination in one's very being. It is to offer all one's 'mental solicitude' in the service of a heavenly ideal of justice: therefore seek first the kingdom of the market, and all other moral values will be added unto you. Yet what is involved in practice in seeking the best possible state of the market? The answer, as I shall explain, is finance. Real markets, as we know, are not perfect: there are limits to inclusion, to the capacity of all to access markets; there are costs on transactions and difficulties in finding the most appropriate partner in any investment or exchange; there are limits to knowledge, on understanding the nature and the future prospects of any product or investment on the market; there are even market failures, when no buyers can be found. In each of these cases, the market fails, and fails to enact justice. Now if all markets expressed perfect competition, with perfect information and perfectly rational participants, then there would be no role at all for finance, as in some of the early models proposed by economists. Yet, in our imperfect world, our imperfect markets can be supplemented by the diverse services offered by finance: enabling financial inclusion by acting as agents or fiduciaries for others; contributing to efficient price-forming mechanisms, by acting as market makers, investors, arbitrageurs, or insurers; counteracting the limits to knowledge by offering specialist financial research and expertise; and regulating and maintaining the existence of markets. In this respect, the entire finance industry, from regulators to speculators, from insurers to advisers, from market makers to researchers, is constructed in service of a moral duty: *perfect the market*. If finance and banking are missing from early economic models, this is because their underlying purpose is to make economic life approximate more fully to the utopian morality of the market that can grant to all the salvation of a clean conscience. As Boatright sums up his approach to financial ethics, 'The best that can be done is perhaps "Contribute to efficient markets and do not take undue advantage of the opportunities provided by market failures"'.[9] This is simply a command to construct or simulate a morally unambiguous world where self-interest conforms to the general interest. The morality of perfecting the market is the primary purpose of finance, and the vast majority of finance professionals regulate their conduct primarily as moral agents in service to an ideal of market justice.

This point becomes clearer when we start to consider the exceptions to moral integrity, the variety of unethical or illegal financial practices that bring public disrepute: each is a violation of an ideal market, where privileged knowledge, deception, or a breach of trust is used to circumvent the conditions of perfect competition. One can cite insider trading, rigging auctions, deceiving about risk, unauthorised trading, operating outside hours, off-balance-sheet activities, violations of accounting principles, lending against insufficient guarantees of creditworthiness, causing spikes or flash crashes through high-frequency trading, and manipulation of interest rates. Each of these involves moving outside the realm of public scrutiny where a competitive market response might restore equilibrium. Financial integrity, then, consists in refusing to take advantage of opportunities to set aside a competitive market.

Financial conduct is therefore regulated primarily by a faith – a faith that the justice of the market is indeed true justice, that it works to the benefit of all despite the consequences for those who lose in its competition, and that it can be approximately realised in this world. Self-interested conduct is justified by faith. Yet the matter of cleaning one's conscience is not quite so simple, for, as Boatright describes, in the conduct of financial affairs the finance professional does in fact encounter moral dilemmas in such areas as conflicts of interest, exploitation of the weakness of others, and the stipulation of rights and obligations. These bear a little closer examination. For even financial markets, close as they are to an ideal, exist within a wider social context consisting of non-market relations.

For example, when a financial adviser agrees to serve a client, he or she undertakes to serve that client's interests without regard for his or her own. Once the contractual relations are agreed, both parties cease to relate as market participants in a buyer-seller relation; they develop an enduring relation of trust, based on moral virtues characteristic of service: honesty, care, loyalty, and confidentiality.[10] The adviser's expertise assists the client in accessing markets that might otherwise prove too dangerous or impenetrable. Problems arise when the finance professional or professional firm operates at the same time as a self-interested economic agent, or provides a variety of services to a variety of parties.[11] Indeed, it is typically pressure from an employer or another client that leads to the moral failures arising from a conflict of interest. Nevertheless, we should note that the problem is structural, not merely a matter of personal integrity: a perfect market is facilitated only by non-market relations. Each finance professional is caught between the moral duty to maximise self-interest for the sake of market efficiency, according to a consequentialist ethic as a participant in financial markets, and the fiduciary duty to serve clients faithfully and transparently, according to a virtue ethic. These are not easily compatible: for example, in a perfect market, all information is public; in fiduciary service, confidentiality is maintained. Moreover, for each market, the more it approaches perfection, the more it is facilitated by a host of finance professionals who regulate and limit the flow of information, so reducing transparency. Conflicts of interest bear witness to an intrinsic tension in finance: an approximation of a perfect market, far from being a natural effect of liberty, is an artificial construct composed from non-market relations. Each finance professional has a duty of service, whether to employers or clients, as a non-market obligation; each finance professional also has a duty to maximise self-interest. Internal conflict and ethical anxiety return.

A second issue is exploitation. One of the key rationales for the efficiency and justice of markets is the principle of the division of labour, linked to comparative advantage: markets are imagined as scenes of barter, where I exchange what I have for what I want. One can certainly find a multitude of examples of such a complementary division of preferences in financial markets, such as between appetites for risk and desires for insurance, or between preferences for long-term investments or short-term profits. Nevertheless, the world of finance differs from our mythical village barter market in one key respect: the only commodity for sale is, as Keynes pointed out, prospective yield.[12] Each market participant is only interested in one utility: market value, or, when considered in anticipation, market value measured against risk. In this respect, financial markets are a zero-sum game: one only profits at the expense of others. While the finance sector of the economy might be fed by other sectors, through dividends and interest rates, and while it might, in turn, feed other sectors through consumption, especially of luxury goods and services, at any one time there remains a finite share of market value to be distributed. Each profit, then, is someone else's loss. In this respect, the voluntary choices that people make in financial markets are often against their own interests. In financial markets, the primary justification for the justice of market equilibrium, that it benefits all, is invalid because of the fallacy of composition: each winner gains at the expense of a loser. This rational deficit has to be compensated by a secondary notion of justice: that the market rewards merit. Profits go to those who are best able to make the most efficient use of resources. But since the most efficient use of resources, in the context of finance, means simply maximising the rate of profit, then such a justification is nothing but a tautology. Unfortunately, this has been widely maintained as a substantive moral insight sufficient to justify profiting from others. Boatright unwittingly illustrates the moral conflict here: 'Little concern should be expressed, perhaps, for investors without the resources or skills for successful trading, but the success of financial markets depends on reasonably wide participation'.[13] Let us observe what is at stake here: financial markets require a continual flow of opportunities for profit in order to exist; without such opportunities, there would be little motive for engaging in financial trading, and society would lack the efficient and inclusive markets that finance is able to facilitate.[14] Nevertheless, in a zero-sum game, these opportunities are only afforded by a continual supply of less knowledgeable and skilful competitors who may be exploited.[15] What is especially problematic here is that it is the wealthy investors who have more options: greater opportunities to diversify, ability to attract greater leverage, ability to gain more from arbitrage through volume, and privileged access to investments closed to small investors. The financial sector seeks to facilitate inclusion; it also seeks to facilitate opportunities to profit from others. In both cases, it is the same marginal people who are included and exploited.[16]

A third area of concern is the stipulation of rights and obligations: the drawing up of contracts. As previously mentioned, any institution approximating to a perfect market depends on a multitude of significant enduring relationships consisting of rights and obligations. Yet in addition, financial markets are the scene for the generation of new rights and responsibilities, whether in the invention of financial instruments or the agreement of new contracts. Here we stand once more on moral ground, for the primary duty in any financial arrangement is to abide by the contract.[17] In this respect, the stipulation of rights and obligations in the formation of contracts is an invention of moral duties. It expresses an extraordinary moral liberty: 'let us pretend that the agreement we have imagined is just'. It invents new bonds and obligations where previously there had been none. This is the heart of the productive force of market relations: contracts establish bonds of cooperation between strangers. Market competition takes place against a backdrop of the more fundamental realm of cooperation. While the finance professional may have been sworn into the faith that the pursuit of self-interest maximises the general welfare, in practice he or she has to live by a subsidiary code of conduct – thou shalt cooperate with others in abiding by the contract.

Once returned to the fold of the ethics of cooperation, a new moral anxiety may take hold: Do contracts freely agreed in the pursuit of self-interest establish truly just rights and obligations? Do they offer a fair basis for cooperation? For not every children's game of 'let's pretend' enacts justice, so why should financial contracts? A libertarian rationale might dismiss such an anxiety as meaningless. For contracts are voluntary: if they are made by rational actors, then surely they are of benefit to both parties. Yet in the context of financial markets, where the only utility is profit, the rational actors that aim at the maximisation of self-interest or utility are simply aiming at profit. They are like the men of Athens questioned by Socrates, who prioritise profit over the state of one's soul. In this respect, the market operates a principle of competitive selection: only those who are truly 'rational', who truly profit, will survive and prosper to increase their influence in financial markets; the mistaken and irrational will lose and be excluded. The active selective principle in the formation of contracts is that those who form the contracts that most advantage them individually or as a group will be the most successful – and they will predominate. Opportunities to profit arise more readily from the imperfections of the market than from perfect competition. Profit may be a sign of injustice rather than justice. To survive and prosper might depend on exploitation of others. In this context, the 'survival of the fittest' amounts to a competition to entice others into a contractual relation in which the counterparty hopes to benefit, but in reality, they are likely to lose. The market selects for precisely such confidence tricks or unjust contracts.

Let us return to the ethical question: How might we know whether the rights and obligations that we invent out of nothing are just? It is not sufficient to presuppose that our economic agents are rational actors; we also have to presuppose that they are moral actors who refuse to take advantage of market failures. Just as rational actors in finance seek to maximise profits, moral actors in finance regulate their conduct by the ideal of perfect market competition. Is this sufficient to guarantee that the rights and obligations invented by moral actors are just? Or is there any meaning to the question: For what could justice possibly mean in this context, beyond the justice of the market?

Now the invention of rights and obligations in the drawing up of contracts between strangers might be an unmitigated good, so long as it does not interfere with any prior bonds or needs. But how often is this truly the case? For each contract involves exposure to risk, and those risks may impact upon others. Contracts are drawn up between two parties as though the conduct and obligations stipulated have no impact upon anyone else, and as though each agent is an expert on their own needs, obligations, and duties. Yet the reality of life is that all relations and activities are intimately connected with others; there are always 'externalities', other parties affected by a contract, whose interests need not be taken into account. In this respect, the presupposition of a free, rational economic agent is a mere fiction, a denial of pre-existing bonds, needs, and obligations, as though market relations could substitute for any of these. It is a blanket denial of moral seriousness, the replacement of life with a game of 'let's pretend'. For in practice, any contract agreed between two parties has a moral ambivalence: it establishes new rights and obligations, but always at some risk or cost to prior needs and moral obligations.

To sum up, then, the ideal of perfect market competition is proposed as a solution to the problems of ethical anxiety, of questioning how a free agent should live. For only here does the natural inclination towards self-interest correspond to the efficient distribution of resources. In reality, however, markets are far from perfect, and the finance sector is required to make good the deficit by facilitating access to markets, by lubricating efficient pricing mechanisms, and by advancing the variety of contractual relations that can be marketised. Moreover, even in finance, 'market failure' or the recurrence of non-market relations is pervasive. For the very institutions that are designed to simulate a perfect market prevent its realisation through conflicts of interest, through the exploitation of weakness, and through the imposition of unfair rights and obligations. As such, the return of moral anxiety is intractable: Should one seek one's own interests or seek to serve others? Should one aim to include others on a level playing field, or seek to exploit their weaknesses? Should one honour all contracts or honour prior needs and obligations?

Now, from the point of view of efficient distribution of resources, the existence of financial market failures generates enormous inequalities and inefficiencies. Yet from the point of view of ethical anxiety, market failure has an extraordinarily reassuring effect: for each failure increases the incentive to renew efforts to make the market perfect. Hence the categorical imperative: perfect the market. The morality of the market is intensified through its failures, just as confessing one's sins leads to renewed spiritual commitment. Yet this faith is merely an illusion. The perfect market cannot exist nor can it be just. Instead, markets are continually created in finance by the provision of liquidity. Insofar as it exceeds the exchange which it makes possible, liquidity constitutes a further ontological layer of the market. It is time to investigate the complex metaphysics of liquidity.

Chapter 19

Liquidity: The Faith of Finance

Liquids flow. Milk, blood, wine, and beer flow. Oil gushes from a well, electricity flows down a wire, gas down a pipe. Paint flows down a brush; sound waves flow from a piano. My cats used to flow out of the door together: a river of just two cats. A heap of coins flows out from an upturned treasure chest. In each case, there is a moving substance. Yet time does not flow, no more than does God, for it is not a substance that moves: it is we who, under the compulsion of time, are the substances compelled to flow.

Does money flow? I press my debit card to a contactless machine, an electronic message flows to a receiver, but money is *transferred*. The message flows but not the money. I watch the ticking of currency values, the momentary transitions of bids and offers: the movement is always discontinuous. Prices change but do not flow. There is this and then that, yet never a smooth transition. At the weekend, the prices seize up completely. But each moment is a momentary weekend, a tiny seizure. For money can be mine or yours; it can be transferred or exchanged; it never flows between us. By purchasing with money, we can capture the flows as property for a period of time: a flow of bricks becomes a house; a flow of metal becomes a car; a flow of ripening fruit becomes a food; a flow of water becomes a month's supply; a flow of thought becomes information. In free market exchange, nothing flows; or, rather, every flow is overcoded as a commodity. We no longer watch the flows; we only count the codes. The entries in an account book or spreadsheet are fixed for a period of time. Similarly, each employee has a code of conduct, a way of dealing with customers professionally. Work is organised by codes, systems, processes, and attainment targets. Everything ticks like clockwork. Movement happens out of sight. Modern economic life is stroboscopic: it illuminates in a flash a world of statues that are stationary when visible yet advance upon us or flee in the blink of an eye. So money does not flow; it has no velocity; it merely has a certain frequency of exchange. Money facilitates exchange, and through this, it facilitates the instantaneous vision that distributes flows into codes and qualities into private property. It illuminates a world frozen into a photograph. At least, in such an instant, the world seems clear for a moment. For the moment one starts to consider life in terms of time rather than of substance, flows rather than codes, one opens a veritable Pandora's box of paradoxes. A momentary peek – or a mention of liquidity – and we are lost.

Finance expresses a faith in liquidity. Woe betide us if exchange itself should ever come to a halt – for then nothing would hold any exchange value. All markets would close. Money would be worthless. Cooperation could no longer proceed upon that basis. Yet strange to say, money itself requires a temporary halt in order to hold value.[1] For money only stores value when it is not exchanged. The moment of seizure is necessary for exchange to work. Like an oil reserve that is left in the ground which gains value from its hoarding, money holds value through the option of not spending it. Just as an oil reserve is both a means of producing other things and an asset or store of value in its own right, money can be advanced as an investment in the means of production or retained as a store of value. Yet paradoxically, at the same time, money that is hoarded and not exchanged has no more value than King Midas' daughter who was turned to gold at his touch. Nothing can be done with money under the mattress except the evocation of anxiety and greed. It is the mere *possibility* of its being exchanged – its liquidity – that gives value to money. Money stores the mere potential of value, a potential that exists only in the suspension of its usage.[2] In finance, then, liquidity is never actual but only imagined: an asset is liquid if it is possible that it might be exchanged.

This much is straightforward, and yet one cannot help but be struck here by an apparent difference between money minted as coin and money created as debt. For one bears an unchanging substance; the other signifies a temporal relation. While money minted as coins retains the possibility of being melted down, sacrificing monetary liquidity for physical, money created as debt actually promises the possibility of its own abolition upon repayment. Indeed, the debt only bears value through the promise of repayment, that is, its own abolition, for a debt that could never be repaid while bearing no interest would hold no intrinsic value in itself. It can only store value and facilitate exchange by promising that it will become as insubstantial as a gossamer veil. After the exchange is complete, we can see that debt money was really nothing; only the exchange it facilitated matters. Yet this apparent nothing of a self-cancelling is what has made all the difference.

If one looks only through this veil of money, it may seem strange that there do in fact exist debts which can never be repaid and earn no interest. They are printed on paper or plastic, and I take care to carry some whenever I leave my house: they are the bank notes which enable us to imagine the 'monetary base'. Whether these particular debts hold value because they are issued by the Bank of England, as in the credit theory of money[3] or hold value because I could use them to pay taxes, as in the state theory of money,[4] or hold value simply because they are priced by foreign exchange derivatives, as in more complex market theories of money,[5] is perhaps beside the point, for each of these dimensions seems to be a condition for the others. In any case, there do exist some permanent debts which can remain liquid. Moreover, they epitomise the most significant paradox to be found in the structure of finance itself: financial assets gain value from their *liquidity*, even as they promise value through their *maturity*. A central bank reserve or note is a debt which never matures. From the point of view of its owner, value is realised when an asset is sold; yet also in relation to its owner, a financial asset that is sold is one that has not yet come to maturity. While maturity is attained by waiting, value is realised by selling. An asset holds value insofar as it is a claim on someone's liability, one that can be effectively realised, resolving the debt; yet an asset also holds value insofar as it can be exchanged, transferred, and so effectively priced. Just as a hoard of coins never realises its purchasing power in exchange, a financial asset that is to be transferred never realises for its owner its capacity to call in the claim. Of course, to sell an asset is to realise part of its maturity value in advance. Yet this value is only realised as money, as the most indefinite promise of future payment. As a transferrable debt, a financial asset is both the promise of its end and an opportunity for deferral.[6] As Keynes would have said, a preference for liquidity is a preference for jam tomorrow.

The point of introducing the question of liquidity is to demonstrate how the drive to complete the market by generating liquidity requires a temporal practice that is sharply at odds with the accounting perspective that records all values as present (or past) values in exchange. This paradox enables us to distinguish two dimensions of financial life on the basis of their temporality: exchange and debt. Exchanges are instantaneous swaps, requiring no more subsequent attention. The photograph of the world has changed, but clarity is restored. Debts, by contrast, endure over time. It would be a mistake to regard debt as merely derivative of exchange, for debts may be created entirely independently of exchange by the imposition of fines, rents, tithes, and taxes. They may also result from exchange without the use of money, such as in the deferral of payment. They may entirely involve money, as in a loan, which is an exchange of money separated over time. They may also take more complex non-monetary forms, such as when one financial asset is swapped for another rather like a peace agreement sealed by offering people to be held hostage, on the understanding that such assets will be returned at a set time. Debts endure through time. In each of these cases, such debts may not be liquid if others know nothing of the character and circumstances of the debtor and the risks they might present. Yet such illiquid debts are an essential part of economic life which takes place over time: time is required for merchants to buy before selling, for investment in capital before producing, or for paying wages in advance of income from sales.[7] Whether such debts are facilitated by an advance of money or by a deferral of payment, economic producers are typically debtors. These debt relations are characterised by risk, uncertainty, and responsibility on both sides – the creditor is responsible for ensuring that they lend to a reliable debtor. If Keynes recommended likening such a bond to a marriage,[8] a pair of his successors, Massimo Amato and Luca Fantacci, have likened the market exchange of such debts to an orgy.[9] For the liquidity of a debt, the capacity to sell it to others, whether in the hope of the early realisation of its value or in the fear of its losing value, offers a means of being absolved of a creditor's risk and responsibility. Exchanges differ from debts insofar as they are instantaneous, leaving no enduring relation in time. But to offer credit is to place oneself at risk; hence to sell a debt for money is to be liberated from the risk, just as to be bought out of debt-slavery is to be redeemed. In this respect, money, imagined as pure liquidity, offers freedom from credit risk just as it offers freedom from debt obligations. It is, quite literally, the means of redemption. Money is a debt that sets us free.

Keynes in his *The General Theory of Employment, Interest and Money* commented on this distinction between debt and exchange: an investment decision is largely irrevocable; its consequences have to be endured. Yet once there is an organised market for investments or debts, then a 'new factor of great importance has entered in', one which facilitates investment but also 'adds greatly' to the instability of the system. The continual valuation of asset prices on the market changes everything: 'It is as though a farmer, having tapped his barometer after breakfast, could decide to remove his capital from the farming business between 10 and 11 in the morning and reconsider whether he should return to it later in the week'.[10] As this example indicates, all investment decisions are in reality irrevocable: someone has invested in the farm, even if it is no longer the farmer. Yet investments which are fixed for the community as a whole can be made 'liquid' for the individual over a short period if they can be sold on to others.[11] The principal problem is that the professional investors and speculators, who help to set the market price, are not mainly occupied with the long-term yield of an investment over its whole life, but with anticipating short-term changes in its market price. And this, noted Keynes, is a purely structural problem:

> This is the inevitable result of investment markets organised with a view to so-called 'liquidity'. Of the maxims of orthodox finance none, surely, is more anti-social than the fetish of liquidity, the doctrine that it is a positive virtue on

the part of the investment institutions to concentrate their resources upon the holding of 'liquid' securities. It forgets that there is no such thing as liquidity of investment for the community as a whole. The social object of skilled investment should be to defeat the dark forces of time and ignorance which envelop our future. The actual, private object of the most skilled investment today is 'to beat the gun', as the Americans well express it, to outwit the crowd, and to pass the bad or depreciating, half-crown to the other fellow.[12]

The unfortunate consequences observed by Keynes include a lack of investment knowledge, excessive volatility, and violent fluctuations in market prices. Nevertheless, liquidity does have some social benefits. For if investment decisions are not irrevocable, if assets can easily be sold, then such investments will prove more attractive and more investments can be made.[13] Risk can be transferred to those who are best able to bear it. Yet the transfer of risks also has its social costs. If risks are reduced by liquidity, then investments seem safer. In that case, more investments will be made, often relying on the insurance provided by liquidity rather than relying on actual knowledge of the security of the investment. Overall risk increases in the system as a result of both the larger overall volume invested and its less prudent direction. The financial system as a whole becomes especially vulnerable in two respects: in the first place, as an interlocking system of credits and debts where any 'money' invested represents the creation of debt upon debt, any significant default at any point in the system risks unravelling a whole system of liabilities leaving all parties insolvent. In the second place, debts are only liquid investments to the extent that they are supported by valuable collateral assets. Any loss of confidence on the part of investors is liable to depress asset values, leading to insufficient collateral, the issuing of margin calls, a need to sell, further asset depreciation, and financial crisis.

Now the moral duty to 'complete the market' may be fulfilled in part by the provision of liquidity. Indeed, the model of an ideal market, with perfect competition and information, is an ideal of complete liquidity for all assets. The banks, as providers of liquidity, achieve this through 'maturity transformation', borrowing in the short-term to make long-term investments. Similarly, through 'securitisation', long-term investments are converted into short-term assets which can easily be sold. The provision of a market is an attempt to subordinate debt to exchange, whether through creating money or through creating securities. Both seem to reduce risk for the individual, while increasing risk for the system as a whole. For liquidity does nothing to modify the initial credit risk of the first investment; indeed, it exposes the initial investment to greater system-wide risks overall. At a time of crisis, those who are able to do so pay down their debts: the amount of investment in the system is reduced. At the same time, those who cannot pay their debts on time are forced to defer payment, if they can do so, or go bankrupt, if they cannot. Debt has a tendency to overflow. Such an overflow signifies viscosity, not liquidity – it is not simply that such assets cannot be instantaneously exchanged, nor that, as a result of radical uncertainty, they do not have a market price, but that their uncertain yield is itself postponed. In the attempt to subordinate debt to exchange, exchange is conquered by temporality.

Overall, then, the creation, monitoring, and settlement of debts each have an intrinsically different temporal structure to the exchange of debts for money. One finds these two kinds of relations, debt and exchange, throughout the financial sector: there are 'primary markets', where investments are agreed, futures and derivatives written and sold, and new kinds of assets are invented, and these operate as a series of over-the-counter transactions between privileged representatives of financial institutions who engage in private business based on their networks of trust.[14] The most useful resource for any broker is their book of contacts.[15] It is important to emphasise that in practice such transactions are nothing like the 'markets' described by economic theory – business is conducted behind closed doors or over the telephone without transparency or publication of prices, and with limited opportunities to compare prices. Credit relations are formed within social relations of prestige, privilege, trust, and patronage. Indeed, many of these transactions are straight swaps, having no need of or recourse to money. Such transactions are irreversible.[16] Only subsequently are these debts and securities bought and sold on the secondary markets, the public financial markets, which approximate more than any other market to those of economic theory because of their liquidity. In the secondary markets, an asset bought yesterday can be sold on at a higher price today; an asset short-sold today can be bought back at a lower price tomorrow. Liquidity is generated by the provision of secondary markets through techniques of pricing.

The essential difference between debt and exchange is that between uncertainty and risk:[17] debt relations are affected by uncertainty, and so rely on privilege and trust to ensure that behaviour will be predictable. Exchange relations, by contrast, enable the pricing of risk, and more accurate levels of insurance – the pricing of options literally turns quantified time and risk into money.[18] To the extent that risk can be priced, then a security has a determinate value: it can be freely bought and sold at that value and advances of money can substitute for temporal commitment. It has *liquidity*. The more confidence in the price, the more liquid the asset; and the more liquid the asset, the more confidence in the price, and the more likely that investments will be made. To the extent that there remains uncertainty, then only the more courageous venture capitalists may invest in the knowledge that the assets may not be liquid. The aim of much financial activity such as securitisation, therefore, is to turn long-term, illiquid investments into liquid assets that can be traded on the market, so attracting far more confidence for investment. Yet, as Amato and Fantacci maintain, 'securitization *undermines* the foundations of economic life, for it changes that fundamental economic relationship which is the link between creditor and debtor, making it not more solid but, literally, more liquid'.[19] If there is a belief system operating in financial markets, it involves a belief in exchange, a belief in accurate pricing by efficient financial markets, a belief that historical volatility is a guide to the future, and a belief in liquidity: risks are only undertaken in the belief that responsibilities can be shed at a moment's notice by selling on the asset. It is the confidence in liquidity that makes a financial market possible. As Edward LiPuma explains, 'Each transaction instantiates and foregrounds the market that it presupposes. . . . The magic of a market is not that it tricks its participants but it makes them believe'.[20] Selling, of course, means exchange of the asset for a more liquid one: money itself. Money is a liquid asset because it is regarded as a safe store of value (apart from the risks of inflation and devaluation); money, in turn, is a safe store of value because it is a liquid asset that can be exchanged for anything else.

Now, even in the case of money, there are degrees of liquidity: the US dollar, the Euro, the Japanese Yen, the British pound sterling, and the Swiss franc are rather easier and quicker to buy and sell on international currency markets than more 'minor' currencies because they are traded more frequently, and there are more complementary orders to match each other. The currency markets are structured as 'over-the-counter' markets, pairing bids and offers, not as secondary markets where assets can always be bought and sold. Even in the case of currency, then, liquidity remains an ideal limit: one cannot entirely turn time into money. Markets cannot entirely eliminate uncertainty. Then just as one kind of market failure results from liquidity preference, leading to a reduction of consumption and investment, another kind of market failure results from aversion to risk, leading to a reduction of borrowing or lending. In both cases, there is a shortage of money, but in a liquidity crisis, this shortage results from storing money for a longer time, whereas in a debt crisis, this shortage results from the insufficient creation of debt. In both cases, there is a lack of confidence, but in a liquidity crisis, there is a lack of confidence in prospective yield, while in a debt crisis, there is a lack of confidence in measures of risk. In both cases, there is an exposure of a measure of illusion, but in a liquidity crisis, the illusion exposed is that of the possibility of barter exchange without money, whereas in a debt crisis, the illusion exposed is the possibility of converting debt into liquidity. A debt crisis discloses the presence of radical uncertainty.

For liquidity is exchangeability, and exchangeability rests upon a set of practices grounded in a belief in an ideal market. To participate in financial markets by buying and selling assets it is necessary to presuppose what other participants are likely to believe: that there is a moral duty to perfect the market, that financial agents are free, that risk can be priced, that wealth is private property, that debts should be repaid, and that markets are efficient. It does not matter if the participant believes all these things personally; it is merely sufficient that the 'market' believes them, that is, that the large number of other participants who one is trying to outwit will behave as if it believes them. No one individual has to believe any of this;[21] it is, as Keynes pointed out, a kind of convention. Continuity and stability may be achieved by relying on this convention. While human decisions affecting the future cannot depend upon expectations derived from strict mathematical calculation, because there is no basis for making such calculations, one only has to behave as though there are such calculations – perhaps made by 'the market', if not known to any individual – and human behaviour becomes stable.[22]

The return of radical uncertainty in a debt crisis exposes this convention as an illusion: it is impossible to offer any accurate pricing of risk. This is not only because 'the market' is never a closed system, insulated from all external and unforeseeable shocks. It is also because the basis for all pricing is merely a convention. Such a convention is held in place by a collective act of faith, but this collective act of faith rests on a fatal flaw: the market is not perfect. Unlike a perfect God, it cannot be conceived without contradiction. For to perfect the market, individuals have at once to pursue the maximisation of their own wealth measured in terms of money as well as contribute to liquidity by participating in exchange, borrowing. and lending. There is a potential practical contradiction here, just as there is a contradiction between contributing to the common good and being a free rider, or between pursuing one's advantage by keeping to the rules and pursuing one's advantage by taking shortcuts. While wealth may be gained through exchanging, borrowing, and lending, wealth may also be preserved by a withdrawal from these. The contradiction lies between venturing and preserving, between taking risks and avoiding risks. The contradiction lies between spending or investing on the one hand or saving on the other. Without taking risks, there is no market at all.

In a sense, then, reliance on convention is an attempt to repress one's own knowledge of radical uncertainty. Such a faith is weak because of its bad conscience. Such a belief is founded on the circular logic of self-assertion: as long as there is confidence, there is liquidity, and as long as there is liquidity, there is confidence. This faith is grounded in nothing outside of itself; it is a pure assertion of the will to believe: it is a nihilistic faith.[23] Even so, it is grounded in internal contradictions. There is the contradiction of money as a store of value: money can only store value and so be a basis for confidence in liquidity if it is not spent; at the same time, money can only be liquid if it is actually spent rather than being used as a store. There is a similar contradiction in the liquidity of a security: ongoing temporal and uncertain investments are only made if they can be easily exchanged for a secure store of value, while investments are only actually sold if one is uncertain about their future value. At some level, even with the most liquid of assets, one desires their liquidity because one is aware that the actual investment underlying the security is a long-term one and is therefore exposed to risk. The basis for an increase in value is long-term investment, while the basis for insurance is short-term liquidity.[24] The quest for liquidity, while founded on confidence alone, actually bears witness to a lack of confidence in the underlying investment. As such, it undermines the underlying confidence which is necessary for economic relations.

This collective faith, while leading to local and temporary stabilities by means of a convention, also leads to its own self-destruction in a return of the repressed. In seeking liquidity, one represses the reality that financial investments are ongoing temporal relations of risk and responsibility, and that the pricing and liquidity of risks merely passes them on, without in any way reducing the underlying uncertainty. In this respect, secondary markets which increase overall investment also increase overall risk; secure risk management increases the capacity to take risks, and so ensures that risks will be undertaken until defaults are realised.[25] One represses the reality that the financial sector is structured by ongoing credit relations rather than simply by private ownership and exchange of assets, so that default does not merely result in a loss of wealth for some, but spreads by contagion. By repressing the reality of contagion, one transfers debts and extends networks of credit in order to profit at the expense of others in a zero-sum game. The ultimate result is to bring about this very contagion, for those who lose in financial markets will eventually either default on their debts or cease their demand for assets. One represses the reality that the market only exists as an act of will, a theological postulate, and that risk is only priced accurately insofar as there remains a market. In a crisis, what remains uncertain is whether there will be any buyers at all, or that an asset will have any price. Ultimately, one represses the reality that there is no real money in the financial sector, including no true store of value and no true market: there are only debts and the swapping of debts issued by one institution for those of another. The illusion of a financial market is maintained only by the operation of banks in their work of maturity transformation. What one has taken as 'money' is in reality an ordering of trust.

Chapter 20

Appropriating Fictitious Capital: Derivatives

These elucidations of the non-market structures which produce approxima-
tions of markets, in the form of the duty to perfect the market and a faith
in liquidity, may enable us to comprehend finance as fictitious capital. In
contrast to standard Marxist treatments of fictitious capital, which start from
labour as the source of all productive power, the approach taken here suggests
that obligations and beliefs are truly productive. Fictions that enable trust and
cooperation have a creative power: they facilitate action and give it orientation. From the outset, I have proposed that human wealth comes in the form
of goods of appropriation, goods of participation, and goods of offering. In
this respect, the duty to perfect the market (a form of participation) and faith
in liquidity (a form of offering) are already features of productive human
wealth. The critical question is whether these forms of wealth are consistently
productive or whether, through their own illusions, they also generate poverty
and constraint.

Fictitious capital itself can be divided into kinds: those generated through
appropriation, such as derivatives which appropriate time and risk; those
generated by participation, such as clearing which enables debts to hold
value by holding out the promise of mutual cancellation; and those generated
by offering, such as deficit spending, which offers goods while taking upon
oneself the risk. The remaining task, for this philosophical investigation of
the theology of finance, is to consider these specific instances: derivatives,
clearing, and deficit spending.

Derivatives, for all their inherent complexity, may now be dealt with quite
briefly for they are a tool for increasing liquidity. The necessary precondition
for enabling liquidity is quantification. Now quantification involves replacing discrete institutions and individuals with partial, quantifiable attributes:
one can only model the aspect of reality which is subject to variation. Arjun

Appadurai illustrates this with two dimensions of owning property: from one perspective, owning a house is a matter of individual possession – it may be counted as a mark of financial adulthood and security to take responsibility for a mortgage and the maintenance of the property, even though one merely owns a piece of paper or property deed. For the financial markets, by contrast, a mortgage itself can be divided, recombined, sold, or used as collateral. From this other perspective, the perspective of finance, all that counts are quantities which predict levels of risk:

> Numbers are attached to consumer purchases, discrete interactions, credit, life chances, health profiles, educational test results, and a whole battery of related life events, so as to make these parts of the individual combinable and customizable in such ways as to render moot or irrelevant the idea of the 'whole', the classical individual.[1]

A massive enterprise of data gathering atomises, partitions, and quantifies each person such that the features become more important than the person as a whole. While it would amount to slavery to physically appropriate a whole person in such a way, it is commonplace to appropriate another's data through monitoring and measurement. In this respect, Appadurai follows Gilles Deleuze in regarding the individual, which had formerly been the basis for modern Western political, economic, and moral thought, as being superseded in significance by the consideration of 'dividuals', partial entities subject to quantification. Deleuze explained the transition from disciplinary societies, based around institutions for containing individuals, to societies of control, based around modifying credit scores as:

> We no longer find ourselves dealing with the mass/individual pair. Individuals have become '*dividuals*', and masses, samples, data, markets, or 'banks'. Perhaps it is money that expresses the distinction between the two societies best, since discipline always referred back to minted money that locks gold as numerical standard, while control relates to floating rates of exchange, modulated according to a rate established by a set of standard currencies. . . . The disciplinary man was a discontinuous producer of energy, but the man of control is undulatory, in orbit, in a continuous network. Everywhere surfing has replaced the older sports.[2]

Finance can monetise all other forms of quantification by associating them with prices. While quantifiable data produces statistical evidence, which may be treated as a set of self-evident facts or checked by further data-gathering, as if this alone constituted knowledge of reality, a further difficulty is found in identifying quantities for future values, events which have not yet happened. Allocating a future price is an act of fictitious appropriation which abstracts a value from an underlying asset. In the case of options, which involve assigning a price to the value of the option to buy an asset in the future at a determinate date and price, a fictional price can be constructed from the past volatility of the asset. It is a way of pricing expectations. Derivatives enable a future arbitrage opportunity: the holder of a call option that closes 'in the money' can profit at the time of closing by buying the asset at the agreed strike price and immediately selling it for the new market price; if it closes 'out of the money', the holder merely loses the price originally paid for the option. In neither case does the buyer of a call option take possession of the underlying asset. In respect of the underlying asset, the entire exchange is a fiction; the real exchange takes place at a derivative level in the buying and selling of options for money.

While buyers of call and put options may use them to hedge against risk, sellers and those who speculate in options only do so because they believe that the current option price will prove inaccurate. As a result, market prices for options, as determined by supply and demand, will deviate from the prices determined by the formula involving past volatility. In other words, the formula for pricing options is initially necessary to price future events, enabling them to be exchanged; yet the formula remains a fiction, and options are exchanged at market prices instead. As LiPuma remarks, to trade in options according to a formula that offers an accurate description of financial reality would be like playing a game of poker where all the cards are dealt face up.[3] The fiction generated by the formula is necessary to generate a trade in options at all: if there were no deviation between the formulaic price and the current market price, or between the option strike price and the actual option price upon expiry, then there would be no arbitrage opportunities, no reason to buy or sell options, no liquidity for options, and no market for them either. The fiction is necessary to enable options to exist at all.

As a result of such deviations between fiction and reality, the option enables hedging and leveraging a position, taking greater risks. Wealth is generated through the asset-leverage spiral when options are successfully traded. Wealth may also be stored in asset forms as derivatives, entirely separate from actual quantities of the underlying assets. For if, on expiry, assets are simultaneously bought and sold, there is no limit to the options which can be created on an underlying asset. The fictitious capital embodied in the value of options consists in expectations of future value.

The fictitious capital of derivatives is not entirely divorced from the underlying economy: it may have effects on prices of the underlying assets. Moreover, insofar as profits are measured in terms of money, the value stored in derivatives can also be spent in the 'real' economy. Nevertheless, it should be noted that any realisation of value in purchasing power returns it to the private property of the autonomous individual. Adapting Marx's formula, one could say that the formula for fictitious capital is, at its simplest, money-fictitious capital-increased money (M-F-M'). Speculation may be a matter of dividuals in relation to dividuals, but when it comes to spending money, this is a task for a modern subject who is an owner of property. Indeed, one can only be composed of 'dividuals' from the perspective of a third party. The active individual, who appropriates and possesses a sum of money through speculation in the undulatory fields of prices and derivatives, remains a modern subject.[4] Even fictitious wealth ultimately has to be reduced to purchasing power: a power to obtain goods and services from others. It would therefore seem to be the case, from the perspective of competitive goods of appropriation, that the entire world of finance is a zero-sum game. Even when realisation of fictitious wealth is not the primary objective, since money is the means of keeping score, it is still a matter of the wealth of individuals.

As LiPuma notes, it is remarkable that fictitious finance has produced individuals whose core of self-esteem is centred around the unending acquisition of monetary value itself, as opposed to the more traditional satisfactions derived from family, lineage, commodities, status, public recognition, intellectual achievement, spiritual peace, or heavenly reward.[5] Fictitious capital, in such speculation on derivatives, gives an orientation which takes leave from individual life, even if the individual reorients their life to serve the accumulation of a fiction. It is not evident that in doing so finance has contributed to the creation of wealth. The problem remains of how surplus wealth is created through appropriation of fictions in money-fictitious capital-increased money (M-F-M'). If financial wealth is a fiction, where does it come from? For it does not come directly from labour, neither is it advanced by the future. Many might assume that quantification itself creates wealth in the form of information. If knowledge is power, information is wealth. Information, insofar as it is valid, offers control over reality, enabling adaptation of reality as a means towards extraneous ends. Nevertheless, in the pricing of derivatives, what is effective is the fiction rather than information. The question is who, guided by a fiction of a wealthy future, will offer to advance wealth. For this, we have to look beyond the individual, as appropriator of assets, fictitious, or otherwise, as well as beyond 'dividuals', the domain of quantifiable entities. It is necessary to turn to one of the lesser noticed aspects of collective behaviour in finance: the creation of wealth through composition via clearing.

Chapter 21

Participating in Fictitious Capital: Clearing

Clearing, the mutual cancelling of debts, is a mode of cooperation which facilitates the creation of wealth. The activities of banking and clearing existed long before industrial capitalism and even coinage; they function as the condition of possibility of both productive and financial capitalism.[1] To understand the wealth-generating effects of clearing, it is helpful to return to Keynes' understanding of composition. The fallacy of composition consists in making a generalisation based on adding up the properties and circumstances of individual units as if these were independent variables. Such generalisations are false when these individual units interact as they are aggregated. In this respect, all attempts to reconstruct the world on the basis of quantification, definition, information, and models are in danger of committing some fallacy of composition, for their starting point is aggregating units assumed to be independent. For quantities are mere surface effects; one cannot assume that some are independent variables in order to extract the dependent variables. To reconstruct the world on the basis of quantified information is like trying to predict market prices through technical analysis. Keynes has taught us how to see through such fallacies by making us aware of the flow of funds. If all individuals seek to save at once in the form of a liquidity preference, hoarding money, then there is no more money in the system for them all to save – some are bound to be disappointed. In reality, the withdrawal of money from consumption and investment reduces production, and with it incomes – if everyone seeks to save, then everyone has less access to money. The effect of composition on saving is the destruction of wealth.

What, then, are we to make of composition in the converse situation, where spending for both consumption and investment exceeds income? While saving is essentially limited, spending may not be so for the system as a whole. Saving is limited to assets that have previously been created and accumulated – saving money is limited by the amount that exists in the banking system. As a result, the preference for liquidity removes liquidity from the financial system, because as bank loans are repaid, money previously created is cancelled out. It is precisely the opposite situation with the tendency to spend or invest in excess of income: with each new loan, money is effectively created. Once this has been spent by the borrower, whether as a consumer or investor, this newly created purchasing power can be spent again and again, boosting both consumption and production, returning a profit. The composite outcome is a multiplier effect.[2] Eventually, however, such profits enter non-productive circuits of exchange, being invested more often in speculative assets than in consumption or production, until they are withdrawn from circulation for longer and longer intervals. Perhaps they sit in the reserve account of a speculator who trades on margin or else are accumulated to pay off a loan, when they are cancelled. What actually happens in economic life is largely determined by the typical life-cycles of sums of created money, for only these hold purchasing power. To understand economic life, one has to follow the money.[3] By contrast, to treat money as a mere veil which conceals value, and to direct one's analysis towards that is to enter into an entirely fictional world. Financial value is an imaginary quantity; money, even if it consists of debts, remains an economic reality facilitating trust and cooperation. If most of the money held in reserve were to be redirected back into investment and consumption, then it could result in a massive increase in economic growth.

There is a substantial difference, then, in the effects of composition on borrowing as compared to saving. In the case of saving, money may be treated like an accumulated stock; in the case of borrowing, money may be freshly created by banks. The difference is between the limited and the unlimited. For while there are certainly constraints on how much an individual can be trusted to borrow, and how much a bank can trust itself to lend within the framework of its capital or reserve requirements, there is no overall limit on the creation of debt in the system as a whole, so long as the banks, as Keynes explained, 'advance together and in step'.[4] For as debt is created in the system as a whole, it is invested in property and financial assets, which, in turn, rise in value. As well as being held as collateral by individual borrowers, such assets may be held as capital by the banks (or exchanged for securities held as capital), increasing the amount they can lend. At the aggregate level, then, borrowing constitutes a 'virtuous cycle', even if at the individual level excessive borrowing is a vice. While the rate of growth of such a system may be constrained, the overall magnitude of its growth is not constrained from within. A growing financial and debt system can be the driving force of production and consumption if money is temporarily extracted from speculative circuits. As a result, incomes can rise, and higher levels of individual, corporate, and government debt can be supported. For such debt signifies the 'saving' of wealth.

This phenomenon has led to credit booms and bank runs over the centuries. Yet it has also supported continuous global economic growth ever since its first stable foundation in the shape of the Bank of England.[5] Nevertheless, in over three centuries, the economic, moral and even religious implications have not been well understood. For example, when individuals, corporations and governments rely on an increasing amount of debt, to whom is all this debt owed? If money were simply an accumulated stock, like a sum of gold, then there would be a clear distinction between creditors and debtors: all debts would be owed to creditors. In this case, morality seems straightforward: where possible, promises should be honoured and debts be repaid. Such creditors would profit at the expense of debtors through interest, while the debtors themselves might profit from investment in their own future. Moreover, the debtors would spend their borrowed money, and this money would, in turn, be deposited in some banking institution. Under such conditions, there might be individual bank runs, yet there could hardly be a credit crisis in the financial system as a whole: all the borrowed money would be sitting in some bank account somewhere, and so could be used as a deposit to underwrite further borrowing. The reality of credit crises demonstrates that the phenomena of composition are already in play between creditors and debtors.

When borrowing, money is created rather than accumulated: there are still creditors and debtors, but the relation is not quite the same. While saving, at least in the short-term, involves seeking to accumulate an existing finite stock, borrowing is normally understood as a transaction in time. For the creation of money by banks through lending is a matter of 'maturity transformation': the borrower gains a short-term asset, the ability to spend immediately, in exchange for a long-term liability, the debt to be repaid in the future; similarly, the bank gains a long-term asset, the loan, in exchange for a short-term liability, honouring the borrower's ability to spend. From a balance-sheet perspective – one that fails to adequately account for composition – assets and liabilities for each party cancel out. The only difference is in time, as if the economic agents deal with their future selves alone. The borrower, as it were, spends out of future income, as if advancing the funds to their present self. The lender, as it were, does the converse: investing now for the sake of future return. Such lending is possible because all such debts cancel out in the aggregate. In this respect, the summation of all balance sheets, which functions as an instantaneous photograph of the entire financial landscape, remains unchanged in the issuing of debt. There seems to be no danger of committing the fallacy of composition if one takes a balance-sheet perspective, for all financial assets and liabilities cancel each other out.

Financial reality seems to be reduced back to the individual level, where debts are obligations to oneself mediated by time. This leaves no way to explain the fictitious mediation of the creation of real wealth.

There is, however, the danger of committing a different fallacy: the fallacy of the rich fool who conceives the future on the basis of the present. This balance-sheet perspective reduces economic life to interacting with one's future self alone. The fallacy consists in imagining an exchange in time, yet time itself is irreversible. For suppose a private debtor should make a pact with their future self: 'I will spend now on your behalf so that you might benefit, but in the future, there's really no obligation to repay – so if I also leave you a debt, I also forgive it: do not pay it at all'. Such a debtor is likely to be pursued by courts and debt-collectors, and be fearful of the bailiff's cry, 'You fool! This very night your house is required of you'. Debt remains a social relation: one can only repay others, not one's past self. An exchange between future and past apart from what actually occurs in the present would be a matter of divination; this is not achieved by either individual promises or the activities of banks.[6] Similarly, such a perspective rules out any aggregate effects, as if this exchange of liabilities had no effect on consumption and production, no multiplier effect. What is true at the microeconomic level, that all economic agents must balance their books, is not the same at the macro-economic level, where a growth in production may be driven by a growth in leverage. In other words, the balance-sheet perspective constitutes the true 'veil of money' previously discussed.

This seems to leave us with a dilemma. If money is treated as an accumu-lated stock, a positive substance without a corresponding negative, then this fiction cannot account for unlimited lending. If money is treated as a balance-sheet phenomenon, as an asset that is cancelled by a corresponding liability, then this fiction cannot account for the real obligation to pay. Both perspec-tives eliminate something essential. How then are we to understand debt? Debt involves a temporal dimension: it is a relation to the future, a promise to pay a certain amount at a certain time. Debt is an obligation; it cannot be reduced to exchange, as in a balance-sheet perspective that looks only at the present; nor can it be reduced to expectation, where it may be given a present value discounted for risk. Debt involves an actual life lived under obligation. Life lived under debt is oriented to achieve settlement. If all share this orien-tation, debtors and creditors alike, then all live under an obligation to achieve settlement of debts. Justice, as Polemarchus affirmed in Plato's *Republic*, would then be taken as 'speaking the truth and repaying what one has bor-rowed'.[7] Settlement is largely achieved through clearing.

While one normally thinks of 'money' as that which is required to settle debts, there are in fact a variety of ways in which debts may be settled without recourse to coins. An obvious case would be payment in kind: the offer of some asset, good, or service which the creditor agrees is sufficient to count the debt as settled. Settlement involves judgement that an equivalent has been paid, or acceptance that a payment should count as an equivalent – this even applies in the case of coins, for if the coins returned are different ones, as they usually are, the creditor will want to be assured that they are indeed good ones. Somewhat less obvious, then, is that debts may be settled by an equivalent in other debts. A first case is settlement with first party debt. A Bank of England £10 note reads, 'I promise to pay on demand the sum of ten pounds'. In other words, it is a promise to pay the Bank's debt with another of its own debts, just as it is possible to meet one's private debt obligations by re-financing. For one can, in principle, pay debts due to expire immediately with debts due to expire later on, simply re-negotiating or postponing settlement. The Bank of England's debt is distinctive here insofar as it is permanent. Another case is settlement with second party debt: if I pay you back in your own debt, which you may have issued to someone else who has transferred it to me in payment for something, then I can return it to you. While the expected time of repayment between such debts may differ, debts may still be settled by offering to a creditor their own IOU. A third case is settlement with third party debt, transferring the debt of another so that, in effect, it is now they who owe you instead of me. This occurs every time a note issued by a bank is used for the purposes of settling debts. In addition to such cases, there are also more complex circumstances that have the effect of partial settlement, even if the nominal debt remains unchanged: inflation, which devalues existing nominal debts, is one such circumstance; currency devaluation relative to other currencies is another. Moreover, a debt may be 'settled' by default, the action of the debtor, or forgiveness, the action of the creditor. Even though the debt is not paid in either case, the matter may have to be regarded as settled.

The settlement of debt has aggregate effects, however, in the case of multilateral clearing systems. While often referred to as 'payment' services, these have a quite different structure from straightforward payment systems, such as Paypal or Bitcoin, that simply transfer an accumulated stock. For in clearing there is a process of 'reckoning', the cancelling of debt against debt. Instead of treating debts as a positive substance like coins, clearing adopts a balance-sheet perspective so that credits and debts cancel each other out. For if clearing were to involve treating money like a stock, so recording each payment from one party to another, and then seeking swaps with the payments from other parties that partially cancel out the first, the entire system would be far too complex to be viable. It would present a problem analogous to the 'non-coincidence of wants' found in barter systems.[8] Instead, the situation is resolved by making each payment to and from a central third party, who matches and cancels out the debt. This is why barter exchange offers a very poor model for market transactions – liquid transactions are at least triadic in structure. For markets for liquid securities are facilitated by a market maker, one who retains a stock of the asset in question and seeks to make bids and offers at prices sufficient to maintain that stock – a third party is required to make a market. Similarly, when bilateral exchanges are facilitated by 'money', then instead of a stock of notes or coins being transferred, the clearing system mediates an exchange of debts. Complex and extended market systems are supplemented by banks.

Banks have been involved in clearing transactions at least since the Middle Ages, ever since they started discounting merchants' bills of exchange – these were effectively receipts, guaranteeing that goods were in transit, which could be exchanged at a discount to the expected worth of the goods, so that the merchant could receive advance payment and continue buying and selling, while the bank would receive the final payment in cash. Similarly, when sending payments to distant cities, merchants could ask their own bank to request that a correspondent bank at the destination make the payment, while the merchant paid the bill at their own bank. The crucial factor here is a difference in numerical scale: while merchants might be numerous, banks function effectively when they are few. In effect, then, problems regarding trust in payment can be overcome by banking, insofar as a bank is primarily concerned with acting in the interest of safeguarding its own reputation for honest dealing. Of course, many similar functions can be provided by a range of financial institutions, but these, in turn, bank with other banks, and the main clearing banks all hold reserve accounts with the central bank for the purposes of clearing.[9] The central banks, in turn, may hold reserve accounts with each other; beyond that, they largely perform clearing operations through the Bank for International Settlements. As a result of mutual cancellation through clearing, the 'base money' held in reserve accounts is far smaller than the total amount spent in daily transactions, as well as far smaller than the total amount held with commercial banks in demand deposits. What is more, this 'base money' never leaves the central bank – it is simply transferred between accounts to make clearing payments. Moreover, such 'reserve money' is simply a debt issued by a central bank: it is normally issued by being swapped for another reliable debt, almost always a treasury bond, with a clearing bank that holds a reserve account. The clearing bank gains a loan of reserves for the purpose of daily clearing transactions; the central bank gains a loan of the treasury bond. The entire monetary base is composed of the swapping of assets and liabilities; there is no need for any public issue of notes and coins apart from those required for minor individual transactions outside the banking system.[10]

Clearing, then, is the effective way in which debts may be settled through aggregation. The principal difference between economic agents and banks is that while the former are separate individual economic units, the banks are united by both a complex network of interlocking credits and debts, being promises of future payment, and by a clearing system that settles them as they fall due. It is clearing which is the secret of 'money creation'. It is possible to regard monetary system as an inverted pyramid, where 'broad money', as used in daily transactions and created as demand deposits, is leveraged on the basis of a narrow 'monetary base'.[11] The advantage of aggregation is achieved by the privileged few institutions that participate in the closed circle of clearing transactions. Only by membership of this privileged circle can they support money creation through offering accounting and clearing services to others. This hierarchical structure, based on privilege, patronage, secrecy, and assessment of the integrity of its members, is rather distant from the egalitarian ideal of open free market exchange. The basis for exchange is not liquidity on an open market, but a closed circuit of privilege. There is no free market without banking, no equality without hierarchy. At the apex of this system, the debts of the central bank can be continually refinanced and never repaid because they are liquid, and therefore not presented for repayment; they remain liquid, however, because they are required for the clearing operations of the clearing banks; and they remain secure because central bank reserves never leave the central banks themselves but are simply transferred between accounts of privileged institutions. So in financial markets, one treats bank debt as if it were money because banks treat central bank reserves as if it were money, even though it only consists in debts that circulate around a privileged circle. Nevertheless, the image of a pyramid is a little misleading insofar as it suggests a single apex, as though a central bank has full control over the quantity and value of money. In fact, the monetary base has a triadic debt structure: reserves, debts of the central bank, are lent to clearing banks, so that they may clear their debts in mutual transactions, in exchange for treasury bills, or government debt. Market, bank, and state exist in mutual presupposition. Should a state pay off its entire national debt, then there would be no treasury bonds for commercial banks to acquire, and no central bank reserves – the monetary framework would break down.

The irony of clearing as a phenomenon of aggregation is that for its effective performance, it requires the fiction of a balance-sheet perspective. This is to treat debt as if it has a present value – which of course it does at the time that it is being cleared. Debts can only be cleared against others if they are given a determinate value in the present moment, discounting any future risk. The balance-sheet perspective does, however, present only a snapshot of what has been agreed. The true action happens elsewhere. There is no explanation visible of the drivers of change: it is as though individuals, banks, government, and central bank were not economic agents, interfering in the market through their own preferences. The illusion created is that 'preferences', while expressed through money, seem entirely exogenous to money, being unaffected by any composition or dynamics in time. Yet it is precisely the composition achieved through clearing, taking a balance-sheet perspective, which enables the growth of 'virtuous cycles' of debt. And, when in debt, one's preferences are constrained by the obligation to balance one's books.

Chapter 22

Offering Fictitious Capital: Deficit Spending

Economic life is largely a matter of necessity. When structured by selective competition, one has to do what one can to stay in the game – survival is a matter of necessity. There is a necessity to seek profits in the form of money. There is a necessity to repay one's debts. There is a necessity to perfect the market. There is a necessity to adopt a balance-sheet perspective, as though all financial assets could be given a present value, as though debts were private property rather than relations. There is a necessity, once money is acquired, to either spend, save, or invest. There are all the dynamic processes that necessarily result from aggregation: the multiplier effect of spending, the liquidity trap of saving, and the intensification of risk from investing. There are the necessary financial crises that result. There is a necessity to preserve a fragile financial system from the system-wide risk of contagion by default. There is a necessity for an indebted government to pursue policies that satisfy the approval and interests of its creditors or bondholders even at the expense of its electorate. This chain of necessities offers a limited context for the exercise of discretion. Of course, all economic decisions concerning the use of money appear to offer complete discretion to the individuals, corporations, and governments involved: as purchasing power, money grants freedom. Yet all the chains of necessity, from the duties to repay debt and perfect the market, through the principles of competitive selection, to the effects of aggregation, provide a context for that freedom: each choice is a challenge to discern what is most in accordance with necessity. Just as a speculator will seek to discern which direction a price will move out of necessity, so also do all economic agents find themselves confronted by a reality far more complex than a market: an economy. At the root of necessity lies human need.

Where, then, is there scope for the exercise of discretion? L. Randall Wray, as one of the pioneers of the 'modern money theory' that describes the creation of money in terms of debt, has attempted to identify the place of discretion among the drivers of economic processes. At the individual level, the overall rate of spending is constrained by income – even if one spends on credit, the amount of credit one can support is determined by one's level of income. At the aggregate level, however, the situation is reversed, for incomes are determined by the spending of firms and governments on wages, profits, and interest. A firm will spend in the expectation of sales – that is, expecting expenditure by other firms, households, governments, or customers abroad. Likewise, a government will spend in the expectation of tax receipts. Overall, then, there is little discretion over income (only in some forms of employment can one choose the hours that one works); there is discretion, however, over deficit spending. At the aggregate level, a society can choose to spend more, but it cannot simply choose to have more income – unless it chooses to produce more, which also requires a decision to spend more.[1] It is the flow of credit that drives and extends economic activity.

In the Keynesian tradition, it is held that only the state has both the motivation and the power to intervene at the aggregate level for the sake of the common good. Wray outlines the unique economic powers of the state: in the first place, it chooses the money of account for official accounts, taxes, and court orders. While it is certainly not the case that all contracts, debts, and exchanges that take place within a sovereign territory have to take place in the state's currency, the very fact of paying taxes in one currency makes it far simpler to perform most transactions in that currency. Second, the state licenses the issue of currency, and prosecutes other issuers as counterfeiters. When banks create demand deposits at will, which are effectively used as currency, then it would seem that the state has given licence to counterfeiting for these are not matched by an equivalent in reserves. Yet the difference, here, is that while a counterfeiter produces a note with no corresponding liability, a bank issues a demand deposit as a promise of future payment. Where a counterfeiter hopes to escape detection, the bank is reasonably transparent – the value promised can be claimed directly from that bank. In the third place, a government imposes tax liabilities to be paid in its money of account. It simply imposes debts – this cannot be reduced to an exchange for the services provided by the state, for the payment of taxes is not a voluntary agreement with the individual, even if the overall level of taxation may be determined by democratically elected representatives. By placing all participants in an economy in debt, a government imposes a demand for the currency it has issued. Finally, the government chooses the money in which it will make its own payments. By spending, the government provides the money with which people can spend their taxes.[2]

Wray therefore subscribes to a version of the 'state theory of money': it is the imposition of taxes that drives demand for a particular currency and so give it value. This is in opposition to the commodity theory of money that a note will only hold value if it represents something of intrinsic value such as gold (which, of course, constrains economic activities arbitrarily by the supply and demand for gold).[3] It is also in opposition to the market theory of money that a note is acceptable in exchange because others will also accept it in exchange – a 'hot potato' theory which relies on an infinite regress, one which would also apply to counterfeit money. Moreover, it is distinguished from those state theories of money that pronounce a currency as legal tender, that it must be accepted in exchange on pain of punishment. Many currencies have not been declared to be legal tender; such a measure would be a last resort to save a currency that is not widely accepted.[4] Historically, it has been through monopolisation of an essential resource, such as land, energy, salt, security from invasion, peace, or religious salvation, and charging rents, fines, tithes, fees, and taxes that a state has imposed the demand for its money.[5] For Wray, the notes of the central bank should actually read, 'I promise to accept this note in payment of taxes'.[6] In this respect, should a state choose to extend its fiscal operations, increasing government spending and taxation, then this has a multiplier effect: once spent by the government, the recipients have higher income and can spend more, the money itself is transferred to others and spent once more, leading to a greater turnover for firms, and more investment as well as more sales and profits leading to higher tax receipts. The crucial point is that while government spending and taxation is one point in the life-cycle of any particular sum of money, its overall effect is multiplied by the number of individual transactions it passes through. Of course, that sum is reduced at each stage by the rate of taxation, whereby it returns to the government, and so the multiplier effect is constrained by the rate of taxation. To reduce this dampening effect, a government may turn to deficit spending – instead of receiving its money back directly from taxpayers, it borrows it back from bondholders who become effective recipients of government spending in the form of interest payments. In either case, government spending, if sufficiently large, can set the entire economic environment for consumption and investment by other economic agents.

The overall picture that emerges of state deficit spending, then, is that it seems to be largely unconstrained by limits. Even in the cases of speculators, firms, and private individuals, any limits set by lenders to deficit spending are somewhat arbitrary. For if interest payments are met by further borrowing, if collateral is provided by the rise in asset prices induced by borrowing, and if debts can be passed on to successors, what is there to stop either an individual or an economy living on an increasing level of debt? Similarly, if government deficits are financed by further borrowing, if deficit spending enhances tax receipts, and if austerity measures reverse the multiplier effect and reduce tax income, then why should not governments spend well in excess of their means – as they are wont to do whenever they go to war?[7] The result of deficit spending would appear to be a complete liberation from the first rule of economic necessity: that spending should be proportioned to income.

Given that the entirety of economic life is premised on scarcity, discipline and austerity, working for an income to provide for one's needs, balancing income and expenditure, and honouring debts and fulfilling obligations, then the notion that somewhere there is 'money for nothing' induces a sense of vertigo. It leads to self-undermining questions: Why should quantitative easing be supplied only to the banks? Why not spend it on investment, creating jobs, or at least on welfare benefits or as a universal citizen's income? Why bother with austerity at all? Why are people not free to invest all their time and energy into intrinsically worthwhile activities, instead of the mindless occupations required by most employers? Is there a fundamental class difference between those who are required to repay their debts and those who can create unlimited amounts of credit by taking on ever-increasing leverage? There appears to be something unreal in the notion that money can be created from nothing. Can a bank really purchase any asset by writing a cheque on its own account without requiring a prior deposit, since the asset purchased will improve its ratio of capital against its liabilities? If such freedom from economic constraint really were to exist, why then have so many banks and states been threatened with insolvency, while most of the super-rich have made their fortunes in more traditional ways – from property, business, land, resources, arbitrage, investment, tax avoidance, and perhaps occasionally a little criminality? What does this privilege of creating money consist in?

The key political question is who holds this power, how it is exercised, and how it is constrained. Wray makes the case for the unique privilege of sovereign states that issue their own currency to be able to borrow and settle debts in it without fear – the US, Japan, and the UK governments can hold far more significant debts than Portugal, Ireland, Italy, Greece, and Spain, which effectively have to balance their books in a foreign currency, the euro. This privilege is held by states who issue strong currencies that are widely in demand; it is not held by those countries that have to borrow and spend in a foreign currency. It derives from the sovereign freedom to impose an obligation upon others: taxation. Since taxes have to be paid in the national currency, that currency will always be in demand for taxed citizens, and therefore will always be in demand in international markets in which those citizens participate. The converse of this is that sovereign governments have a unique privilege of unconstrained spending within their own currencies. Wray's argument goes like this: when a government spends, the results are both fiscal and monetary. If one considers the monetary effects, reserves are transferred from its own account at the central bank to the reserve accounts of the banks of the recipients of its payments. There are now excess reserves in the private sector banks, who offer these for loan to each other in daily operations, and the result is that the interest rate falls. The central bank, however, has a target for the interest rate, and will seek to reduce the excess reserves – it sells treasury bills into the open market in exchange for reserves. The monetary effect of government spending, then, is that excess reserves released from the government's account at the central bank are reabsorbed again by the central bank. On the other hand, when one considers the fiscal dimension, a government also borrows by selling treasury bills onto the open market, and these too are bought in exchange for central bank reserves. The result of this is to reduce the reserves available in private sector banks. To restore equilibrium, the central bank will borrow these treasury bills in exchange for newly created reserves. Monetary and fiscal effects then cancel out; the overall effect is that the treasury borrows from the central bank. The money that the government 'borrows' is therefore created by the central bank, even if this is mediated through the private sector.[8] The central bank is constrained by economic necessity: Wray's argument is that while central banks are given the roles of maintaining an interest rate and preventing inflation, they adjust the economy to equilibrium, while it is solely the government that decides on the level of spending, and thus the level of financial assets in the economy. 'From inception, taxpayers and financial markets can only supply to the government the "money" they received *from* government'.[9] Even if a rising government deficit leads to inflation by pumping more money into the economy than is invested in new production, inflation itself increases nominal tax revenues, and the nominal rate of growth will rise above the interest rate, both of which decrease the deficit. In the meantime, the central bank can control the interest rate by swapping reserves and treasury bills, effectively inviting the private banks to move money between a current account (consisting of reserves) and a time deposit that pays a higher rate of interest (consisting of treasury bills).

There is a risk of confusion here: when the government spends in such a modern monetary system, it does not create 'money' in a form that is widely used in exchange. It does not mint fresh coins or print additional bills. It does not directly add to the demand deposits in the overall banking system. It does not increase central bank reserves. Instead, it prints treasury bonds, so that, once held by commercial banks, such treasury bonds function as a capital asset against which further liabilities may be issued. Similarly, when taxes are paid, the government does not directly receive notes or even demand deposits from commercial banks. Instead, to meet the payment of taxes, reserves are transferred at the central bank back to the government's account. So in government spending, reserves are transferred from the government's account back to the commercial banks. In government borrowing, central bank reserves are credited to the government's account in exchange for treasury bills, and it is such reserves that are spent in deficit spending. It is essential to distinguish three different, and practically inconvertible, kinds of money: the issue of notes and coins; demand deposits; and central bank reserves. Having clarified these distinctions, the government can effectively increase the amount of demand deposits in the system by deficit spending.

So long as this argument holds, then the political ramifications are extraordinary. Why should local and national government departments work within budgets? Why pay taxes at all, if the government can create the money it spends at will? Why repay debts, when more money can be created? Why work for a living, if the government can afford welfare payments for all? Why have a functioning economy at all? An answer was once given by the leading American economist of the Keynesian generation, Paul Samuelson, in an interview:

> I think there is an element of truth in the view that the superstition that the budget must be balanced at all times [is necessary]. Once it is debunked [that] takes away one of the bulwarks that every society must have against expenditure out of control. There must be discipline in the allocation of resources or you will have anarchistic chaos and inefficiency. And one of the functions of old fashioned religion was to scare people by sometimes what might be regarded as myths into behaving in a way that the long-run civilized life requires.[10]

Samuelson exposes directly the secret that economic life is grounded in faith. There are three levels of fiction here. There is the fictional wealth of future tax receipts which is pledged as collateral to enable government deficit spending. Here, the government spending itself provides the money which will return in tax receipts. There is the political fiction that budgets must be balanced, a fiction invoked to maintain work, discipline, and efficiency. It is, of course, an economic necessity that someone should do the work; but it is a political fiction which motivates those who work to do so. Now, one might take Samuelson to be confessing a political secret here: that government books do not need to balance, and that government spending can be unlimited. Yet the purport of his statement is that there is an element of truth in the superstition. For, at another level, that government spending could be unlimited is also fictional, for this spending power does depend on a circuit of taxation, based on efficient productive work. If the government spends too much, people may start to work too little to generate the goods and services upon which the money is to be spent, or to generate sufficient taxes to repay government deficits. Among all these fictions, it is difficult to discern the source of wealth in deficit spending; for this wealth is not simply free wealth since it is constrained by necessary conditions. In truth, the only goods and services that a society has are those that are produced by work and cooperation; if all gained income without work, such money would be worthless as there would be no goods or services to purchase. The underlying threat embodied in excess government spending is really that of stagnation: a failure to produce goods and services at all. People are motivated to work and cooperate by the 'old-fashioned religious myth' that expenditure should be proportioned to income – this keeps up the circular flow. Production in the aggregate depends on belief. In short, the superstitions of austerity are a matter of social control and morality. Without them, the political compact between state and people is broken – one has to behave as though money is a stock, as though books must be balanced, as though each is subject to market forces, in order for there to be an economy at all.[11] This is one reason why quantitative easing might be restricted to lending reserves to banks, who participate in the central bank monetary framework, so that the cancer of unlimited leverage does not leak out into the wider economy. Society still functions on the basis of a religious faith – now a faith in the market, in the value of money, and in paying one's debts. This economic theology motivates work, profits, and taxation. A debt-based economy is ultimately grounded on a somewhat Puritan ethos, for all its excesses in consumption.

There are, of course, limits even to the power of the state. These limits are imposed by the exercise of discretion by private firms and individuals. A first limit, as we have just seen, is the willingness of the populace to work and cooperate; some accounts suggest that a failure at this level brought down the Soviet system. A second limit is their willingness to be taxed.[12] Populations, following their immediate perceptions of self-interest, do not like to be taxed, and so may express their democratic choices by electing representatives that promise lower rates of taxation. When such electorates make self-contradictory demand for better government services and lower taxes, or better security to be achieved through more wars, there is no choice but for a government to engage in deficit spending. Moreover, the higher the rate of taxation, the higher the rate of tax evasion and tax avoidance, sending capital abroad to tax havens, or the higher the rate of emigration by the wealthy and the more skilled or educated workers who might otherwise have to pay higher taxes. A third limit is set by capital flight, whether from foreign investors, or to foreign investment, or from investment in government bonds, in response to perceptions of the likely effects of government policy. In the long run, then, deficit spending leads to a thorough subordination of government policy to the interests of capital against the interests of voters and taxpayers – until the compact between government and people is broken, and the people elect a populist government. Even so, such populist governments inherit the economic constraints of their predecessors. In short, political discretion is still constrained by economic necessity. Yet, since this is a moral constraint, it is difficult to discern the threshold beyond which deficit spending leads to stagnation. Far from achieving the euthanasia of the rentier, the capitalist, or the usurer, the economic system empowers them as it lurches further and further from equilibrium.

Deficit spending, while apparently promising freedom, in fact yields further constraint. In the system as a whole, debt has to be financed with further debt. Under further constraint from debt, the laws of competitive selection are tightened: each are under further compulsions to repay debts and seek profits, and to do whatever is required to achieve sufficient levels of income to manage the debt. As a result, inequality increases. Horizons are narrowed to the short-term: immediate survival requires 'business as usual', while long-term preventative measures cannot be afforded. An economy driven by deficit spending lurches towards financial, political, and ecological crisis. Where, then, is there hope for redemption? How might one stop this impersonal spiral of debt?

It would seem that debts might be reduced in three possible ways: at the level of individuals and corporations, by deleveraging through paying down the debt; at the collective level, by inflation or devaluation of the currency; or at the spiritual level, by default, for forgiveness of debt seems equivalent in its economic effects to settlement by default. Adair Turner has argued that none of these options are desirable on a large scale.[13] While large public sector debts were reduced massively between 1945 and 1970 (in the UK from 250% to 50% of GDP, in the United States from 120% to 35%) by a combination of inflation and significant GDP growth, the technological opportunities for increased productivity no longer seem to be present.[14] Moreover, the new circumstance is the large private sector debt. For whether the deleveraging is public or private, the result is a reduction of effective demand and an inversion of the multiplier effect.[15] The ultimate consequence would be a debt-deflationary spiral. Moreover, even this would be ineffective in reducing private or public sector debt, since incomes and tax receipts would thereby be reduced, making overall deleveraging impossible. By contrast, the opposite approach of encouraging a higher rate of inflation by holding interest rates extremely low would encourage precisely the kind of debt growth for speculation that has produced the financial crisis. Whether in inflation or deflation, the overall size of debt grows. The only alternative, then, would appear to be some kind of debt default, write-down, or debt forgiveness. This is simply an unavoidable necessity for debts that cannot be paid. Yet while it can be managed successfully on a small-scale, the effects of large-scale default or forgiveness would spread through contagion throughout the financial system. Most creditors are also debtors; forgiving the debts of others requires forgiveness from others of one's own debts. The result of such a system-wide collapse would be the destruction of money in demand deposits, the loss of knowledge of the creditworthiness of all economic participants, default on all existing contracts, and the destruction of all cooperation based on existing networks of trust. Suddenly reduced for the first time to a set of isolated individuals and surviving firms, economic life would have to be rebuilt from scratch.

In the meantime, then, the only viable course of action to address a debt crisis would seem to be that which was in fact taken in response to the crisis of 2007–2008: government recapitalisation of failing financial institutions, central bank purchase of bad loans and toxic assets, and a programme of quantitative easing to increase lending and investment. What is striking about such measures is their sheer arbitrary contingency and lack of accountability in their endeavour to restore the faith.[16] Of course, regulatory and structural reforms can contribute to the stability of the system, prolonging the time until the next crisis, but each of these only strengthens a system constrained to pursue ever-increasing debt. If deficit spending offers the illusion of freedom, the spectre of anarchy, or an anxious maintenance of shrinking islands of stability, in practice it delivers only tightening constraint.

The creation of fictitious forms of wealth, whether in the form of derivatives, clearing, or deficit spending, is ultimately only a strategy of deferral which increases overall constraint. In conclusion, then, if a debt-based economy is already subject to conflicting constraints, compelled towards growth yet having external limits, increasing inequality while turning the wealthy against each other, advancing short-term interests while undermining long-term prospects, then the creation of fictitious wealth merely offers a promise of freedom while tightening the constraints. For one person's financial wealth is another's financial obligation. The creation of fictitious wealth, even by a state for the sake of redistribution, either tightens the constraint of debt, interest, or taxation payments, or else threatens to undermine the economic theology upon which trust and cooperation rest. Since fictitious wealth is funded by the creation of more fictitious wealth, the world lurches ever deeper into ecological, economic, social, and spiritual crisis.

Conclusion

Economic science is largely concerned with aspects of human behaviour which can be quantified – such matters as rates of productivity, numbers employed, trade balances, import tariffs and quotas, discount rates, capital reserves, and rates of default or bankruptcy. Such quantifications offer useful snapshots on economic life, enabling interventions to modify quantities and enabling measurements to evaluate interventions. It enables the construction of models of an immensely complex machine which, if understood well enough, could be mastered and adapted for the ends of human welfare. At the same time, human persons are key components of this complex machine, and the very existence of the machine depends on human behaviour being consistent, regular, and reliable when measured over large numbers of interactions. In this latter respect, the condition of possibility of an economic science, and thus of limited mastery over the economy, is that the machine exerts mastery over us, integrating us into its circuits. While economic science provides a useful overview for managers who seek to exercise their freedom and discretion, another discipline is required to understand human conditioning by autonomous, machinic processes.

If, from one perspective, economic life can be quantified, from another, economic life is conducted through the use of words, documents, and contracts which construct the reality to which they refer. Such words order time and attention, care and evaluation, trust and cooperation, ensuring that not only a particular kind of life is propagated in this way but also awareness is focused on a particular aspect of such life. Moreover, the quantifiable does not have priority: constructive words are the preconditions for quantification. There are no immediately given quantities in economic life: everything has first to be produced by words, documents, standards, and agreement. Economics can only approximate to an empirical science. It is one matter to turn one's attention solely to the quantities. It is quite another matter to turn one's attention to the forces which direct human attention in this way.

While there are many accounts of social and cultural conditioning, the aim of this book has been to contribute an account in terms of economic theology. In one respect, the subject matter is theological because it concerns people's secret thoughts, thoughts taken for granted and not usually available to the subjects themselves. While one might infer from people's behaviour what perspective they may have adopted or how they may have invested their trust and hopes, there is no science of trust, credit, or faith: such matters are neither quantifiable nor available for empirical investigation. The method adopted here, by contrast, is philosophical: it consists in the elaboration of concepts, forming a perspective upon perspectives. It is a matter of unfolding that which is implicit in our thought. As Hegel, the great critic of 'mere empiricism' put it:

> Moreover, this dialectic is not an activity of subjective thinking applied to some matter externally, but is rather the matter's very soul putting forth its branches and fruit organically. This development of the Idea is the proper activity of its rationality, and thinking, as something subjective, merely looks on at it without for its part adding to it any ingredient of its own. To consider a thing rationally means not to bring reason to bear on the object from the outside and so to work on it, but to find that the object is rational on its own account.[1]

Of course, the philosophy pursued here is not the same as Hegel's: the mind is not composed of universal ideas; it is made of flesh and blood – it is local, temporal, and partial, and any grasp it has of eternal or universal ideas is mediated by its own particular concepts, language, and habits of thought. The method developed here is far less systematic: it has been the recollection of selected contingent and particular perspectives in order to bring to light the dimensions of offering trust and collective participation which are often over-looked. By adding fresh perspectives, which are themselves transformed by that upon which they are brought to bear, one can invert what is counted as significant and suspend dominant judgements. This procedure is not intended to discover the eternal truths of reason nor the inner rationality of objects. Instead, it is intended to put the mind back in contact with the multiple dimen-sions of the world in order to affirm them. Yet, in one respect, Hegel is right: the value that the mind feels and honours is not contributed by the subjective act of thinking; instead, given appropriate conditions, value may put forth its branches and fruit organically, and the mind may even digest its fruit and offer it to others. Such an offering of value, however, can never be appropri-ated for exchange, for this is already to substitute an imagined or anticipated value for that which has been digested. The mind can feed on value, orient itself by value, and point towards value; it cannot directly master, produce, or even state value. In order to sense value, the mind must submit to it.

Nevertheless, human words do indeed have a certain creative power. The creative power of money evokes trust and cooperation where otherwise these may be lacking. Money, which itself is created by the words of trusted authorities, facilitates cooperation where there are a diversity of goals, perspectives, and values. When one trusts the power of money and sells, labours, or lends in order to receive it, one trusts that, in the future, it will enable one to exercise effective demand on one's own account. Money harnesses the social power of effective cooperation in a way which far exceeds any merely individual exercise of leadership. It is not the will by itself which has creative power, but money lends the will its own power of turning imagination into reality. The possession of money functions as a sign that one has previously offered something of value to society, some resource, product, service, or even money itself. Yet, for any individual who seeks money, there is no need to believe that the money that backs up demand faithfully reflects a definite amount of value previously offered. Instead, one only has to have faith in the effective power of money itself. Likewise, for one who creates or lends money, there is no need to believe that the debtor has previously rendered any service to society; one merely needs to believe that the debtor has a credible plan to render such future service as is necessary to acquire enough money to repay loan and interest. It is the act of offering credit which facilitates creation, enabling ideas and plans to become realised through cooperation. The theological dimension of economic life consists in the creative power of ordering trust.

For money functions as a token of accountability. Most people acquire money through offering some good, service, or labour to those who require these, receiving money in return. Others acquire money by investing or lending property or money to those who have need. As such, these have done some service to others, and the money that they possess may be treated as an indicator that they are in credit, that they have fulfilled their obligations to society, and that they deserve to be treated with recognition and respect, having their requirements fulfilled in turn. Of course, everyone knows that money can be acquired in other ways which do not contribute to the common good, such as theft, exploitation, inheritance, speculation, fraud, and forgery. Nevertheless, imperfect as this system of accountability is, it is adopted for the sake of its convenience. Possessing money is an imperfect way of demonstrating one's accountability before others. Yet since the quantity of money that changes hands in any transaction is that agreed at a given moment, it can bear little relation to what has gone before or will come after. In this respect, having money is only evidence that one has received or taken it; it is no evidence that one has contributed or will contribute to the satisfaction of human needs, the fulfilment of social obligations or the cultivation of values. The convenience of money as a token of value comes at the expense of its accuracy. A quantity of money agreed may reflect certain perspectives on what is to be counted as significant, yet it offers no overall evaluation of what has been done or will be done in order to receive it. In this system of account-ability and trust, the immediate viewpoint of the one with money to spend is the only one that counts. Economic action has conditions and consequences, orientations and values, experiences and possibilities, which far exceed any-thing specified in a contract. In particular, one can only purchase the things that may be appropriated. Goods that only exist in and through participation, such as the recognition through which concrete ethical life is formed, and goods that are only received insofar as they are offered, such as time, care, and trust, cannot strictly be bought and go unnoticed when counting quanti-ties. Of course, one can endeavour to sell one's time and agree a sum of money; yet what one in fact sells is the outcome of one's conduct during that time – no employer purchases the lived experience of any worker.

In these respects, there is no possible commensurability between value cre-ated and value extracted. There is no possible way of agreeing equivalence in exchange. Once such broader dimensions of life are taken into account, there is no possible conception of market justice nor any possible approach to equilibrium. Economic activity is at once extractive and creative: any attempt to render these commensurate or equivalent rests on quantification, requiring abstraction, appropriation, substitution, and anticipation, leaving the reality to be measured largely out of account. It is not simply that money possessed is a poor measure of what matters in life; what matters in life cannot be measured. As Nietzsche might have put it, in order to evaluate a preference accurately, one would have to be situated outside life so as to view it as a whole, including the entire past and future, and yet at the same time to know it as thoroughly as any, as many, as all who have experienced it, in order to be able to touch on the problem of the value of the preference at all: a sufficient reason for regarding this as an inaccessible problem for us.[2] Yet one cannot live without valuing: in all cases, one has to proceed on trust. In reality, time is irreversible: the future is not equivalent to the past. Life is constituted by inequality. Human activity cannot commensurate what it receives with what it offers. Nor can human activity refuse to receive or offer. Equality in exchange is incoherent both as presupposition and as goal; economic equality is meaningless as formal situation or as outcome. Instead, all one can hope to do is receive well, participate well, and offer credit well. Inclusion in eco-nomic life; recognition of physical, social, and cultural needs; and offering credit to those who may be trusted are far more significant aspirations than maximising technological inventions, overall output, or levels of equality.

Moreover, reforms aimed at realising an ideal market, whether through the extension of market relations, regulatory measures, or currency reforms, have misconstrued the multidimensional nature of economic life. Economic life consists in more than just exchange: politics, debts, and faith cannot be simply wished, regulated, or reformed away. In this respect, one may distinguish three levels to economic reality: there are those things that can be quantified and appropriated, if only in imagination. These may be regulated, exchanged, and distributed according to the logic of money and markets. Even the collective power of society can be appropriated and quantified as the right of private property to increase; even the future can be appropriated and quantified through the use of options and derivatives. Even debts can be treated as individual responsibilities subject to payment, rollover, or default. This level is at once an object of economic science as well as an object of faith: faith in quantification, money, and markets leads to their extension as far as possible for the sake of management. Yet, at another level, there are also those things that only exist in and through participation. There is the productive power of social cooperation. There are trusted records of accounts and institutions which record them. There is the clearing of debts which facilitates their payment and transfer. There are the aggregate economic phenomena which bear especially on finance and saving. There are all the politically agreed regulations and ideals that make a market possible. This level is at once an object of political economy as well as an object of faith: faith in the kinds of institutions we seek to construct makes their existence possible. Yet, finally, there are those things which exist only insofar as they are offered. The economy is an ordering of time and attention, care and evaluation, trust and cooperation. Money itself only realises its power when it is offered in exchange. Money is only created by a kind of deficit spending. Credit is the spiritual precondition enabling all production. Trust in the market ideal enables its operation and extension. Taking up an orientation towards the future is an irreducible dimension of economic life. Debts and assets only hold value to the extent that they are trusted. All financial assets are debts or liabilities, created through an act of faith. The global financial system expresses faith in its ordering of faith.

There are reasons to suspect that this faith in debt-driven capital is merely a temporary bubble. The foundation of a market system on the exchange of debts builds into the system the necessity of meeting conflicting constraints. The payment of debt is necessary; yet since debt expands exponentially, the non-payment of debt is also necessary. The logic of appropriation is subject to incompatible constraints: appropriation must increase exponentially; yet appropriation has insuperable limits. Once these limits are reached, the economy turns cannibalistic, consuming the environmental and social resources of its own wealth until trust evaporates and only naked power remains. The market logic of competition and substitution is also subject to incompatible constraints: inequality must increase progressively; yet inequality depletes the wealth of those from whom wealth is extracted. Those who benefit from exploitation have no other resource but to substitute each other for those who were previously exploited. Competition, no longer balanced with cooperation, turns into naked conflict. The logic of anticipation is also subject to incompatible constraints: short-term interests are prioritised above all else, yet, as time advances, short-term interests cannot be met unless long-term interests are served. In each of these respects, the debt-based economy devours itself. The overall result is demand destruction, ecological destruction, and spiritual destruction.

Finance offers no genuine possibilities for saving and redemption; it simply uses its fictions to offer the costly pledge of an increasingly constrained future. In order to 'build larger barns', it repeatedly pulls down its present ones, while at the same time, its fictitious promises constrain the future just to maintain the present. In this respect, it may be necessary to rethink the meaning of 'redemption'. If this has been presumed to have been primarily an economic term, a matter of payment or exchange, it now seems that it is primarily a religious term: redemption from the sacrifice of the future for the sake of the present. It will be necessary in the next volume to turn from the internal conversations of the world of finance to relations with the realms above, beyond, and deep within the human subject of credit and faith. For only such realms, beyond knowledge and control, can offer a genuine return on investment.

Recent centuries have witnessed the globalisation of two quite different frameworks for trust: for want of better terms, these may be designated as the capitalist economy and world religions. In many ways, these frameworks have been made compatible, but where tensions arise, these are often due to local factors or specific teachings. In some localities, the insecurities and instabilities generated by the capitalist system intensify the need to find assurance and cooperation in religious faith; in other localities, the security and stability granted by the institutions that service the capitalist economy have been sufficiently successful as to make religious faith seem irrelevant. Where religious life seems to predominate, a critical philosophy of religion is needed to guard against misplaced trust. Where economic life seems to predominate, religion may be ignored as irrelevant in favour of a critique of misplaced trust in economic life under the heading of 'neoliberalism'. The view expressed in these pages is that we have arrived at a historic juncture where 'anthropogenic' economic globalisation is coming to be replaced by a variety of quasi-automatic processes, like crossing the 'tipping point' of climate change beyond its anthropogenic triggers.[3] If the economy is no longer governed by politics, the time for the critique of neoliberalism is over; historical changes will take their course that no government or people can control. A key element of this transition is a loss of faith in economic globalisation, with its free movement of goods, services, people, and capital, as hope for future prosperity expires. As faith in debt-driven capitalism collapses, along with the benefits of globalisation, peace, and prosperity that it brings, there will be a change in where people place their faith. Initially, loss of faith may lead to the behaviour of a desperate debtor who endeavours to postpone future settlement as far as possible, funding debt with more debt. Attention becomes focused upon opportunities to make money in the here and now, while others come to be regarded primarily as competitors in a market that scarcely feeds us all. In short, debt-driven capitalism promotes the psychological dynamics of an investment bubble, involving practical denial of the future, inattention to reality, and a purely extrinsic relation to others. These dynamics are intensified for those from whom value is extracted, just as they are intensified for those who draw a profit. Nevertheless, under modern conditions of fragmentation, a route out of chaos has often been offered by religion, for religions offer a framework for self-discipline, mutual trust, and cooperation. If the developed world loses faith in a cooperative and prosperous future, if the wealth of the many is extracted by the few, and if globalisation collapses into fragmentation and conflict, then the world may well see a resurgence of religious commitment in currently secular countries. For world religions offer to save us from ourselves. Where globalisation offered the salvation of future prosperity through the cooperation that overcomes individual differences, world religions may offer salvation from isolation and anarchy. Such religions may not often take a form of which modern, critical theologians could approve. They might found trust on a wilful denial of patent reality; they might deny ecological concerns and promote war. Yet they might also offer some defence against economic catastrophe and a universal loss of trust by offering a basis for human cooperation. For where economic globalisation is based on an exchange of mere promises and debts that are treated as collateral for other debts, religious life offers the substance of a life regulated by religious piety. Prior to the financial revolution, this was the basis for economic life. Following the crisis of debt-driven capitalism, it may become so once again. Once more there will be an urgent need for a critical philosophy of religion in order to expose misplaced trust.

Notes

PREFACE

1. J.M. Keynes, 'My Early Beliefs (1938)', in *The Essential Keynes* (London: Penguin Random House, 2015), 13–27.
2. Gilles Deleuze and Félix Guattari, *Anti-Oedipus*, trans. Robert Hurley, Mark Seem, and Helen R. Lane (London: Athlone, 1983), 2.
3. Simone Weil, *Notebooks*, trans. Arthur Wills (London: Routledge, 1956), 454.

CHAPTER 1. GLOBAL MODERNITY: ECONOMICS AND THEOLOGY

1. Dani Rodrik outlines the preconditions for trade as follows: 'There must be some way – a marketplace, bazaar, trade fair, an electronic exchange – to bring the two parties to a transaction together. There must be a modicum of peace and security for them to engage in trade without risk to life and liberty or concern for theft. There must be a common language for the parties to understand each other. In any form of exchange other than barter, there must be a trusted medium of exchange (a currency). All the relevant attributes of the good being exchanged (for example, its durability and quality) must be fully observable. There must be sufficient trust between the two parties. The seller must have (and be able to demonstrate) clear property rights over the goods being sold and must have the ability to transfer these rights to the seller. Any contract that the two sides enter must be enforceable in a court of law or through other arrangements. The parties must be able to take on future commitments ("I will pay you so much upon the delivery of . . .") and do so credibly. There must be protection against third parties trying to block the exchange or impede it'. *The Globalization Paradox* (Oxford: Oxford University Press, 2011), 13–14.
2. Niklas Luhmann, *Trust and Power*, trans. Howard Davis, John Raffan, and Kathryn Rooney (Chichester: John Wiley, 1979).

3. These were the starting assumptions for modern economics with William Petty in the seventeenth century.

4. Margaret Schabas, *The Natural Origins of Economics* (Chicago, IL: Chicago University Press, 2005).

5. For example, see Karl Polanyi, *The Great Transformation: The Origins of Our Time* (London: Gollancz, 1945); Martin Khor, *Rethinking Globalization* (London: Zed Books, 2001); Joseph Stiglitz, *Globalization and Its Discontents* (London: Allen Lane, 2002); Rodrik, *The Globalization Paradox*.

6. Shashi Tharoor, *An Era of Darkness: The British Empire in India* (New Delhi: Aleph, 2016), 252.

7. The logic of such a cleansing of conscience, via the medium of Locke's theory of rights, has been dissected by Ulrich Duchrow and Franz Hinkelammert, *Property for People, Not for Profit* (London: Zed Books, 2004).

8. Newton's laws of mechanics were the paradigm, as explored in depth by Philip Mirowski, *More Heat Than Light: Economics as Social Physics, Physics as Nature's Economics* (Cambridge: Cambridge University Press, 1989).

9. John Cassidy, *How Markets Fail: The Logic of Economic Calamities* (London: Penguin, 2010).

10. This idea has undergone considerable development in my work since its first formulation in terms of the organisation of the investment of desire by means of its repressing representation, in *Deleuze and Guattari: An Introduction to the Politics of Desire* (London: SAGE, 1996). Drawing on the influence of Marx, Deleuze and Alliez, I later formulated the role of paper money as defining the structure of thought in modernity in *Capitalism and Religion: The Price of Piety* (London: Routledge, 2002). This was then fused with a theory of money creation drawn from C.H. Douglas, Michael Rowbotham and Frances Hutchinson to produce a dynamic social theory of debt in *Theology of Money* (London: SCM, 2007). For the present work, my own thinking has developed through engagement with other attempts to offer a social theory of debt, such as those of Richard Dienst, Maurizio Lazzarato, David Graeber, and Elettra Stimilli, as well as with the contemporary stream of alternative monetary economics espoused by Randall Wray, Steve Keen, Michael Hudson, Richard Werner, and Andrew Jackson.

11. Rodrik cites a rise of average government expenditure as a proportion of GDP from around 11% in 1870, to 20% in 1920, to 28% in 1960, to around 40% in 1978. *The Globalization Paradox*, 17.

12. For the political history of the era of financialisation, see Giovanni Arrighi, *The Long Twentieth Century* (London: Verso, 1994); Peter Gowan, *The Global Gamble* (London: Verso, 1999); Robert Brenner, *The Boom and the Bubble* (London: Verso, 2002); and Greta R. Krippner, *Capitalizing on Crisis* (Cambridge, MA: Harvard University Press, 2011).

13. Kathryn Tanner, *Christianity and the New Spirit of Capitalism* (New Haven: Yale University Press, 2019), 191.

14. Michael Hudson, *Finance as Warfare* (London: College Publications, 2015), 16.

15. For an overview of 'wreckage economics' in the UK, see Peter Fleming, *The Death of Homo Economicus: Work, Debt and the Myth of Endless Accumulation* (London: Pluto, 2017).

16. See John Quiggin, *Zombie Economics: How Dead Ideas Still Walk among Us* (Princeton, NJ: Princeton University Press, 2010).

17. 'Curve-fit back-testing' involves modifying a model to fit past data, usually in the technical analysis of price movements, in order to achieve an optimal outcome; it is distinguished from 'forward-testing' which takes a given model and tests its predictive capacity against real-world data as they occur.

18. On the role of models in economics, see Dani Rodrik, *Economics Rules* (New York: W. W. Norton, 2015).

19. See Jason W. Moore, *Capitalism in the Web of Life: Ecology and the Accumulation of Capital* (London: Verso, 2015).

20. This understanding of capitalism as an ordering of the inner life was first proposed by Pierre Klossowski, and developed significantly by Michel Foucault, Gilles Deleuze and Félix Guattari, before being taken up by various Italian Marxists. My own reception of this tradition shifted the terms of analysis from drives, power or desire to the ordering of attention and evaluation.

CHAPTER 2. A PRECURSOR

1. Simone Weil, *Oppression and Liberty*, trans. Arthur Wills (London: Routledge & Kegan Paul, 1958), 124.

2. A pertinent example here is embarrassment: unexpected and involuntary exposure may be interpreted by the mind as embarrassing; the thought of embarrassment, in turn, may cause the face to blush. The relation between mind and world here is not simply a factual one, a matter of representing what is the case; it is better understood in terms of appropriateness: Is embarrassment appropriate in this situation? The dichotomy of fact and value may be inappropriate for explaining this notion of 'appropriateness'.

3. The metaphysics of such an affirmed relation between mind and reality has been introduced under the heading of 'value' in *Credit and Faith*; it will be explored in the next volume in terms of appropriation, participation, and offering: see *Metaphysics of Trust*.

4. Weil, *Oppression and Liberty*, 113.

5. This is not to claim that contemporary reasoning is not motivated by moral conscience; what is lacking is a coherent understanding of how clashing moral intuitions can be integrated into a system of value.

6. Friedrich Nietzsche, *The Will to Power*, trans. Walter Kaufman (New York: Vintage, 1974) especially sections 1–14; Martin Heidegger, 'Nietzsche's Word: "God is Dead"', in *Off the Beaten Track*, trans. Julian Young and Kenneth Haynes (Cambridge: Cambridge University Press, 2002); Martin Heidegger, *Nietzsche: Volume IV: Nihilism*, ed. David Farrell Krell (San Francisco: HarperSanFrancisco, 1991), 199–249.

7. Weil, *Oppression and Liberty*, 117–8.

8. Weil, *Oppression and Liberty*, 118.

9. Weil, *Oppression and Liberty*, 119.

10. Weil, *Oppression and Liberty*, 115.

11. Weil, *Oppression and Liberty*, 113.

12. Weil, *Oppression and Liberty*, 106–7. Weil identified predominantly literary authors as the modern bearers of such an insight into the primacy of work: Rousseau, Goethe, Shelley, Proudhon, and Tolstoy – a tradition where Marx can be located. It should be noted that in this volume, this relation to the tool will be treated as a mere symbol of the more fundamental relation of credit; Bacon's 'new Bible' will be replaced by the philosophy extracted from the New Testament in *Credit and Faith*.

13. Likewise, Henri Bergson rejected approaches to philosophy grounded in epistemology as impossible since 'we are studying thought before the expansion of it which it is the business of knowledge to obtain', as well as approaches to metaphysics starting with general concepts since these too simple concepts are unenriched by experience. By contrast, the effort to engage with material reality draws out from the self more than it has already, where material reality is at once obstacle, instrument and stimulus. 'Life and Consciousness', in *Mind-Energy*, trans. H. Wildon Carr (London: Macmillan, 1920), 2–3, 22–23. What is of interest here is the dimension of life which is 'more than' the given.

14. Weil, 'Science and Perception in Descartes', in *Formative Writings 1929–1941*, trans. Dorothy Tuck McFarland and Wilhelmina van Ness (London: Routledge & Kegan Paul, 1987), 53.

15. Weil, *Lectures on Philosophy*, trans. Hugh Price (Cambridge: Cambridge University Press, 1978), 72.

16. G.W.F. Hegel, *Lectures on the Philosophy of World History: Introduction: Reason in History*, trans. H.B. Nisbet (Cambridge: Cambridge University Press, 1975), 75.

17. It is notable that this analogy epitomises the three stages of Hegel's dialectical method: the given situation consists in the prior injustice, the natural properties of fire and the impulse towards revenge; a particular and determinate will then chooses to act on the situation, disclosing a point of view; a synthesis of points of view can then rise once more to the rational level of universal truth: arson is a crime. Likewise, in the study that follows, the aim is to rise above the given by means of particular perspectives, and rise once more by exploring how much trust to invest in them. The method is synthetic. Yet, unlike with Hegel, what is sought is an orientation towards value rather than a universal, rational knowledge. This distinctive synthetic method, introduced in *Credit and Faith*, will be elaborated further in *Metaphysics of Trust*.

18. As Gilles Deleuze put it: 'Mediators are fundamental. Creation's all about mediators. Without them nothing happens. . . . Whether they're real or imaginary, animate or inanimate, you have to form your mediators. It's a series. If you're not in some series, even a completely imaginary one, you're lost'. *Negotiations*, trans. Martin Joughin (New York: Columbia University Press, 1995), 125.

19. Deleuze, *Negotiations*, 129–30.

CHAPTER 3. ECONOMIC THEOLOGY

1. For a range, see Stefan Schwarzkopf (ed.), *The Routledge Handbook of Economic Theology* (London: Routledge, 2020).

2. A previous attempt, inspired by Jacques Derrida's *Spectres of Marx* and Gilles Deleuze's *Difference and Repetition*, may be found in Philip Goodchild, *Capitalism and Religion: The Price of Piety* (London: Routledge, 2002), ch. 3.

3. Karl Marx, *Economic and Philosophic Manuscripts of 1844* (London: Lawrence & Wishart, 1977), 120–3; emphasis in original.

4. Marx, *Economic and Philosophical Manuscripts of 1844*, 63–64.

CHAPTER 4. A RECAPITULATION

1. For example, I am broadly in agreement with the economic diagnoses and programmes offered by David Boyle and Andrew Simms, *The New Economics: A Bigger Picture* (London: Earthscan, 2009); Tim Jackson, *Prosperity without Growth* (London: Routledge, 2011); Ross Jackson, *Occupy World Street* (Dartington: Green Books, 2011); Brian Davey, *Credo: Economic Beliefs in a World in Crisis* (Cloughjordan, Ireland: Feasta, 2015); and Kate Raworth, *Doughnut Economics* (London: Random House, 2017).

2. An insightful summary of the political decision-making is offered by Yanis Varoufakis, *The Global Minotaur: America, Europe and the Future of the Global Economy* (London: Zed, 2015).

CHAPTER 5. ALCHEMY: THE CREATION OF MONEY

1. Nobuhiro Kiyotaki and John Moore, 'Evil is the root of all money', Clarendon Lectures, Oxford, 26 November 2001.

2. Mervyn King, *The End of Alchemy: Money, Banking and the Future of the Global Economy* (London: Little, Brown 2016), 4.

3. Cited in King, *The End of Alchemy*, 10.

4. King, *The End of Alchemy*, 84.

5. King, *The End of Alchemy*, 131.

6. King, *The End of Alchemy*, 301.

7. King, *The End of Alchemy*, 129.

8. King, *The End of Alchemy*, 320.

9. King, *The End of Alchemy*, 302.

10. King, *The End of Alchemy*, 42.

11. King, *The End of Alchemy*, 155.

12. King, *The End of Alchemy*, 301.

13. King, *The End of Alchemy*, 91.

14. While this model was accurate in describing the banking process in the United States in the nineteenth century, where all banks were small since legally restricted to one state, it bears no relation to the founding of credit currency with the Bank of England in 1694 nor current practice. An official publication of the Bank of England has stated emphatically that this model is incorrect: see Michael McLeay, Amar Radia and Ryland Thomas, 'Money creation in the modern economy', *Bank of England Quarterly Bulletin* Q1 2014, 14–28.

15. In fact, this only occurred in London after King Charles had seized a shipment of merchants' bullion stored in the Tower of London. In most cities, merchants would keep their bullion in a central and guarded location.

16. Glyn Davies, *A History of Money from Ancient Times to the Present Day* (Cardiff: University of Wales Press, 2002), 251–2.

17. King, *The End of Alchemy*, 59.

18. For a nuanced account of the influence of alchemy leading to the founding of the Bank of England and a stable credit currency, see Carl Wennerlind, *Casualties of Credit: The English Financial Revolution* 1620–1720 (Cambridge, MA: Harvard University Press, 2011).

19. King, *The End of Alchemy*, 8. King takes the obvious image of alchemy, turning base metals into gold, from Hans Binswanger's commentary on Goethe's *Faust*; the use of alchemy to describe the creation of paper money goes back at least as far as Marco Polo's reports on the mint of Kublai Khan. See Richard A. Werner, *A New Paradigm in Macroeconomics* (Basingstoke: Palgrave Macmillan, 2005), 166.

20. King, *The End of Alchemy*, 37.

21. Adair Turner, *Between Debt and the Devil: Money, Credit and Fixing Global Finance* (Princeton: Princeton University Press, 2016), 6.

22. Turner, *Between Debt and the Devil*, 58.

23. Turner, *Between Debt and the Devil*, 59.

24. Turner, *Between Debt and the Devil*, 58.

25. Knut Wicksell, *Interest and Prices*, trans. R.F. Kahn (London: Macmillan, 1936), 68; emphasis in original.

26. As discussed in *Credit and Faith*.

27. Joan Robinson, 'What Has Become of the Keynesian Revolution', in Robinson (ed.) *After Keynes* (Oxford: Blackwell, 1973), 5.

CHAPTER 6. MORAL EQUILIBRIUM

1. Adam Smith, *A Theory of Moral Sentiments* (Cambridge: Cambridge University Press, 2002), IV.1.8 210–3.

2. Smith, *Theory of Moral Sentiments*, IV.1.10 215–6.

3. For Smith's inconsistent attitude to classes as the occasion suits, see Michael Perelman, *The Invention of Capitalism: Classical Political Economy and the Secret History of Primitive Accumulation* (Durham, NC: Duke University Press, 2000), ch. 8.

4. Smith, *Theory of Moral Sentiments*, IV.1.9 214.

5. Smith, *Theory of Moral Sentiments*, IV.1.1 209.

6. By 'police', Smith intended the administrative functions of regulation, surveillance, enforcement and discipline on behalf of the state, including the regulation of markets. See Bernard E. Harcourt, *The Illusion of Free Markets: Punishment and the Myth of Natural Order* (Cambridge, MA: Harvard University Press, 2011), 20.

7. Smith, *Theory of Moral Sentiments*, IV.1.11 216. For further discussion, see Pierre Manent, *The City of Man*, trans. Marc A. LePain (Princeton, NJ: Princeton University Press, 1998), 99–100.

8. Smith, *Theory of Moral Sentiments* V.2.6 363.

9. Smith, *Wealth of Nations*, volume 1 (Oxford: Clarendon Press, 1976), I.8.24 89.

10. Smith, *Wealth of Nations*, I.8.39 97–98.

11. Smith, *Wealth of Nations*, I.8.36 96.

12. Smith, *Wealth of Nations*, I.8.26 91.

13. Smith, *Wealth of Nations*, I.8.57 104.

14. Smith, *Wealth of Nations*, I.1.1. 13.

15. Smith, *Wealth of Nations*, I.1.5 17.

16. See further Harcourt, *The Illusion of Free Markets*, who shows that such a market is constructed on the basis of regulation, discipline and punishment.

17. Smith, *Wealth of Nations* I.11.b.1 162.

18. Smith, *Wealth of Nations* I.8.52 103.

19. Ricardo, *On the Principles of Political Economy and Taxation* (Cambridge: Cambridge University Press, 1813).

20. For the contemporary significance of value theory, see Mariana Mazzucato, *The Value of Everything: Making and Taking in the Global Economy* (London: Penguin, 2018).

CHAPTER 7. CHOICE

1. Thorstein Veblen, *The Place of Science in Modern Civilization and Other Essays* (New Brunswick, NJ: Transaction, 1990), 73–74. The incorporation of utilitarianism into economics was formulated by James Mill to keep one feature constant while another could vary: 'Man is compounded of a fixed and a flowing quantity; the principles of his constitution are eternal as the heavens, and the modes of their development not less diversified than the appearances of cloud and sunshine. Nature always makes him the same, and events always make him different'. Quoted in Mirowski, *More Heat Than Light*, 171.

2. Smith, *Wealth of Nations* I.2.2 26. Note that examples of dogs using money for exchange can be found on YouTube.

3. One is reminded of Hannah Arendt's account of total domination in concentration camps: 'Total domination, which strives to organize the infinite plurality and differentiation of human beings as if all of humanity were just one individual, is possible only if each and every person can be reduced to a never-changing identity of reactions, so that each of these bundles of reactions can be exchanged at random for another'. *The Origins of Totalitarianism* (New York: Schocken, 2004), 565.

4. This inconsistency is explored by Tony Lawson, *Economics and Reality* (London: Routledge, 1997), 8–11.

5. Cited in Joan Robinson, *Economic Philosophy* (Harmondsworth: Penguin, 1964), 49; on Marshall's handling of this problem, see further.

6. Robinson, *Economic Philosophy*, 48.

7. Alfred Marshall, *Principles of Economics*, eighth edition (London: Macmillan, 1920) I.ii.2 18.

8. Paul Ormerod, *The Death of Economics* (London: Faber, 1994), 111. See further John Cassidy, *How Markets Fail: The Logic of Economic Calamities* (London: Penguin, 2010).

9. Arendt explains how economics can only become a science when people become social beings who follow patterns of behaviour. Hannah Arendt, *The Human Condition* (Chicago, IL: University of Chicago Press, 1998), 42.

10. John Milbank and Adrian Pabst, *The Politics of Virtue* (London: Rowman and Littlefield International, 2016), 57.

11. Pope Francis, *Laudato si'* (Vatican, 2015), para 189.

12. For a notable example, influential in Catholic social teaching, see the work of Luigino Bruni and Stefano Zamagni, *Civil Economy* (New York: Columbia University Pres, 2017) with its attempt to replace the legacy of Adam Smith with that of Antonio Genovesi.

13. The literature here is too vast to cite; for a range of recent theological criticisms, see, for example, Leonardo Boff, *Cry of the Poor, Cry of the Earth*, trans. Philip Berryman (Maryknoll, NY: Orbis, 1997); Paul F. Knitter and Chandra Muzaffar (eds.), *Subverting Greed: Religious Perspectives on the Global Economy* (Maryknoll, NY: Orbis, 2002), Ulrich Duchrow and Franz Hinkelammert, *Property for People, Not for Profit* (London: Zed Books, 2004); Kathryn Tanner, *Economy of Grace* (Minneapolis, MN: Augsburg Fortress, 2005); Jung Mo Sung, *Desire, Market and Religion* (London: SCM, 2007); Daniel M. Bell Jr, *The Economy of Desire: Christianity and Capitalism in a Postmodern World* (Grand Rapids, MI: Baker Academic, 2012); Peter Dominy, *Decoding Mammon: Money as a Dangerous and Subversive Instrument* (Eugene, OR: Wipf and Stock, 2012); and Peter Selby, *An Idol Unmasked: A Faith Perspective on Money* (London: DLT, 2014).

14. Mazzucato, *The Value of Everything*, 66–69.

CHAPTER 8. MONEY AS MORAL MEASURE

1. Alfred Marshall, *Principles of Economics*, I.ii.1 14–15.

2. Marshall, *Principles of Economics*, II.ii.2 57.

3. Marshall, *Principles of Economics*, I.iv.1 39. The phrasing raises a host of complications: Is it the force of human motives that works or money? If riches are measured by money, but also need to be taken into account when considering the conditions under which money works, are we not caught between mutually dependent variables? Marshall is referring, here, to the marginal utility of money for those who are rich (see III.iii.4 96) – but that would imply that rich people are likely to spend most of their money and become like everyone else.

4. Marshall, *Principles of Economics*, I.ii.5 24.

5. Marshall, *Principles of Economics*, I.ii.4 23.

6. Marshall, *Principles of Economics*, I.ii.7 27.

7. Marshall, *Principles of Economics*, I.ii.4 22.

8. Nietzsche's judgement that science is a prejudice is especially relevant here: 'That the only justifiable interpretation of the world should be one in which *you* are justified because one can continue to work and do research scientifically in *your* sense (you really mean, mechanistically?) – an interpretation that permits counting, calculating, weighing, seeing, and touching, and nothing more – that is a crudity and naivete, assuming that it is not a mental illness, an idiocy'. *The Gay Science*, section 373.

9. Mazzucato, *The Value of Everything*, 12.

10. Erik S. Reinert, *How the Rich Countries Got Rich* (London: Constable, 2007).

11. Thomas Piketty, *Capital in the Twenty-First Century*, trans. Arthur Goldhammer (Cambridge, MA: Harvard University Press, 2014).

12. Michel Chossudovsky, *The Globalisation of Poverty: Impact of IMF and World Bank Reforms* (Penang: Third World Network, 1997).

13. Smith, *Wealth of Nations*, I.ii.2 26–27.

14. Craig Muldrew, *Economy of Obligation* (Basingstoke: Palgrave, 1998).

15. Gorz, *Critique of Economic Reason*, trans. Gillian Handyside and Chris Turner (London: Verso, 1989), 121–2; emphasis in original.

16. Smith, *Wealth of Nations* is quoted in E. Ray Canterbery, *A Brief History of Economics* (Singapore: World Scientific, 2001), 58.

17. See Timothy K. Kuhner, *Capitalism V. Democracy: Money in Politics and the Free Market Constitution* (Stanford, CA: Stanford University Press, 2014).

18. As previously discussed in Volume 1 (*Credit and Faith* chapter 8), section 2.3, the concept of ends may itself mask the fulfilment of basic needs, social obligations, and the cultivation of values.

19. Nietzsche once remarked: 'what is here called "utility" is ultimately also a mere belief, something imaginary, and perhaps precisely that most calamitous stupidity of which we shall perish some day'. *The Gay Science*, section 354.

20. Weil, *Notebooks*, 495.

CHAPTER 9. MONEY AS THEOLOGY

1. Robert H. Nelson, *Economics as Religion: From Samuelson to Chicago and Beyond* (Philadephia, PA: Pennsylvania State University Press, 2001), 268.

2. Robinson, *Economic Philosophy*, 11–15.

3. Fukuyama, *Trust: The Social Virtues and the Creation of Prosperity* (New York: Free Press, 1996), 11.

4. Fukuyama, *Trust*, 37.

5. John Atherton, *Transfiguring Capitalism* (London: SCM, 2008).

6. As described by Karl Polanyi, *The Great Transformation: The Origins of Our Time* (London: Gollancz, 1945).

7. See Slavoj Žižek, *The Sublime Object of Ideology* (London: Verso, 1989), 28.

8. Nelson, *Economics as Religion*.

9. See Graeber's discussion of the conquistadors: *Debt*, 311–25.

10. Aquinas, *Summa Theologiae*, II.2 66.7.

11. Lazzarato, *The Making of Indebted Man*, 29–30.

12. Cited in Geoffrey M. Hodgson, *Economics and Evolution: Bringing Life Back into Economics* (Cambridge: Polity, 1993), 218.

13. Marx, *Economic and Philosophic Manuscripts of 1844*, 123–4.

14. On money as a means becoming an absolute end due to enabling of all possibilities, see Simmel, *The Philosophy of Money*, ed. David Frisby (London: Routledge, 1990), 232.

15. Nietzsche, *On the Genealogy of Morality*, II.19 65–66.

16. Karl Marx, 'Excerpts from James Mill's *Elements of Political Economy*' in *Early Writings*, trans. Rodney Livingstone and Gregor Benton (London: Penguin, 1975), 260–1.

17. Philip Goodchild, *Theology of Money* (London: SCM, 2007), 1.

18. Marx, 'Excerpts from James Mill', 265.

19. Marx, 'Excerpts from James Mill', 263.

20. Marx, 'Excerpts from James Mill', 264.

CHAPTER 10. SIN

1. Wolfhart Pannenberg, *Systematic Theology*, volume 2, trans. Geoffrey T. Bromiley (Edinburgh: T & T Clark, 1994), 262.

2. Pannenberg, *Systematic Theology* 2, 263.

3. Pannenberg, *Systematic Theology* 2, 260.

4. Søren Kierkegaard, *Sickness unto Death*, trans. Alastair Hannay (London: Penguin, 1989), 55–57.

5. Weil, *Notebooks*, 37.

6. Peter Selby, *Grace and Mortgage* (London: DLT, 1997), 106.

PART III. EXPLOITATION AND CONSTRAINT: DYNAMICS OF CONDUCT

1. For this alternative account of money, see Philip Goodchild, *Theology of Money* (London: SCM, 2007).

2. Here I would especially recommend Wolfgang Streeck, *Buying Time: The Delayed Crisis of Democratic Capitalism* (London: Verso, 2017); and Yanis Varoufakis, *The Global Minotaur* (London: Zed, 2015).

CHAPTER 11. APPROPRIATION

1. Pierre-Joseph Proudhon, *What Is Property?*, ed. and trans. Donald R. Kelley and Bonnie G. Smith (Cambridge: Cambridge University Press, 1994), 164.

2. Josh Ryan-Collins, Toby Lloyd and Laurie Macfarlane, *Rethinking the Economics of Land and Housing* (London: Zed Books, 2017), 18.

3. Jeremy Waldron, *The Right to Private Property* (Oxford: Clarendon, 1988), 28.

4. Proudhon, *What Is Property?* 118.

5. For a fuller discussion of the implications of such arguments, see Waldron, *The Right to Private Property*, 432–9.

6. Proudhon, *What Is Property?* 150.

7. Proudhon, *What Is Property?* 105.

8. In Marxist terminology, exploitation, as the extraction of surplus value from the worker, is distinguished from primitive accumulation, which might include plunder, enclosure, and slavery. Our aim in this discussion is to draw an alternative account of exploitation as appropriation from Proudhon.

9. Rousseau, *Discourse on Inequality*, quoted in Proudhon, *What Is Property?* 67.

10. Proudhon, *What Is Property?* 150–1.

11. Proudhon, *What Is Property?* 71.

12. Proudhon, *What Is Property?* 114.

13. Proudhon, *What Is Property?* 181.

14. Proudhon, *What Is Property?* 177.

15. Proudhon, *What Is Property?* 116.

16. Proudhon, *What Is Property?* 91.

17. Marx's formulation expresses a simple category error: time cannot be extracted or directly appropriated; it can only be ordered. Likewise, while products can be in surplus or extracted, value itself can neither be in surplus nor extracted. For value, insofar as it is recognised, is a good of participation, not one of appropriation. It is neither mine nor yours, but it only exists insofar as recognition is shared.

18. For a multidimensional exploration of how such appropriation of the commons has been deployed in English history and the present, see Guy Standing, *Plunder of the Commons* (London: Penguin, 2019).

19. Proudhon, *What Is Property?* 126.

20. For a survey of how English property law, through acts of enclosure, has been a key part of capitalism, colonialism, and neocolonialism, see The Ecologist, *Whose Common Future?* (London: Earthscan, 1992).

21. Proudhon, *What Is Property?* 156.

22. Proudhon, *What Is Property?* 136.

23. Proudhon, *What Is Property?* 163.

24. Weil, 'On Bankruptcy', in *Selected Essays 1934–43*, trans. Richard Rees (London: Oxford University Press, 1962), 146.

25. Weil, 'On Bankruptcy', 149.

CHAPTER 12. SUBSTITUTION

1. Weil, *Oppression and Liberty*, 1.

2. Weil, *Oppression and Liberty*, 50.

3. Roger Perlman et al. cite the world reserve base life of key minerals under current rates of usage, including reserves not yet discovered under reasonable expectations of future price, costs, and technology possibilities: silver twenty-seven years, tin thirty-three years, zinc forty-four years, lead forty-five years, copper sixty years, sulphur sixty-six years, and fluorspar eighty-two years. The figures for deposits already discovered and recoverable under current prices, costs, and technologies are, of course, rather shorter. See Roger Perlman Yue Ma, Michael Common, David Maddison, and James McGilvray, *Natural Resource and Environmental Economics* (Harlow: Pearson, 2011), 512.

4. Joan Robinson wrote that 'The essence of "development" is the application of power to production and transport, which raises output per man-hour of labour above what human muscle (aided by some animal muscle) can achieve'. *Freedom and Necessity* (London: George Allen & Unwin, 1970), 105.

5. There is evidence that it does not function in this way: see Timothy Mitchell, *Carbon Democracy* (London: Verso, 2011).

6. For a fuller discussion, see Ross Jackson, *Occupy World Street: A Global Roadmap for Radical Economic and Political Reform* (Totnes: Green Books, 2012), 66–73. Models of production which incorporate energy use, rather than labour and capital alone, explain the 75% of GDP growth which is missing from other models.

7. Weil, *Oppression and Liberty*, 48.

8. For a discussion of the complexities surrounding this, see Davey, *Credo*, 222–7.

9. Weil, *Oppression and Liberty*, 47.

10. See Perlman et al., *Natural Resource and Environmental Economics*, 489.

11. In Joseph A. Tainter's theory, energy flow and complex sociopolitical organisation are mutually dependent, yet the greater proportion of energy devoted to maintaining a complex hierarchy leads to diminishing returns, and eventually collapses. See Tainter, *The Collapse of Complex Societies* (Cambridge: Cambridge University Press, 1988); Jared Diamond, by contrast, places more emphasis upon absolute depletion of resources, such that a civilisation starts to collapse at the height of its strength. See Diamond, *Collapse: How Societies Choose to Fail or Survive* (London: Penguin, 2011).

12. A fundamental advance within Marxist economics in this regard has been articulated by Jason W. Moore: capitalism is not simply a process of commodification and exploitation of labour-power, but one of imperial appropriation of cheap sources of labour, food, energy and raw materials through imposing order on new spaces. The rate of profit depends on keeping the commodified dimensions of capital and markets small relative to the unpaid labour extracted from subsistence and reproduction and the unpaid 'ecosystem services' of producing resources and absorbing waste. Yet there remains a tendency for this ecological surplus to fall: entropy and the production of waste, growth in accumulated capital relative to unpaid production, the pursuit of short-term profit at the expense of sustainability, and growing energy inefficiency of production (e.g. in agriculture) all lead capitalism towards crisis. See *Capitalism in the Web of Life: Ecology and the Accumulation of Capital* (London: Verso, 2015).

13. This list is extracted from UNEP, *GEO – 2000* (UNEP, 1999), 13.

14. Elmar Altvater, *The Future of the Market: An Essay on the Regulation of Money and Nature after the Collapse of 'Actually Existing Socialism'*, trans. Patrick Camiller (London: Verso, 1993), 69.

15. Altvater, *The Future of the Market*, 226.

CHAPTER 13. ANTICIPATION

1. Weil, *The Need for Roots*, 41.

2. Weil, *The Need for Roots*, 19.

3. Weil, *The Need for Roots*, 43.

4. Weil, *The Need for Roots*, 42.

5. Weil, *The Need for Roots*, 48–9.

6. Theology is perhaps the only remaining intellectual discipline where one can still encounter any understanding of this requirement – witness Pope Francis' call for an 'integral ecology'; yet even theology may be in danger of uprooting.

7. Weil, *Oppression and Liberty*, 143.

8. Weil, *Oppression and Liberty*, 144.

9. Weil, *Oppression and Liberty*, 143.

10. Weil, *Oppression and Liberty*, 13.

11. Karl Marx, *Grundrisse*, trans. Martin Nicolaus (Harmondsworth: Penguin, 1973), 693.

12. Gorz, *Critique of Economic Reason*, 32.

13. Hence, Smith's famous (yet ironic, considering his title) remark following his only appeal to the invisible hand in *The Wealth of Nations*: 'every individual necessarily labours to render the annual revenue of the society as great as he can. He generally, indeed, neither intends to promote the publick interest, nor knows how much he is promoting it. . . . By pursuing his own interest he frequently promotes that of the society more effectually than when he really intends to promote it. I have never known much good done by those who affected to trade for the publick good. It is an affectation, indeed, not very common among merchants, and very few words need be employed in dissuading them from'. *Wealth of Nations* IV. 2.9 456.

14. Gorz, *Critique of Economic Reason*, 35.

15. Gorz, *Critique of Economic Reason*, 86.

16. Gorz, *Critique of Economic Reason*, 118.

17. Gorz, *Critique of Economic Reason*, 119–20.

CHAPTER 14. DEBT DYNAMICS AND INEQUALITY

1. See Mary Mellor, *The Future of Money: From Financial Crisis to Public Resource* (London: Pluto, 2010); Ann Pettifor, *The Production of Money: How to Break the Power of the Bankers* (London: Verso, 2017).

2. L. Randall Wray, *Modern Money Theory: A Primer on Macroeconomics for Sovereign Monetary Systems* (Basingstoke: Palgrave Macmillan, 2012), 1.

3. Werner, *New Paradigm in Macroeconomics*, 177–9.

4. Knut Wicksell, *Interest and Prices*, 110.

5. Werner, *New Paradigm*, 214.

6. Andrew Jackson and Ben Dyson report that in the UK in 2010, bank credit was extended in the following proportions: 45% as loans to individuals secured on property; 15% to real estate companies; 20% for financial intermediation; 7% unsecured personal debt; 1% to insurance and pension funds; 9% to public and other services, and only 8% to productive businesses. *Modernising Money* (London: Positive Money, 2012), 114.

7. Werner, *New Paradigm*, 228. One countervailing factor is that rising house prices may result in increasing house-building, as was notable in Ireland and Spain prior to the Great Financial Crisis. In places where land is scarce, however, the rising price of land drives up costs for builders, so restricting their profits; this prevents new building from functioning as a limit on property bubbles. In the case of share values, increasing borrowing by companies to buy back their own shares also drives up their value, making the shares themselves more scarce. This commits the company to paying the rate of interest instead of a dividend – which may, overall, weaken its financial position, especially when profits are used for buy-backs in place of new investment.

8. For a good explanation of the asset-leverage spiral, see Turner, *Between Debt and the Devil*, ch. 4.

9. For example, in 2011, £109 billion in interest was repaid to the banks in the UK, about 6.7% of GDP – well in excess of GDP growth rates. Jackson and Dyson, *Modernising Money*, 156n.

10. Ryan-Collins, Lloyd, and Macfarlane, *Rethinking the Economics of Land and Housing*, ch. 5.

11. The works of contemporary economists, such as Steve Keen, *Debunking Economics* (London: Zed Books, 2012); Werner, *New Paradigm*; Michael Hudson, *The Bubble and Beyond* (Dresden: ISLET, 2012); Jackson and Dyson, *Modernising Money*; and Turner, *Between Debt and the Devil* stand out for offering money-creation-based accounts of Irving Fisher's debt-deflationary spiral.

12. Werner, *New Paradigm*, 230.

13. Turner, *Between Debt and the Devil*, ch. 7.

14. Michael Hudson, *Killing the Host: How Financial Parasites and Debt Destroy the Global Economy* (Dresden: ISLET, 2015).

15. John Maynard Keynes, *A Treatise on Money*, volume 1 (London: Macmillan, 1930), 26.

CHAPTER 15. CONSTRAINTS

1. For a summary of Campbell's views, see 'The Assessment and Importance of Oil Depletion', in Andrew McKillop with Sheila Newman (eds.), *The Final Energy Crisis* (London: Pluto, 2005).

2. Energy returned on energy invested for oil is estimated to have declined from around 1000:1 in 1919 to around 5:1 in 2010; by contrast, the figure for Canadian tar sands has improved in recent years due to improved extraction technologies.

3. Gail Tverberg, 'Oil supply limits and the continuing financial crisis', *Energy* 37 (1) January 2012: 27–34; see especially her blog http://ourfiniteworld.com where her analysis is further refined and updated.

4. A similar conclusion is reached by Brian Davey, drawing on the work of Charles Hall: *Credo*, 230.

5. See the extended discussion in Steve Keen, *Can We Avoid Another Financial Crisis?* (Cambridge: Polity, 2017).

6. See Peter Fleming, *The Death of Homo Oeconomicus: Work, Debt and the Myth of Endless Accumulation* (London: Pluto, 2017).

7. For the significance of unrestricted capital flows, see Jackson, *Occupy World Street*, 107–9.

CHAPTER 17. SAVING: THE SPIRIT OF FINANCE

1. Keynes, 'Economic Possibilities for our Grandchildren', *The Essential Keynes*, 84.

2. Keynes, 'The Political Doctrines of Edmund Burke', *The Essential Keynes*, 5.

3. Keynes, 'Political Doctrines', 6.

4. Keynes, 'The End of *Laissez-faire*', *The Essential Keynes*, 50.

5. Keynes, Correspondence 23 December 1925, *The Essential Keynes*, 75.

6. In a similar vein, Simmel noted, 'Money, as the *absolute* means, provides unlimited possibilities for enjoyment, while at the same time, as the absolute *means*, it leaves enjoyment as yet completely untouched during the stage of its unused ownership. In this respect, the significance of money coincides with that of power; money, like power, is a mere potentiality which stores up a merely subjectively anticipatable future in the form of an objectively existing present'. *The Philosophy of Money* 242; emphasis in original.

7. Keynes, 'Economic Possibilities', 84.

8. Keynes, 'The Economic Consequences of the Peace', in *The Essential Keynes*, 31.

9. Keynes, *The General Theory of Employment, Interest and Money* (London: Macmillan, 1973), 374.

10. Keynes, *The General Theory of Employment, Interest and Money*, 210.

11. Keynes, *The General Theory of Employment, Interest and Money*, 83.

12. Keynes, *The General Theory of Employment, Interest and Money*, 24.

13. Malthus' letter to David Ricardo of 16 July 1821, cited by Keynes in 'Thomas Robert Malthus', *The Essential Keynes*, 501.

14. Keynes, 'Economic Possibilities', 84–85.

15. Keynes, 'Economic Possibilities', 85.

16. Keynes, 'Economic Possibilities', 81.

17. Randy Martin saw here the basis for a new political imaginary: 'Economy promised a wealth while it naturalized scarcity. Derivatives pose a wealth already to hand that, with proper investment and sense of return, would render scarcity unnecessary. The money is there, the mutuality exists; the means to make what is desired are to hand'. *Knowledge LTD: Toward a Social Logic of the Derivative* (Philadelphia, PA: Temple University Press, 2015), 78. While I share this vision of the possibility of imagining wealth in mutuality, I do not locate this in derivatives, whether in finance or as a social logic.

18. Keynes, *The General Theory of Employment, Interest and Money*, 83.

19. Simmel explains how money has the greatest possible number of uses and so possesses the maximum value in this respect. *The Philosophy of Money*, 212. There is little opportunity cost in holding money, little reason not to prefer it.

20. For finance as ritual performance, see Arjun Appadurai, 'The Wealth of Dividuals', in Benjamin Lee and Randy Martin (eds.), *Derivatives and the Wealth of Societies* (Chicago, IL: University of Chicago Press, 2016).

21. Marx, *Capital*, volume 3 (New York: International Press, 1967), chs 13–15.

22. Søren Kierkegaard, when commenting on this parable, suggested that the idea of a future need is a snare in which only a free person entraps themselves: it substitutes an idea for presently felt needs. *Upbuilding Discourses in Various Spirits*, trans. Howard V. Hong and Edna H. Hong (Princeton, NJ: Princeton University Press, 1993), 175–6.

23. Søren Kierkegaard, *Christian Discourses*, trans. Walter Lowrie (London: Oxford University Press, 1939), 23.

CHAPTER 18. PERFECT MARKETS: THE DUTY OF FINANCE

1. Plato, *Apology*, 29d-e.
2. Plato, *Apology*, 30a.
3. John Boatright, *Foundations of Business Ethics: Ethics in Finance* (London: John Wiley, 2013), 27.
4. On the link between the invention of coinage and philosophy, see Seaford, *Money and the Early Greek Mind* (Cambridge: Cambridge University Press, 2004).
5. Randy Martin, *Financialization of Daily Life* (Philadelphia, PA: Temple University Press, 2002).
6. Søren Kierkegaard, *Christian Discourses*, trans. Howard V. Hong & Edna H. Hong (Princeton, NJ: Princeton University Press, 1997), 115–6.
7. Boatright repeats these three commonplace points: *Ethics in Finance*, 30.
8. As Keynes describes the gospel of laissez-faire: 'The political philosopher could retire in favour of the business man – for the latter could attain the philosopher's *summum bonum* by just pursuing his own private profit'. Keynes, 'The End of *Laissez-faire*', in *The Essential Keynes*, 43; for Keynes' account of the false assumptions of *laissez-faire*, see 55.
9. Boatright, *Ethics in Finance*, 38.
10. Boatright, *Ethics in Finance*, 40.
11. See the discussion of agency theory in Eve Poole, *Capitalism's Toxic Assumptions: Redefining Next Generation Economics* (London: Bloomsbury, 2015), ch. 4.
12. Keynes also observed that money differs from other commodities in crucial respects: its production cannot be increased to meet demand; there is no tendency to substitute for it as it rises in value; and there are no carrying costs of a stock of money. *The General Theory of Employment, Interest and Money*, 228–35.
13. Boatright, *Ethics in Finance*, 181.
14. Boatright, *Ethics in Finance*, 178.
15. See Stephen Davis, Jon Kukomnik and David Pitt-Watson, *What They Do with Your Money* (New Haven: Yale University Press, 2016).
16. If this picture seems a little pessimistic, note that the asset-leverage bubble of rising prices, as discussed in the previous part, is a 'rising tide that lifts all boats'. Then the question of exploitation also concerns the matter of growing inequality between those who have financial assets and those who do not.
17. Boatright, *Ethics in Finance*, 17.

CHAPTER 19. LIQUIDITY: THE FAITH OF FINANCE

1. 'Everything stops dead for a moment, everything freezes in place – and then the whole process will begin all over again. From a certain point of view it would be better if nothing worked, if nothing functioned'. Deleuze and Guattari, *Anti-Oedipus*, 7.

2. For this general structure of potentiality, see Giorgio Agamben, *Potentialities: Collected Essays in Philosophy*, trans. Daniel Heller-Rosen (Stanford, CA: Stanford University Press, 1999).

3. Geoffrey Ingham, *The Nature of Money* (Cambridge: Polity, 2004).

4. L. Randall Wray (ed.), *Understanding Modern Money* (Cheltenham: Edward Elgar, 1998).

5. Dick Bryan and Mark Rafferty, *Capitalism with Derivatives: A Political Economy of Financial Derivatives, Capital and Class* (New York: Palgrave, 2006).

6. This is the central paradox explored in Massimo Amato and Luca Fantacci, *The End of Finance* (Cambridge: Polity Press, 2012).

7. Amato and Fantacci, *The End of Finance*, 28.

8. Keynes, *The General Theory of Employment, Interest and Money*, 159.

9. Amato and Fantacci, *End of Finance*, 32.

10. Keynes, *The General Theory of Employment, Interest and Money*, 150.

11. Keynes, *The General Theory of Employment, Interest and Money*, 152.

12. Keynes, *The General Theory of Employment, Interest and Money*, 154.

13. Keynes, *The General Theory of Employment, Interest and Money*, 159.

14. Edward LiPuma, 'Ritual in Financial Life', in Lee and Martin, *Derivatives and the Wealth of Societies*, 61.

15. Brett Scott, *The Heretic's Guide to Global Finance: Hacking the Future of Money* (London, Pluto Press, 2013).

16. Former derivatives market maker turned philosopher, Elie Ayache, has emphasised that derivatives trading is an irreversible act of writing derivatives, not a reversible act of imagining possible futures. See Ayache, *The Blank Swan* (London: John Wiley, 2010), 25.

17. Frank Knight, *Risk, Uncertainty and Profit* (Washington DC: Beard Books, 2002).

18. It is notable that the formula for options pricing contains the interest rate so that the marginal cost of risk in any option can be compared to the zero-risk investment in a treasury bond. One result is that the creation of derivatives is partially restricted by the creation of treasury bonds as safe collateral. For the politics of derivatives, see Robert Meister, 'Liquidity', in Lee and Martin, *Derivatives and the Wealth of Societies*.

19. Amato and Fantacci, *The End of Finance*, 71.

20. LiPuma, 'Ritual in Financial Life', 64.

21. Ole Bjerg treats this feature as an essential aspect of the way in which money holds value. *Making Money: The Philosophy of Crisis Capitalism* (London: Verso, 2013), 145.

22. Keynes, *The General Theory of Employment, Interest and Money*, 151.

23. Amato and Fantacci, *The End of Finance*, 220.

24. Amato and Fantacci, *The End of Finance*, 19.

25. A mathematical model of the asset-inflation and debt-leverage vicious circle (initially described by Keynes, Schumpeter and Minsky) has been constructed by Steve Keen, *Debunking Economics*, second edition (London: Zed Books, 2011).

CHAPTER 20. APPROPRIATING FICTITIOUS
CAPITAL: DERIVATIVES

1. Appadurai, 'The Wealth of Dividuals'.
2. Gilles Deleuze, *Negotiations*, trans. Martin Joughin (London: Athlone, 1992), 180.
3. LiPuma, 'Ritual in Financial Life', 69.
4. Appadurai, 'The Wealth of Dividuals', 31.
5. LiPuma, 'Ritual in Financial Life', 44.

CHAPTER 21. PARTICIPATING IN FICTITIOUS
CAPITAL: CLEARING

1. Marx identified the phenomenon of clearing, but too late in the development of his theory to explore its significance as a foundation for capitalism. See *Capital*, volume 3, part V, ch. 29, 470. The theory of primitive accumulation is not sufficient alone here. See further Geoffrey Ingham, *The Nature of Money* (Cambridge: Polity, 2004); and Michael Hudson, . . . *And Forgive Them Their Debts: Lending, Foreclosure and Redemption from Bronze Age Finance to the Jubilee Year* (Dresdon: ISLET, 2018).
2. The magnitude of this effect may vary with the marginal propensity to consume, the marginal propensity to invest, and the existing overall level of debt within an economy (which affects the marginal propensity to repay debt). See Keen, *Can We Avoid Another Financial Crisis?*
3. Unfortunately, it is difficult to trace the movements of a sum of money, for with each transaction it is added into an account as a droplet of rain falls into a pond, before the aggregate is divided with each successive purchase, since only a portion of this aggregate is utilised with each subsequent transaction. Just as the genes of one's ancestors are halved in each successive generation, so also the presence of any particular sum of money is heavily diluted with each transaction. The fate of money is splicing and dicing.
4. Keynes, *A Treatise on Money*, volume 1(London: Macmillan, 1930), 26.
5. Even here, as John Hicks remarked in 1938, 'One cannot repress the thought that perhaps the whole Industrial Revolution of the last two hundred years has been nothing else but a vast secular boom'. *Value and Capital: An Inquiry into Some Fundamental Principles of Economic Theory* (Oxford: Clarendon Press, 1946), 302.
6. Although there may seem to be elements of divination even here: see Joshua Ramey, *Politics of Divination* (London: Rowman and Littlefield International, 2015).
7. Plato, *Republic*, 331d.
8. Robinson maintains that the non-coincidence of wants in a barter system is not a problem, since any durable object that is generally desired is as such a vehicle for purchasing power. Robinson, *Freedom and Necessity*, 32. Likewise, clearing solves this problem by selecting a unique agent who is generally in receipt of payments and making payments.

9. The Bank of England states that there are 183 participants in the Sterling Monetary Framework as on 15 September 2016 – a rapid increase in recent years.

10. For a clear exposition of the architecture of the monetary system in the UK, see Josh Ryan Collins et al. *Where Does Money Come From?* (London: New Economics Foundation, 2012); for the United States, see L. Randall Wray, *Modern Money Theory* (Basingstoke: Palgrave Macmillan, 2012); for Japan, see Werner, *A New Paradigm in Macroeconomics*.

11. Wray, *Modern Money Theory*, 86.

CHAPTER 22. OFFERING FICTITIOUS CAPITAL: DEFICIT SPENDING

1. Wray, *Modern Money Theory*, 13.

2. Wray, *Modern Money Theory*, 42.

3. Amato and Fantacci point out that not only has the gold standard only been in operation for limited historical periods in modernity, but also it was not effectively functioning that way even when it was nominally in operation.

4. Wray, *Modern Money Theory*, 46.

5. Wray, *Modern Money Theory*, 51.

6. Wray, *Modern Money Theory*, 49.

7. The traditional view is that money is an accumulated stock: in this case, under tight credit restrictions, governments, individuals and corporations are in competition for a limited amount of credit, and government spending can 'crowd out' private investment, unless it attracts capital from overseas through high interest rates. According to modern money theory, government spending is financed through treasury bills which are private saving, while private saving of treasury bills in the banking system functions as a reserve for the creation of new money. In other words, the money spent by the government is private debt, while the money saved in the private sector is government debt. For this reason, individual, corporate, financial and government debt can all increase at the same time in reality. For an account of how deregulation changed the US economy, still expressed in terms of the traditional view of money, see Greta R. Krippner, *Capitalizing on Crisis: The Political Origins of the Rise of Finance* (Cambridge, MA: Harvard University Press, 2011).

8. Wray, *Modern Money Theory*, 106–7.

9. Wray, *Modern Money Theory*, 198.

10. Wray, *Modern Money Theory*, 200.

11. This is not to deny that government spending can stabilise at a variety of different levels as a proportion of GDP, or that social spending for wealth redistribution may not contribute to economic growth and wellbeing. It is merely to assert that, whatever the policy, it has to be bounded by the fiction of balanced budget, even when budgets are never balanced.

12. Howard Davies and David Green, *Banking on the Future: The Fall and Rise of Central Banking* (Princeton, NJ: Princeton University Press, 2010), 20.

13. Turner, *Between Debt and the Devil*, 222–7.

14. While this is how Turner states the problem, I would agree for different reasons: the prospects for utilisation of cheap, abundant, and transportable energy sources are no longer present. David Graeber sheds an alternative light on lack of productivity growth over the past four decades in *The Utopia of Rules: On Technology, Stupidity and the Secret Joys of Bureaucracy* (New York: Melville, 2016).

15. Steve Keen has demonstrated that the rate of acceleration or deceleration of overall debt directly drives GDP. See *Developing an Economics for the Post-Crisis World* (World Economics Association, 2016).

16. Martin, *Knowledge LTD*, 17–26.

CONCLUSION

1. G.W.F. Hegel, *Outlines of the Philosophy of Right*, trans. T.M. Knox (Oxford: Oxford University Press, 2008), para 31.

2. Nietzsche, *Twilight of the Idols*, trans. R.J. Hollingdale (London: Penguin, 1990), 55.

3. Recent biogeophysical science estimates that the tipping point could lie around a 2°C temperature rise above pre-industrial levels. See Will Steffen et al., 'Trajectories of the earth system in the Anthropocene', *Proceedings of the National Academy of Sciences* (August 2018), 115 (33): 8252–9. It is harder to estimate how the human economic system is currently operating: the account of its operation put forward here is that of a positive feedback mechanism operating through extraction. Levels of debt may well have crossed a tipping point, inevitably leading to the triggering of future tipping points; it remains to be seen whether there are thresholds of distrust which constitute further tipping points restoring negative feedback.

Index

About the Author

Philip Goodchild is the Professor of Religion and Philosophy at the University of Nottingham, UK. His most influential books include *Deleuze and Guattari: An Introduction to the Politics of Desire* (1996), *Capitalism and Religion: The Price of Piety* (2002), *Theology of Money* (2007/2009) and *Philosophy as a Spiritual Exercise: A Symposium* (2013). He is currently producing a trilogy consisting of *Credit and Faith*, *Economic Theology*, and *Metaphysics of Trust* (2019–2021).
ORCID No. 000-0002-8326-6721